New Perspectives on

MICROSOFT®
INTERNET
EXPLORER 5

Introductory

SANDRA POINDEXTER
Northern Michigan University

JOAN CAREY
Carey Associates, Inc.

COURSE
TECHNOLOGY

Thomson Learning™

ONE MAIN STREET, CAMBRIDGE, MA 02142

Australia • Canada • Denmark • Japan • Mexico • New Zealand • Philippines
Puerto Rico • Singapore • South Africa • Spain • United Kingdom • United States

New Perspectives on Microsoft® Internet Explorer 5—Introductory is published by Course Technology.

Senior Product Manager	Rachel A. Crapser
Product Manager	Catherine V. Donaldson
Associate Product Manager	Karen Shortill
Editorial Assistant	Melissa Dezotell
Developmental Editor	Sandra K. Kruse
Production Editors	Melissa Panagos, Ellina Beletsky
Text and Cover Designer	Meral Dabcovich

© 2000 by Course Technology—I⟨T⟩P®

For more information contact:

Course Technology
One Main Street
Cambridge, MA 02142

ITP Europe
Berkshire House 168-173
High Holborn
London WCIV 7AA
England

Nelson ITP, Australia
102 Dodds Street
South Melbourne, 3205
Victoria, Australia

ITP Nelson Canada
1120 Birchmount Road
Scarborough, Ontario
Canada M1K 5G4

International Thomson Editores
Seneca, 53
Colonia Polanco
11560 Mexico D.F. Mexico

ITP GmbH
Konigswinterer Strasse 418
53227 Bonn
Germany

ITP Asia
60 Albert Street, #15-01
Albert Complex
Singapore 189969

ITP Japan
Hirakawacho Kyowa Building, 3F
2-2-1 Hirakawacho
Chiyoda-ku, Tokyo 102
Japan

ISBN 0-7600-7122-5

Printed in the United States of America

3 4 5 6 7 8 9 10 BM 04 03 02 01 00

PREFACE

The New Perspectives Series

About New Perspectives

Course Technology's **New Perspectives Series** is an integrated system of instruction that combines text and technology products to teach computer concepts, the Internet, and microcomputer applications. Users consistently praise this series for innovative pedagogy, use of interactive technology, creativity, accuracy, and supportive and engaging style.

How is the New Perspectives Series different from other series?

The **New Perspectives Series** distinguishes itself by **innovative technology**, from the renowned Course Labs to the state-of-the-art multimedia that is integrated with our Concepts texts. Other distinguishing features include **sound instructional design, proven pedagogy**, and **consistent quality**. Each tutorial has students learn features in the context of solving a realistic case problem rather than simply learning a laundry list of features. With the **New Perspectives Series**, instructors report that students have a complete, integrative learning experience that stays with them. They credit this high retention and competency to the fact that this series incorporates critical thinking and problem-solving with computer skills mastery. In addition, we work hard to ensure accuracy by using a multi-step quality assurance process during all stages of development. Instructors focus on teaching and students spend more time learning.

Choose the coverage that's right for you

New Perspectives applications books are available in the following categories:

Brief
2-4 tutorials

Brief: approximately 150 pages long, two to four "Level I" tutorials, teaches basic application skills.

Introductory
6 or 7 tutorials, or Brief + 2 or 3 more tutorials

Introductory: approximately 300 pages long, four to seven tutorials, goes beyond the basic skills. These books often build out of the Brief book, adding two or three additional "Level II" tutorials. The book you are holding is an Introductory book.

Comprehensive
Introductory + 4 or 5 more tutorials. Includes Brief Windows tutorials and Additional Cases

Comprehensive: approximately 600 pages long, eight to twelve tutorials, all tutorials included in the Introductory text plus higher-level "Level III" topics. Also includes two Windows tutorials and three or four fully developed Additional Cases.

Advanced
Quick Review of basics + in-depth, high-level coverage

Advanced: approximately 600 pages long, covers topics similar to those in the Comprehensive books, but offers the highest-level coverage in the series. Advanced books assume students already know the basics, and therefore go into more depth at a more accelerated rate than the Comprehensive titles. Advanced books are ideal for a second, more technical course.

Office Office suite components + integration + Internet

Custom Editions Choose from any of the above to build your own Custom Editions or CourseKits

Office: approximately 800 pages long, covers all components of the Office suite as well as integrating the individual software packages with one another and the Internet.

Custom Books The New Perspectives Series offers you two ways to customize a New Perspectives text to fit your course exactly: *CourseKits*™ are two or more texts shrinkwrapped together, and offer significant price discounts. *Custom Editions*®, offer you flexibility in designing your concepts, Internet, and applications courses. You can build your own book by ordering a combination of topics bound together to cover only the subjects you want. There is no minimum order, and books are spiral bound. Contact your Course Technology sales representative for more information.

What course is this book appropriate for?

New Perspectives on Internet Explorer 5—Introductory can be used in any course in which you want students to learn all the most important topics of Internet Explorer 5, including using the Internet Explorer browser and the Outlook Express e-mail and newsreader program, as well as downloading new versions of Internet Explorer and developing Web pages with FrontPage Express. It is particularly recommended for a short-semester course on Internet Explorer 5. This book assumes that students have learned basic Windows navigation and file management skills from Course Technology's *New Perspectives on Microsoft Windows 95—Brief*, or the equivalent book for Windows 98 or NT.

Proven Pedagogy

CASE

Tutorial Case Each tutorial begins with a problem presented in a case that is meaningful to students. The case turns the task of learning how to use an application into a problem-solving process.

45-minute Sessions Each tutorial is divided into sessions that can be completed in about 45 minutes to an hour. Sessions allow instructors to more accurately allocate time in their syllabus, and students to better manage their own study time.

1.
2.
3.

Step-by-Step Methodology We make sure students can differentiate between what they are to do and what they are to read. Through numbered steps – clearly identified by a gray shaded background – students are constantly guided in solving the case problem. In addition, the numerous screen shots with callouts direct students' attention to what they should look at on the screen.

TROUBLE?

TROUBLE? Paragraphs These paragraphs anticipate the mistakes or problems that students may have and help them continue with the tutorial.

"Read This Before You Begin" Page Located opposite the first tutorial's opening page for each level of the text, the Read This Before You Begin Page helps introduce technology into the classroom. Technical considerations and assumptions about software are listed to save time and eliminate unnecessary aggravation. Notes about the Data Disks help instructors and students get the right files in the right places, so students get started on the right foot.

QUICK CHECK

Quick Check Questions Each session concludes with meaningful, conceptual Quick Check questions that test students' understanding of what they learned in the session. Answers to the Quick Check questions are provided at the end of each tutorial.

RW

Reference Windows Reference Windows are succinct summaries of the most important tasks covered in a tutorial and they preview actions students will perform in the steps that follow.

TASK REFERENCE

Task Reference Located as a table at the end of the book, the Task Reference contains a summary of how to perform common tasks using the most efficient method, as well as references to pages where the task is discussed in more detail.

REVIEW

CASE

LAB

Explore

End-of-Chapter Review Assignments, Case Problems, and Lab Assignments Review Assignments provide students with additional hands-on practice of the skills they learned in the tutorial using the same case presented in the tutorial. These Assignments are followed by three to four Case Problems that have approximately the same scope as the tutorial case but use a different scenario. In addition, some of the Review Assignments or Case Problems may include Exploration Exercises that challenge students encourage them to explore the capabilities of the program they are using, and/or further extend their knowledge. Finally, if a Course Lab accompanies a tutorial, Lab Assignments are included after the Case Problems.

Microsoft® Internet Explorer 5 Instructor's Resource Kit for this title contains:

■ Electronic Instructor's Manual
■ Data Files
■ Solution Files
■ Course Labs
■ Course Test Manager Testbank
■ Course Test Manager Engine
■ Figure files

These supplements come on CD-ROM. If you don't have access to a CD-ROM drive, contact your Course Technology customer service representative for more information.

The New Perspectives Supplements Package

Electronic Instructor's Manual. Our Instructor's Manuals include tutorial overviews and outlines, technical notes, lecture notes, solutions, and Extra Case Problems. Many instructors use the Extra Case Problems for performance-based exams or extra credit projects. The Instructor's Manual is available as an electronic file, which you can get from the Instructor Resource Kit (IRK) CD-ROM or download it from **www.course.com**.

Data Files Data Files contain all of the data that students will use to complete the tutorials, Review Assignments, and Case Problems. A Readme file includes instructions for using the files. See the "Read This Before You Begin" page/pages for more information on Data Files.

Solution Files Solution Files contain every file students are asked to create or modify in the tutorials, Review Assignments, Case Problems, and Extra Case Problems. A Help file on the Instructor's Resource Kit includes information for using the Solution files.

Course Labs: Concepts Come to Life These highly interactive computer-based learning activities bring concepts to life with illustrations, animations, digital images, and simulations. The Labs guide students step-by-step, present them with Quick Check questions, let them explore on their own, test their comprehension, and provide printed feedback. Lab icons at the beginning of the tutorial and in the tutorial margins indicate when a topic has a corresponding Lab. Lab Assignments are included at the end of each relevant tutorial. The Labs available with this book and the tutorials in which they appear are:

Tutorial 1

Tutorial 3

Appendix B

Figure Files Many figures in the text are provided on the IRK CD-ROM to help illustrate key topics or concepts. Instructors can create traditional overhead transparencies by printing the figure files. Or they can create electronic slide shows by using the figures in a presentation program such as PowerPoint.

Course Test Manager: Testing and Practice at the Computer or on Paper Test Manager is cutting-edge, Windows-based testing software that helps instructors design and administer practice tests and actual examinations. Course Test Manager can automatically grade the tests students take at the computer and can generate statistical information on individual as well as group performance.

Online Companions: Dedicated to Keeping You and Your Students Up To Date Visit our faculty sites and student sites on the World Wide Web at **www.course.com**. Here instructors can browse this text's password-protected Faculty Online Companion to obtain an online Instructor's Manual, Solution Files, Data Files, and more. Students can also access this text's Student Online Companion, which contains Data Files and all the links that the students will need to complete their Review Assignments.

More innovative technology

Course CBT Enhance your students' Office 2000 classroom learning experience with self-paced computer-based training on CD-ROM. Course CBT engages students with interactive multimedia and hands-on simulations that reinforce and complement the concepts and skills covered in the textbook. All the content is aligned with the MOUS (Microsoft Office User Specialist) program, making it a great preparation tool for the certification exams. Course CBT also includes extensive pre- and post-assessments that test students' mastery of skills. These pre- and post-assessments automatically generate a "custom learning path" through the course that highlights only the topics students need help with.

Course Assessment How well do your students *really* know Microsoft Office? Course Assessment is a performance-based testing program that measures students' proficiency in Microsoft Office 2000. Previously known as SAM, Course Assessment is available for Office 2000 in either a live or simulated environment. You can use Course Assessment to place students into or out of courses, monitor their performance throughout a course, and help prepare them for the MOUS certification exams.

WebCT is a tool used to create Web-based educational environments and also uses WWW browsers as the interface for the course-building environment. The site is hosted on your school campus, allowing complete control over the information. WebCT has its own internal communication system, offering internal e-mail, a Bulletin Board, and a Chat room.

Course Technology offers pre-existing supplemental information to help in your WebCT class creation, such as a suggested Syllabus, Lecture Notes, Figures in the Book/Course Presenter, Student Downloads, and Test Banks in which you can schedule an exam, create reports, and more.

Acknowledgments

We wish to thank Inge Schmitt, Notre Dame College of Ohio, Janis Cox, Tri-County Technical College, and Glenda Kennedy, University of Arkansas at Pine Bluff, for their suggestions for improving the tutorials. Many thanks to the New Perspectives team at Course Technology, particularly Marjorie Hunt, Publisher; Christine Burmeister, Acquisitions Editor; Donna Gridley, Senior Editor; Rachel Crapser, Senior Product Manager; Catherine Donaldson, Product Manager; Karen Shortill, Assistant Product Manager; Melissa Dezotel, Editorial Assistant; Nancy Ludlow, Chris Greacen, Scott Rezek, Web Services; John Bosco, Li-Juian Jang, Greg Bigelow, Jeff Schwartz, John Freitas, Alex White, Quality Assurance Testers; and Melissa Panagos and Ellina Beletsky, Production Editors.

Joan Carey and Sandra Poindexter

Without the assistance of Martin Eskelinen, Helen Heck, Jane Phillips, Mike Bradley, and Steve and Anna Poindexter this book could not have been written. Finally, my thanks to Peter Heck who gave me the drive not just to finish, but to succeed.

Sandra Poindexter

Thanks also to my husband Patrick and my five little sons, Stephen Andrew, Michael Joseph, Peter Francis, Thomas James, and John Paul, for the joy you bring to my life.

Joan Carey

BRIEF CONTENTS

TABLE OF CONTENTS

Tutorial 3   IE 3.01

Corresponding with Outlook Express

Communicating over the Internet at Carey Outerwear

Appendix A   IE A.01
Downloading and Installing Internet Explorer

Using Windows Update to Download the Internet Explorer Software

Appendix B   IE B.01
Web Pages & HTML

Reference Window List

New Perspectives on

MICROSOFT®
INTERNET
EXPLORER 5

Read This Before You Begin

To the Student

Data Disk

To complete the Brief tutorials, Review Assignments, and Case Problems in this book, you need 1 Data Disk. Your instructor will either provide you with a Data Disk or ask you to make your own.

If you are making your own Data Disk, you will need **1** blank, formatted high-density disk. You will need to copy a set of folders from a file server or standalone computer or the Web onto your disk. Your instructor will tell you which computer, drive letter, and folders contain the files you need. You could also download the files by going to **www.course.com**, clicking Data Disk Files, and following the instructions on the screen.

The following table shows you which folders go on your disk, so that you will have enough disk space to complete all the tutorials, Review Assignments, and Case Problems.

Data Disk

Write this on the disk label:
Student Disk 1: Level I Tutorials 1-3

Put these folders on the disk:
Tutorial.01
Tutorial.03

When you begin each tutorial, be sure you are using the correct Data Disk. See the inside front or inside back cover of this book for more information on Data Disk Files, or ask your instructor or technical support person for assistance.

Course Labs

The tutorials in this book feature 2 interactive Course Labs to help you understand the World Wide Web, e-mail concepts and how to create Web pages. There are Lab Assignments at the end of Tutorials **1 and 3** and in Appendix 2, that relate to these Labs.

To start a Lab, click the **Start** button on the Windows taskbar, point to **Programs**, point to **Course Labs**, point to **New Perspectives Applications**, and click the name of the Lab you want to use.

Using Your Own Computer

If you are going to work through this book using your own computer, you need:

- **Computer System** Microsoft Internet Explorer 5 and Windows 95/98 must be installed on your computer. This book assumes a complete installation of Internet Explorer 5.

- **Data Disk** You will not be able to complete the tutorials or exercises in this book using your own computer until you have a Data Disk.

- **Course Labs** See your instructor or technical support person to obtain the Course Lab software for use on your own computer.

Visit Our World Wide Web Site

Additional materials designed especially for you are available on the World Wide Web. Go to **http://www.course.com**.

To the Instructor

The Data files and Course Labs are available on the Instructor's Resource Kit for this title. Follow the instructions in the Help file on the CD-ROM to install the programs to your network or standalone computer. For information on creating Data Disks or the Course Labs, see the "To the Student" section above. Also, please note that students will need an Internet connection in order to complete the tutorials in this book.

You are granted a license to copy the Data Files and Course Labs to any computer or computer network used by students who have purchased this book.

OBJECTIVES

In this tutorial you will:

- Investigate the structure of the Internet and the World Wide Web

- Identify Internet Explorer tools

- Start, customize, and exit Internet Explorer, and view and hide Explorer toolbars

- Open a Web page from your Data Disk

- Navigate links and frames

- Open a Web page with its URL, abort a connection, and attempt to connect to a defunct site

- Move among Web pages

- Print a Web page

- Get online help

LABS

The Internet: World Wide Web

NAVIGATING
THE WEB WITH INTERNET EXPLORER

Conducting Teacher Workshops at Northern University

CASE

Northern University

Michelle Pine, an education student at Northern University, is researching the use of the Internet as a teaching tool in the classroom and as an aid for preparing class lessons. She uses the Northern University Internet connection regularly to keep in contact with her friends and professors. She also uses an online service at home to communicate with her family members in New Mexico.

Michelle has been amazed at the wealth and variety of information she has found freely available on the Internet, especially the amount geared toward educators. At forums, educators can share ideas, advice, and encouragement. Teachers can find current information about every subject that can be incorporated into the curriculum. Geography and history, for example, come alive with multimedia travel through various time periods and lands. Physical equipment no longer limits scientific inquiry; in virtual labs students can conduct experiments that would not be possible in many classrooms. Humanity studies become more vibrant as students tour world-famous museums, and listen to music and view video clips from particular artists, styles, or times. The more Michelle looks, the more resources she finds. What's more, she has discovered that information is updated and added daily.

As a special project for one of her education courses, Michelle is planning a two-hour workshop for teachers on Internet basics and Internet Explorer. The 25 educators enrolled in the workshop have little working knowledge of the Internet and Internet Explorer but are interested in its possibilities. Michelle asks you to help her facilitate the workshop. She'd like to give the talk while you help at the computer keyboard. Michelle wants to begin by giving the educators an overview of the Internet and the World Wide Web. Then she'll teach them Internet Explorer basics using a presentation she created especially for the workshop. Finally, she'll demonstrate how to connect to and navigate through pages on the Web.

SESSION 1.1

In this session, you will learn about the Internet, the World Wide Web, and the Internet Explorer suite. You will also learn how to start and exit Internet Explorer, identify components of the Internet Explorer window, work with Internet Explorer toolbars, view Web pages, activate a link, and work with frames.

The Internet

The Internet:
World Wide
Web

Michelle wants to begin her talk with an overview of the technology that enables people to communicate with each other using their computers. She also wants to familiarize her audience with common network terms that will help them understand how the Internet operates. Two or more computers linked together so that they can exchange information and share resources create a structure known as a **network**. Some computers, called **servers**, provide specific resources for the network, such as print capabilities or file storage. Figure 1-1 shows a small network consisting of a single server, a shared printer, and a handful of computers.

| Figure 1-1 | SMALL NETWORK |

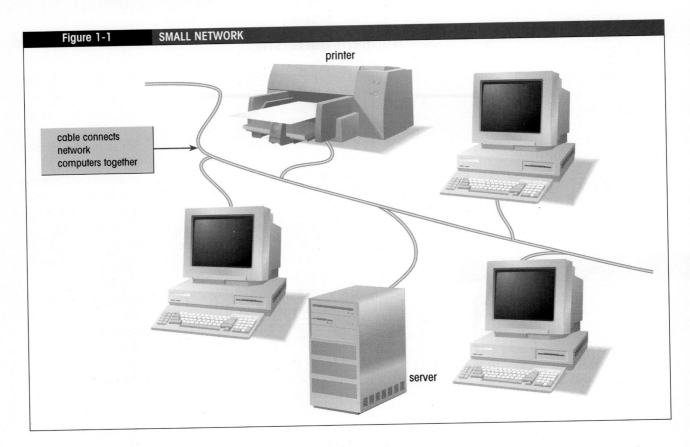

Networks can also be connected to each other so computers on different networks can share information. The **Internet**, the largest and most famous example of a "network of networks," is made up of millions of computers and networks all over the world. Fiber optic cables, satellites, phone lines, and other communication systems connect computers and networks on the Internet, as shown in Figure 1-2. Computers on a network are often called **hosts**, and thus computers on the Internet are sometimes called **Internet hosts**.

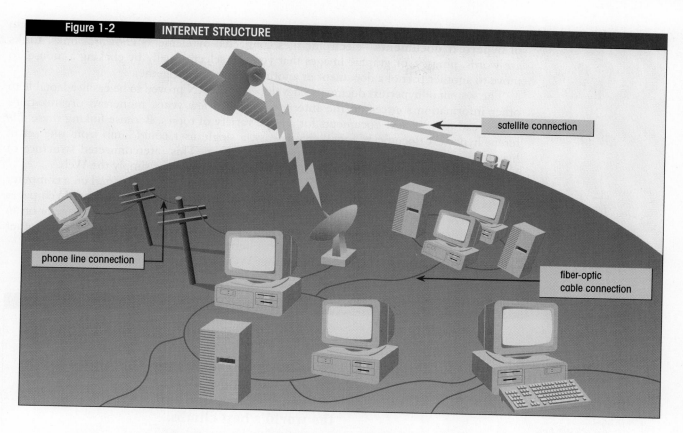

Figure 1-2   **INTERNET STRUCTURE**

satellite connection

phone line connection

fiber-optic cable connection

The Internet, by design, is a decentralized structure. There is no Internet "company." Instead, the Internet is a collection of different organizations, such as universities and companies, that organize their own information. There are no rules about where information is stored, and no one regulates the quality of information available on the Internet. Even though the lack of central control can make it hard for beginners to find their way through the Internet's resources, decentralization offers some advantages. The Internet is open to innovation and rapid growth because different organizations and individuals are free to test new products and services and make them quickly available to a global audience. One such service is the **World Wide Web**, an Internet service that makes finding information and moving around the Internet easy. Other services on the Internet include

- **FTP**, short for **File Transfer Protocol**, which provides an efficient means of file transfer.
- **Telnet**, which lets you connect to other computers and use their services, such as a public library's card catalog.
- **Gopher**, which organizes a server's resources via easy-to-use menus. (Gopher, however, is almost obsolete on today's Internet.)
- **E-mail**, or electronic mail, which allows the electronic transfer of messages between people who have Internet access.

Some Web sites incorporate these services into their Web pages. When this is the case, the Internet Explorer suite accesses the services without requiring any action on your part.

The World Wide Web

In 1989 Timothy Berners-Lee and other researchers at the CERN research facility near Geneva, Switzerland, laid the foundation of the World Wide Web. They wanted a method that would make it easy for researchers to share data electronically, so they created a system of **hypertext documents**—electronic files connected by elements known as links. **Links** are words, phrases, or graphic images that you can select, usually by clicking a mouse, to move to another part of a document or another document altogether.

The system of hypertext documents developed at CERN proved to be easily adaptable to other information sources on the Internet. Within a few years, numerous organizations were creating hypertext documents for a large variety of topics. Because linking these different hypertext documents together was easy, a single user could jump from one set of hypertext documents to another without much effort. This interconnected structure of hypertext documents became known as the World Wide Web, or simply the Web.

Each hypertext document on the Web is called a **Web page** and is stored on a computer on the Internet called a **Web server**. A Web page can contain links to other Web pages located anywhere on the Internet—on the same computer as the original Web page or on an entirely different computer halfway across the world. The ability to cross-reference other Web pages with links is one of the Web's most important features.

Figure 1-3 shows how you move to another Web page when you click a link.

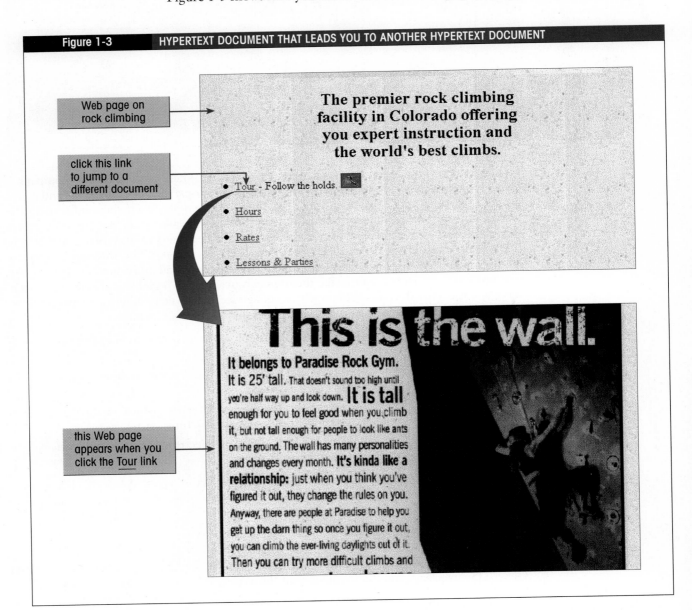

Figure 1-3   HYPERTEXT DOCUMENT THAT LEADS YOU TO ANOTHER HYPERTEXT DOCUMENT

Web page on rock climbing

click this link to jump to a different document

The premier rock climbing facility in Colorado offering you expert instruction and the world's best climbs.

- Tour - Follow the holds.
- Hours
- Rates
- Lessons & Parties

this Web page appears when you click the Tour link

This is the wall.

It belongs to Paradise Rock Gym. It is 25' tall. That doesn't sound too high until you're half way up and look down. **It is tall** enough for you to feel good when you climb it, but not tall enough for people to look like ants on the ground. The wall has many personalities and changes every month. **It's kinda like a relationship:** just when you think you've figured it out, they change the rules on you. Anyway, there are people at Paradise to help you get up the darn thing so once you figure it out, you can climb the ever-living daylights out of it. Then you can try more difficult climbs and

Some links point to files other than Web pages, such as scanned photographs, graphic images, film clips, sounds, and computer programs. A link could lead you to a discussion group called a **forum** or **newsgroup** whose users share information on topics of common interest. Another link might point to an individual's e-mail address.

Navigating Web pages using hypertext is an efficient way of accessing information. Michelle points out that when you read a book, you follow a linear progression, reading one page after another. With hypertext, you progress through the pages in whatever order you want, skipping from one topic to the next, as Figure 1-4 shows.

Figure 1-4   FOLLOWING HYPERTEXT LINKS

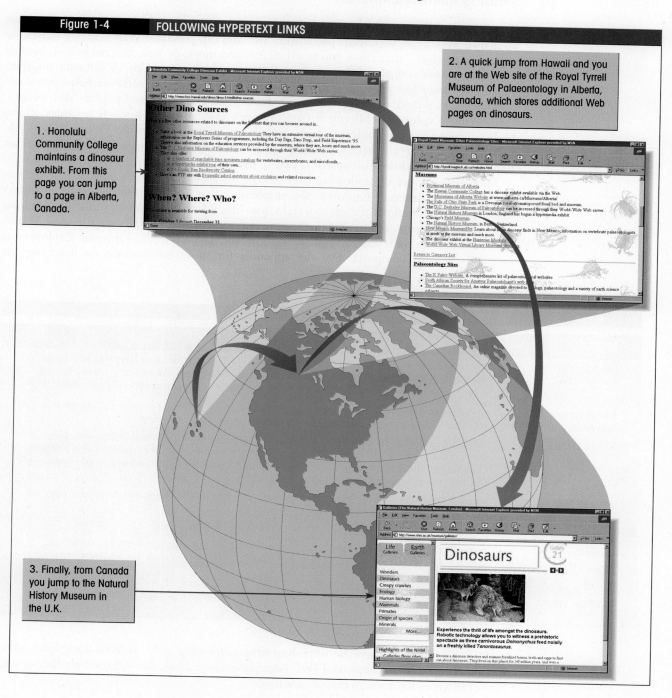

1. Honolulu Community College maintains a dinosaur exhibit. From this page you can jump to a page in Alberta, Canada.

2. A quick jump from Hawaii and you are at the Web site of the Royal Tyrrell Museum of Palaeontology in Alberta, Canada, which stores additional Web pages on dinosaurs.

3. Finally, from Canada you jump to the Natural History Museum in the U.K.

In addition to the ease with which you can access documents on computers all over the world, the Web also makes sharing your ideas with others easy. All you need is an account on a computer connected to the Internet. The account lets you store your Web page and make it available for others to read. Many companies, called **Internet Service Providers** or **ISPs**, sell access to the Internet and also provide you with the opportunity to place pages on the Web as part of their service.

What is Internet Explorer?

To access documents available on the Web, to communicate with others, and to publish your own Web page, you need special software. You can purchase Web software **suites**, or groups of products, that allow you to do all this and more, or you can purchase individual software components that help you with certain tasks on the Web. A software program called a **browser** lets you view and work with Web pages. Other software helps you communicate with e-mail, participate in group discussions, and create and publish Web pages.

Internet Explorer is Microsoft Corporation's Web software suite. It provides all the tools you need to communicate, share, and access information on the World Wide Web. For this reason it is Northern University's product of choice. Michelle plans to use Internet Explorer at the workshop because it is easy to use and understand.

Michelle provides the following overview of the tools available in various installations and versions of Internet Explorer. She emphasizes that you shouldn't worry if you don't understand the functions of each tool right now. You'll learn more about individual Internet Explorer tools later. Figure 1-5 lists some services Internet Explorer provides. Which Internet Explorer tools your computer has, however, depends on how Internet Explorer was installed on your computer. See the appendix for more information on installing the Internet Explorer tools.

Figure 1-5	INTERNET EXPLORER TOOLS
SERVICE	**DESCRIPTION**
Internet Explorer and Internet Tools	Browser that retrieves, displays, and organizes documents. These documents are retrieved from Web servers and appear on your computer monitor. Internet Explorer includes searching and organizing features that help you keep track of information on the Web and built-in intelligence that automates many common Web tasks.
Internet Explorer Web Accessories	Kit that makes Web browsing even easier. Includes ability to view single frames, simplify searches, zoom in and out of Web page images, highlight text, view all the links on a page, and more.
Outlook Express	E-mail and newsgroup manager that lets you send, receive, compose, edit, search, and sort e-mail. **E-mail**, or electronic mail, is a note you write and send across the Internet. Outlook Express can handle e-mail containing practically any file type—graphics, sounds, videos, and so on. Outlook Express also functions as a newsgroup manager that helps you participate in a discussion group.
Windows Media Player	Windows Media Player lets you receive and play most media types on the Internet, including audio, video, and mixed-media files.
Chat	Microsoft Chat is an Internet chat program that lets you chat inside a comic strip.
NetMeeting	NetMeeting lets you participate in online conferences in which you can share documents over the Internet.
Wallet	Stores credit card and address information in a secure "wallet" on your computer so you can easily and safely shop on the Internet.
FrontPage Express	FrontPage Express is a Web-page editor that lets you create and format Web pages without having to learn HTML programming first.

Michelle wants to keep the workshop simple, focusing only on Web navigation rather than on e-mail, newsgroups, and Web page publishing. Thus, she will use only the browser tool of Internet Explorer in her presentation.

With the Internet Explorer browser, you can visit sites around the world; view multimedia documents; transfer files, images, and sounds to your computer; conduct searches for specific topics; listen to radio broadcasts; and run software on other computers.

When a user tries to view a Web page, the user's browser, in this case Internet Explorer, locates and retrieves the document from the Web server and displays its contents on the user's computer. As shown in Figure 1-6, the server stores the Web page in one location, and browsers anywhere in the world can view it.

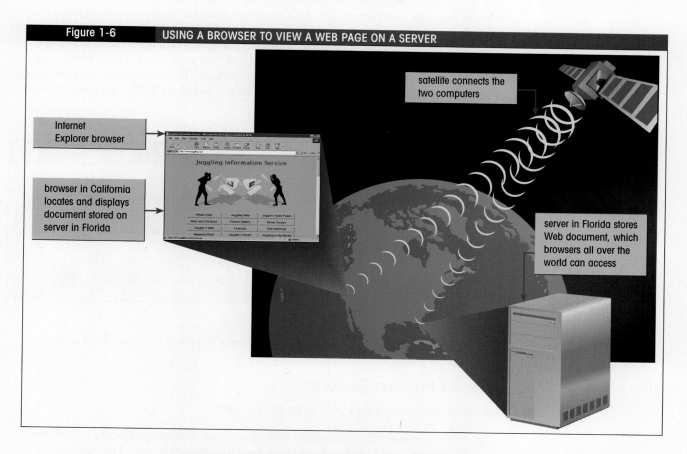

Figure 1-6   USING A BROWSER TO VIEW A WEB PAGE ON A SERVER

Here, a browser in California is retrieving a document stored on a Web server in Florida, which it saves in a temporary folder. You might retrieve such a page without knowing or caring on which Web server it is stored. You can view a document stored on a Web server across the room or across the world using the same technique. Information stored on a server in Cairo is just as accessible as information stored on one in Cleveland. Is there any doubt why the Web has been called the "Information Superhighway"?

Starting Internet Explorer

Before you can start using Internet Explorer to explore the Web, you must have an Internet connection. In a university or institutional setting your connection might come from the campus or company network on which you have an account. If you work on a home computer, your connection might come over the phone line from an account with an ISP.

Michelle explains that, unlike many other software applications, Internet Explorer does not open with a standard start-up screen. Instead, you see a document called the **home**

page—the Web page that appears when you start Internet Explorer. Internet Explorer lets each computer installation specify what home page users see when they start Internet Explorer. When you launch Internet Explorer, you may see:

- Your school's or institution's home page
- A page your technical support person has set as the default
- The Microsoft Corporation home page

A home page can also refer to the Web page that a person, organization, or business created to give information about itself. A home page might include information about the host, links to other sites, or relevant graphics and sounds. When Michelle starts Internet Explorer from home, she connects to the Microsoft Network home page, which provides fundamental information about Microsoft and its software. When she starts it in the university's lab, she sees Northern University's home page, stored on a Web server at Northern University.

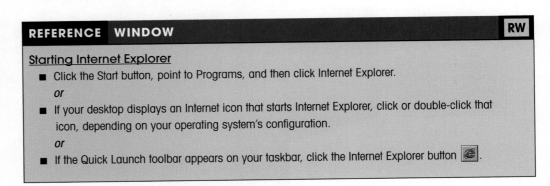

REFERENCE WINDOW   **RW**

Starting Internet Explorer
- Click the Start button, point to Programs, and then click Internet Explorer.
  or
- If your desktop displays an Internet icon that starts Internet Explorer, click or double-click that icon, depending on your operating system's configuration.
  or
- If the Quick Launch toolbar appears on your taskbar, click the Internet Explorer button.

These instructions show you how to start Internet Explorer from the Start menu.

To start Internet Explorer:

1. If necessary, connect to your Internet account.

   TROUBLE? If you are in a university setting, you are probably already connected and can skip Step 1. If you don't know how to connect to your Internet account, ask your technical support person for help or call your Internet Service Provider's technical support line.

   TROUBLE? If you are using a dial-up connection, your computer or ISP may disconnect you if the browser is idle for a designated period of time. If this happens, Internet Explorer prompts you to choose either to work offline or to connect again. Click the Connect button and proceed with the tutorial.

2. Click the **Start** button 🏁 Start on the Windows taskbar.

3. Point to **Programs** with the mouse pointer. After a short pause, the Programs menu opens with a list of programs available on your computer.

4. Click **Internet Explorer** to start the program, as shown in Figure 1-7. The home page specified by your site's installation opens.

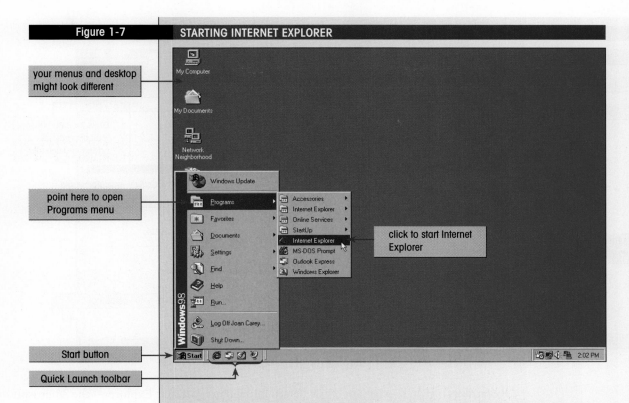

Figure 1-7   STARTING INTERNET EXPLORER

your menus and desktop
might look different

point here to open
Programs menu

click to start Internet
Explorer

Start button

Quick Launch toolbar

TROUBLE? If you don't see Internet Explorer on the Programs menu, ask your instructor or technical support person for assistance. If you are using your own computer, make sure Internet Explorer is installed.

TROUBLE? If another menu opens, you probably clicked the Internet Explorer program group that contains other Internet Explorer suite tools. Locate and click the Internet Explorer option, either on the Programs or Internet Explorer menu, which displays the Internet Explorer icon 🦋.

TROUBLE? If this is the first time Internet Explorer has been used on your computer, you might be prompted to establish a connection or other settings. If you are using a computer that is not your own, ask your technical support person for assistance. If you are using your own computer, read the instructions, proceed through the dialog boxes that appear, providing information where requested (such as your e-mail address), and then click Next when you finish each step. If you don't understand a dialog box, check your ISP documentation or call your ISP's technical support line for assistance.

5. Click the **Maximize** button 🗖 in the upper-right corner of the Microsoft Internet Explorer window if the window is not maximized. Figure 1-8 shows the Microsoft Network home page.

TROUBLE? If your screen shows a different home page, don't worry. Also don't worry if your title bar or activity indicator is different.

Figure 1-8	INTERNET EXPLORER WINDOW

Regardless of which page appears when you first start Internet Explorer—the Microsoft Network home page, your university's home page, or a different home page—your window should share some common components with the one in Figure 1-8. Michelle points out the most important parts of the Internet Explorer window, shown in Figure 1-9. Don't worry if you don't see all these components. You'll soon learn how to make them appear.

Figure 1-9	INTERNET EXPLORER WINDOW COMPONENTS

WINDOW COMPONENT	DESCRIPTION
Title bar	Identifies the active Web page.
Menu bar	Groups Internet Explorer commands by menu name. You click a menu name to open a menu, and then click the command you want.
Standard toolbar	Offers single-click access to the more common menu commands.
Address bar	Identifies the address of the active Web page—the one currently appearing in the Internet Explorer document window.
Go button	Connects you to the Web address displayed in the Address bar.
Links toolbar	Displays buttons that you can click to jump immediately to individual Web pages. You can add buttons for your personal favorites.
Document window	Displays the active Web page.
Scroll bars	Lets you move through the active page content. Click the up and down arrows on the vertical scroll bar to move the page up and down, or less frequently, the left and right arrows on the horizontal scroll bar to move the page left and right. You can also drag the scroll box or click above and below it to move through a page.
Activity indicator	Displays a graphic that rotates when a page is loading and rests when the browser is idle. If the activity indicator is idle but the page doesn't seem to have been successfully retrieved, you know there is a problem with the connection. The appearance of the activity indicator depends on how you installed Internet Explorer.
Status bar	Indicates the status of the document you are retrieving from the Web server, as well as site security information.

Customizing the Internet Explorer Window

The Internet Explorer window looks different depending on what toolbars or Explorer bars are displayed. You can easily drag toolbars to different locations so that more of the document window is available, or you can hide toolbars you aren't likely to use. You can also customize toolbars to display buttons you frequently use and hide buttons you rarely use. For now, you want to display only the Standard toolbar and the Address bar, with the Links bar off to the side.

To customize the placement of the Internet Explorer toolbars:

1. Click **View** to open the View menu, and then point to **Toolbars**. The options on the menu let you control the appearance of the Internet Explorer window. A check mark indicates that the feature is enabled. For example, a check mark next to the second command in the View menu, Status Bar, indicates that the status bar is visible. Figure 1-10 shows that the status bar and Standard, Address, and Links toolbars are all visible in the Internet Explorer window. Notice that all these menu options have check marks next to them.

   TROUBLE? If fewer toolbars appear on your screen or if they are organized differently, don't worry. You'll learn to control the position of the toolbars in the next steps.

Figure 1-10	VIEWING STATUS OF INTERNET EXPLORER DISPLAY

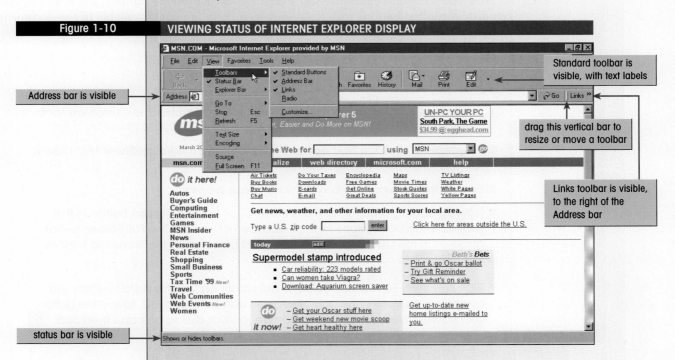

2. Now you'll experiment with hiding a toolbar. Look at the Toolbars submenu, which should still be open, and note whether Links has a check mark next to it. If it does, click **Links**. The Links toolbar disappears.

3. Click **View**, point to **Toolbars**, and again click **Links**, which should not have a check mark next to it. The Links toolbar reappears in its previous position.

4. Now practice dragging the Links toolbar to a new location. To drag a toolbar, drag the vertical bar that precedes it, as shown in Figure 1-10. Point to the vertical bar in front of the Links toolbar. The pointer changes from ⇖ to ↔. Now drag the Links toolbar below the Address bar. As you drag, the pointer changes to ⊣⊢.

TROUBLE? If the Links toolbar is already below the Address bar, drag it above the Address bar so that it is to the right of the Standard toolbar.

TROUBLE? If your Address bar isn't visible, click View, point to Toolbars, click Address Bar, and then repeat Step 4.

5. Drag the Links toolbar to the right of the Address bar.

6. Now resize the Links toolbar. Point at the vertical bar preceding the Links toolbar. Drag the vertical bar to the left. The Links toolbar is enlarged. The Address bar shrinks.

7. Resize the Links toolbar so that only the word "Links" appears, as in Figure 1-10.

8. Click **View** once more, point to **Explorer Bar**, and click any checked Explorer bar to hide it.

Now you'll learn to customize the appearance of the toolbar buttons. For example, you can display toolbar buttons with icons only to make more space available in the document window. Because you want the workshop attendees to see the buttons clearly, you'll display both icons and text labels.

To modify the toolbar button display:

1. Click **View**, point to **Toolbars**, and then click **Customize**. The Customize Toolbar dialog box opens.

2. If necessary, click the **Text options** list arrow, and then click **Show text labels**. Text labels appear on the buttons.

3. Be sure the Icon options box displays **Large icons**.

4. Now try adding a button to the toolbar. Click the **Full Screen** button in the Available toolbar buttons list box, and then click **Add**. The Full Screen button appears in the Current toolbar buttons list box and on the Standard toolbar. See Figure 1-11.

TROUBLE? If the Full Screen button is not visible on the Standard toolbar, you have more buttons on your toolbar than can be displayed. To see the button, you would have to close the Customize Toolbar dialog box and then click ⟩⟩ .

Figure 1-11 ADDING A TOOLBAR BUTTON

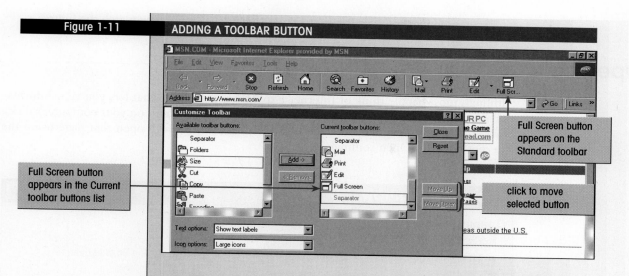

Full Screen button appears in the Current toolbar buttons list

Full Screen button appears on the Standard toolbar

click to move selected button

5. Now change the button's position on the toolbar by clicking the **Full Screen** button in the Current toolbar buttons list box and then clicking the **Move Up** button several times. As you click the Move Up button, the Full Screen button moves to the left on the Standard toolbar.

TROUBLE? If the Full Screen button is at the top of the list, click the Move Down button several times, and observe how it moves to the right on the Standard toolbar.

6. Now remove the Full Screen button, which is still selected, from the Standard toolbar. Click the **Remove** button. The Full Screen button disappears from the Standard toolbar.

7. Click **Close** to close the Customize Toolbar dialog box. Compare your screen to Figure 1-12.

Figure 1-12 FINAL DISPLAY

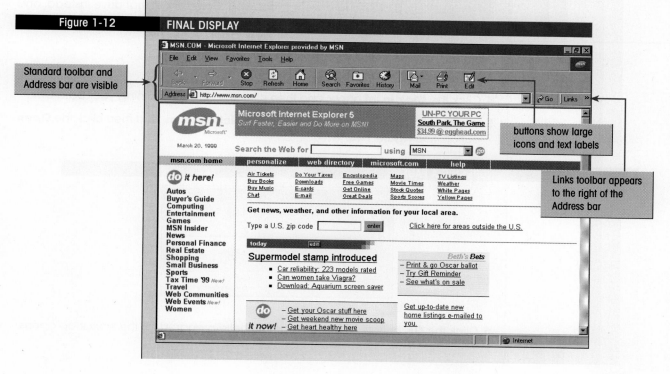

Standard toolbar and Address bar are visible

buttons show large icons and text labels

Links toolbar appears to the right of the Address bar

The components of your Internet Explorer window should now match the figures.

Opening a Web Page from a Disk

Although most people think of Internet Explorer as a program that lets you view information on the Internet, you can also use it to view Web pages stored on your computer's disks. If you have a Web page in the form of a file on a disk, you can open that page using the Internet Explorer Open command.

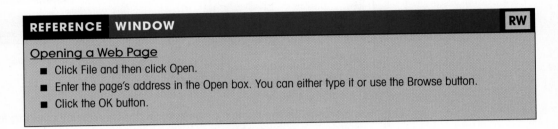

REFERENCE WINDOW   RW

Opening a Web Page
- Click File and then click Open.
- Enter the page's address in the Open box. You can either type it or use the Browse button.
- Click the OK button.

Michelle prepared a Web page that she will use at the workshop to demonstrate how to activate a link. It's on your Data Disk. You'll open it in the Internet Explorer browser. Keep in mind that you are opening Michelle's file on your Data Disk, not on the Web. You'll learn how to view Web documents on the Internet in Session 1.2.

To open a specific Web page:

1. Place your Data Disk in drive A. See the "Read This Before You Begin" page to make sure you are using the correct disk for this tutorial.

   TROUBLE? If you are using drive B, place your Data Disk in that drive instead, and for the rest of these tutorials, substitute drive B wherever you see drive A.

2. Click **File** and then click **Open**.

3. Click the **Browse** button.

4. Click the **Look in** list arrow, and then click the drive containing your Data Disk.

5. Double-click the **Tutorial.01** folder, click **Michelle.htm**, and then click the **Open** button. See Figure 1-13.

| Figure 1-13 | OPENING A PAGE |

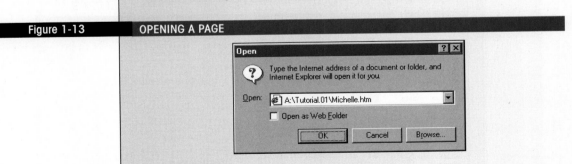

6. Click the **OK** button. The Web page Michelle prepared for the workshop opens. See Figure 1-14.

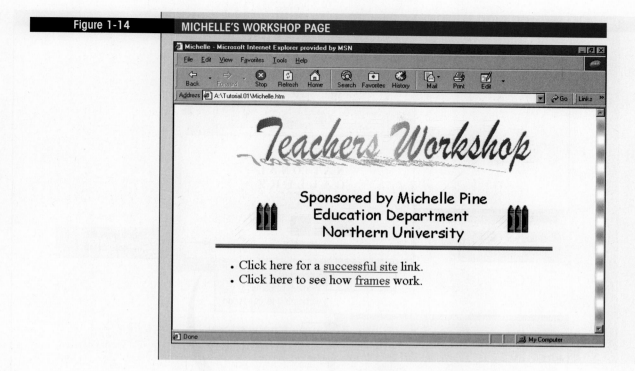

Figure 1-14   **MICHELLE'S WORKSHOP PAGE**

Activating a Link

A hypertext link on the Web, like a link in a chain, connects two points. Links can appear in two ways: as text that you click or as a graphic that you click. A **text link** is a word or phrase that usually appears in a different color or underlined. A **graphic link** is a graphic image that you click to jump to another location. When you aren't sure whether text or a graphic image is a link, point to it with the mouse pointer. When you move the mouse pointer over a text or graphic link, it changes shape from ⯈ to ☝. The ☝ pointer indicates that when you click, you will activate that link and jump to the new location. The destination of the link appears in the status bar, and for some graphic links a small identification box appears next to your pointer.

As you'll see, Michelle's workshop pages contain both text and graphic links. The text links are underlined and colored. Each link gives Internet Explorer the information needed to locate the page. When you activate a link, you jump to a new location, called the **target** of the link. The target can be either another location on the active Web page (for example, the bottom of a Web page often contains a link that targets the top), a different document or file on your computer, or a Web page stored on a remote Web server anywhere in the world. The amount of time necessary to link to the target, called the **response time**, varies, depending upon the number of people trying to connect to the same site, the number of people on the Internet at that time, and the site design.

Activating a link starts a multi-step process. Although Internet Explorer does the work for you, following the sequence of events is important: it helps you recognize problems when they occur and understand how to resolve them.

Figure 1-15 illustrates the string of events that occur when you link to a site. When you point to a link, the status bar displays the address of the link's target. When you click a link, the activity indicator animates, and the status bar displays a series of messages indicating that Internet Explorer is connecting to the file targeted by the link, is transferring data, and finally, is done.

Figure 1-15   ACTIVATING A LINK

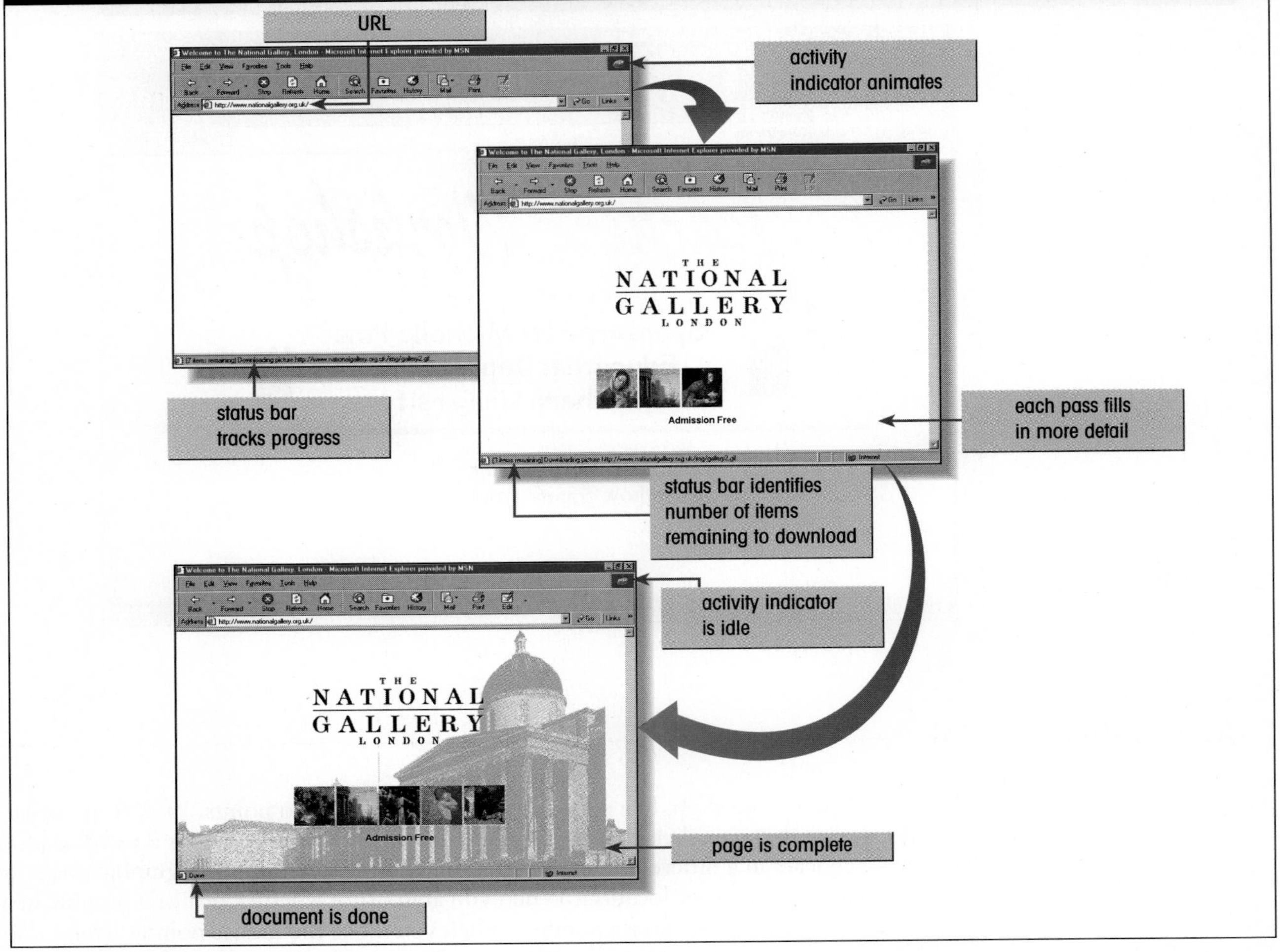

URL

activity
indicator animates

status bar
tracks progress

each pass fills
in more detail

status bar identifies
number of items
remaining to download

activity indicator
is idle

page is complete

document is done

You can see the Web page build as Internet Explorer transfers information to your screen in multiple passes. The first wave brings a few pieces to the page; with each subsequent pass, Internet Explorer fills in more detail until the Web page is complete. The progress bar fills in to indicate how much of the Web page has transferred. The vertical scroll box scrolls up as Internet Explorer adds more information and detail to the page. Although you don't need to wait until the page is complete before scrolling or clicking another link, it might be difficult to determine links and other information until the page is mostly filled in. Try activating one of the links on Michelle's page.

To initiate a link to a Web page:

1. Point to the **successful site** link. Notice that the pointer changes shape from ⟍ to 👆, indicating that you are pointing to a hypertext link. The status bar shows the target for that link. See Figure 1-16.

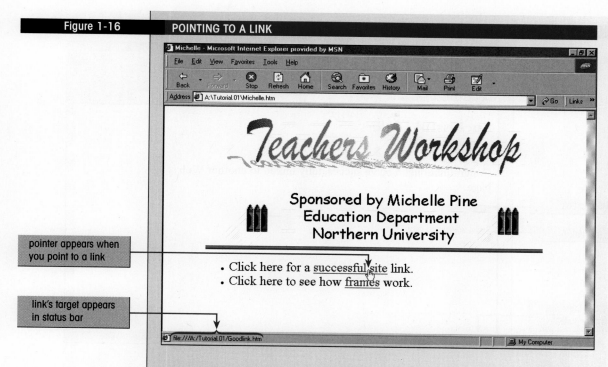

Figure 1-16   **POINTING TO A LINK**

pointer appears when you point to a link

link's target appears in status bar

TROUBLE? If the status message area is blank, slowly move your pointer over the underlined words. When you see the link's target in the status message area, the pointer is positioned correctly.

2. Click the **successful site** link to activate the link. The status bar notes the progress of the link, although this might happen so fast that you can't see it. When the status bar displays, "Done," the link is complete and the Web page that is the target of the link appears. See Figure 1-17.

TROUBLE? If a message dialog box opens, the link was not successful. Click the OK button to close the dialog box, and repeat Steps 1 and 2. After you click the hypertext link, be sure not to click anywhere else on the page until Internet Explorer completes the link.

Figure 1-17   **COMPLETED LINK**

graphic link

text link

status bar indicates
link is complete

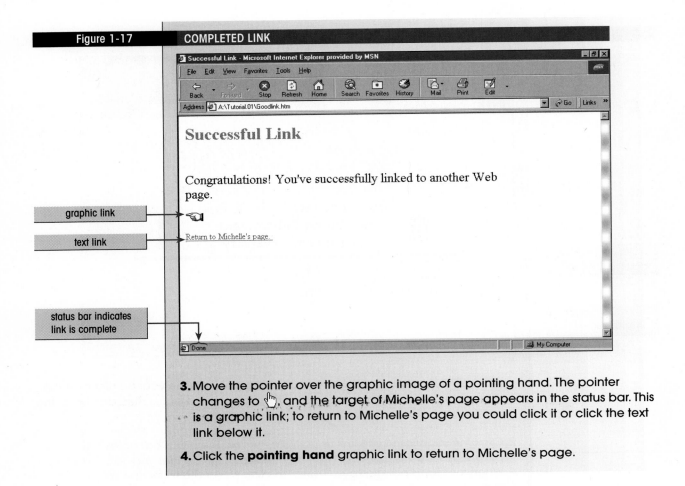

3. Move the pointer over the graphic image of a pointing hand. The pointer changes to ⬆, and the target of Michelle's page appears in the status bar. This is a graphic link; to return to Michelle's page you could click it or click the text link below it.

4. Click the **pointing hand** graphic link to return to Michelle's page.

You connected to a Web page with a single click, and then you used the graphic link on that page to return to Michelle's page. Using hypertext links is a simple way to move from one Web page to another. Notice that the successful site link on Michelle's page changed color. Internet Explorer displays text links you've already visited, or activated, in a different color so you know which links you've already tried.

Working **with Frames**

Michelle wants to illustrate one more navigational concept. Web page designers often divide their pages into parts, called frames, to organize their information more effectively. A **frame** is a section of the document window. Each frame can have its own set of scroll bars and can display the contents of a different location. Often the top frame displays the Web site's title, the left frame contains links that form a "table of contents" for the site, and the right frame displays the content of the current page. Many Web sites employ frames because they let the user see different areas of information simultaneously. When you scroll through the contents of one frame, you do not affect any other frames.

Michelle wants to demonstrate frames using a page that she is designing for Northern University and its Education Department, listing available degree programs. She's included a link for this page on her main page.

To scroll through a frame:

1. If necessary, scroll down Michelle's page until you see the sentence "Click here to see how frames work."

2. Click the **frames** link. Figure 1-18 shows the page that opens. It contains three frames. The top frame identifies the page as that of the Education Department. The frame on the left identifies the two types of undergraduate programs—certification and non-certification—and the right frame displays information about the programs.

| Figure 1-18 | WEB PAGE WITH FRAMES |

BANNER
top frame identifies page

NAVIGATION
left frame contains links

STUFF
right frame contains
information

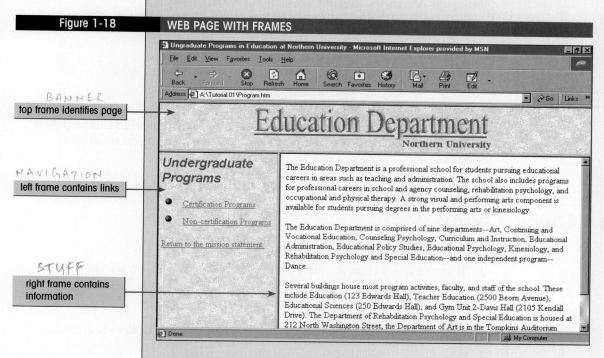

3. First, scroll through the information displayed in the right frame. Notice the scroll bar appears only in that frame, not in the other two. Moreover, the other two frames remain static while the right frame changes.

TROUBLE? If no Scroll bar appears on the right side of the screen, your monitor resolution is so high that it displays the entire information page. Skip Step 3 and continue with Step 4.

4. To change the display in the right frame and view certification programs, click the **Certification Programs** link in the left frame. Notice that the right frame now displays the certification program list. Scroll through this list and again notice that the other frames are static.

5. Click the **Non-certification Programs** link in the left frame. Now the right frame displays the non-certification program list. Scroll through this list.

6. Click the **Return to the mission statement** link. The right frame now shows its original contents.

Using frames, Michelle has enabled users to examine only information of interest to them. Knowing how to recognize and navigate frames is increasingly important because many Web pages now use them.

Exiting Internet Explorer

Michelle decides to take a break in the workshop. Before you leave the computer, you need to close Internet Explorer. The next time you start Internet Explorer, the window will show the home page designated for your installation. To return to a site you visited in this session, you will need to reopen the Web page and link to the sites you want to see.

> ### To exit Internet Explorer:
>
> 1. Click the **Close** button ⊠ to close Internet Explorer.
>
> TROUBLE? If you are working in a lab and are prompted to choose whether or not to stay connected to the Internet, click the Stay Connected button unless your instructor or technical support person has instructed you otherwise.

Session 1.1 QUICK CHECK

1. What is an ISP?

2. True or False: When you start Internet Explorer, you always see the same screen, no matter what computer you use.

3. What is a home page?

4. How does Internet Explorer display a text link that you've already activated?

5. Why do Web page designers often use frames?

SESSION 1.2

In this session, you will learn about URLs and how to open a Web page using its URL, how to navigate the Web with Internet Explorer using toolbar buttons, how to print Web pages, and how to use the online Help feature.

Connecting to a Web Site with a URL

Clicking a hypertext link is just one way of connecting to a Web page. Clicking links, often called "surfing," is an easy way to navigate the Web when you don't have a specific destination in mind and just want to follow links. To connect to a particular site, however, you need to know its address, called its **Uniform Resource Locator** or **URL**. A URL is composed of a protocol identifier, a server address, and a file pathname. If the file is stored in a folder, the folder name appears as part of the file pathname. For example, when Michelle saves the undergraduate program list she is creating for the Education Department, it will have the following URL:

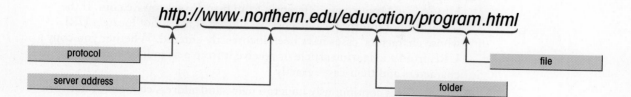

Computers use standardized procedures, called **protocols**, to transmit files. Web documents travel between sites using **HyperText Transfer Protocol** or **HTTP**, so the URL for a Web page usually begins with "http://" to identify its type. Another common protocol you might see is File Transfer Protocol, or FTP, a protocol that facilitates transferring files over the Web.

The server address contains the domain name and tells the exact location of the Internet server and the type of organization that owns and operates it. For example, in the domain name "www.northern.edu" the "www" indicates that the server is on the World Wide Web, "northern" indicates the name of the organization that owns the server (Northern University), and "edu" indicates that it's an educational site. The entire domain name tells you that Northern is an educational site on the Web. Outside the United States, domain name types include a two-letter country code. For example, "fi" identifies a server located in Finland. Figure 1-19 lists common domain name types.

Figure 1-19	DOMAIN NAME TYPES				
DOMAIN	**DESCRIPTION**	**DOMAIN**	**DESCRIPTION**	**DOMAIN**	**DESCRIPTION**
au	Australia	fr	France	net	Networking organizations
ca	Canada	gov	Government agencies	org	Nonprofit organizations
com	Commercial sites	int	International organizations	tw	Taiwan
de	Germany	jp	Japan	uk	United Kingdom
edu	Educational institutions	mil	Military sites	za	South Africa

All files stored on a network server must have a unique pathname, just as files on a disk must. The pathname includes the folder or folders the file is stored in, plus the filename and its extension. The filename and extension are usually the last items in the pathname, although if a URL targets a specific location within the file, that target name may also appear. The filename extension for Web pages is usually "html" (or just "htm"), which stands for hypertext markup language. Michelle's file for the Education Department program, for example, is named program.html and is located in the education folder on the Northern server.

Remembering two important facts about a URL makes using a URL to access an Internet site significantly easier:

- Some servers are case-sensitive, and they might interpret the URL http://www.Mysite.com differently from http://www.mysite.com. If the server cannot interpret case-sensitive addresses, it cannot locate a URL whose characters' cases have been incorrectly entered. Whether you copy a URL from a magazine article or receive it from a friend, be sure to copy the characters and their cases exactly.

- Internet sites continuously undergo name and address changes. A network server might have changed names, the file might be stored in a different folder, or the page you want may no longer be available. Remember no one person or organization controls the Internet. Organizations and individuals can add, rename, and delete files at will. Often when a URL changes, you can find the forwarding address (URL) at the old URL. Other sites will simply vanish from servers, leaving no forwarding information.

Before you actually enter a URL in the Address bar, you should be aware of the Internet Explorer **AutoComplete** feature, which remembers Web addresses and other information that you previously entered. When you type a URL you've entered before, Internet Explorer attempts to complete it for you. As you type, a list of suggested matches appears. If no suggestions match the address you want to enter, for now simply ignore the suggestion list and continue typing the URL.

Internet Explorer also attempts to complete URLs that you only partially type. For example, if you type the incomplete URL "www.whitehouse.gov," Internet Explorer connects you to http://www.whitehouse.gov/WH/Welcome.html, the Welcome page at the White House Web site.

REFERENCE WINDOW   **RW**

Entering a URL
- Type a URL into the Address box, and click the Go button.
- *or*
- Type a URL into the Address box, and press Enter.

Michelle wants to show the workshop attendees how to connect to a specific site on the Web. She has placed a page on a server on the Web for you to use during the workshop demonstration. Its URL is http://www.course.com/NewPerspectives/IE5. You will type this URL directly in the Address box on the Address bar.

To connect to a Web page using a URL:

1. Launch Internet Explorer and be sure the Standard and Address toolbars are visible and the buttons display icons with text labels.

   TROUBLE? If you need help starting Internet Explorer or setting its options, refer to the appropriate sections earlier in this tutorial.

2. Click the **Address** box to highlight the current entry, which should be the URL for your home page.

TROUBLE? If the current entry is not highlighted, highlight it manually by dragging the mouse from the far left to the far right of the URL. You must highlight the entire entry so that the new URL you type replaces the current entry.

3. Type **http://www.course.com/NewPerspectives/IE5** in the Address box. Be sure to type the URL exactly. Notice that two forward slashes always follow the protocol identifier.

TROUBLE? If Internet Explorer displays an Address list that contains the URL you are typing, someone has already entered that URL on the computer you are using. For now, ignore the list and type the correct URL in the Address box.

4. Click the **Go** button. Internet Explorer connects you to the Web page at the address you typed. The status bar tracks the progress of the connection and informs you when the page finishes loading. See Figure 1-20.

TROUBLE? If you cannot connect to the Web page, you may have typed the URL incorrectly. Repeat Steps 2 through 4, and be sure that the URL in the Address box matches the one shown in Figure 1-20. You can correct a minor error by double-clicking in the Address box, using the arrow keys to move to the error, and then making the correction. If the URL matches Figure 1-20 exactly, or if you see a different error message, press the Enter key to try connecting to the Web page again. The server storing the Web page may be busy, so keep reading to learn what may have happened.

Figure 1-20	OPENING A WEB PAGE WITH ITS URL

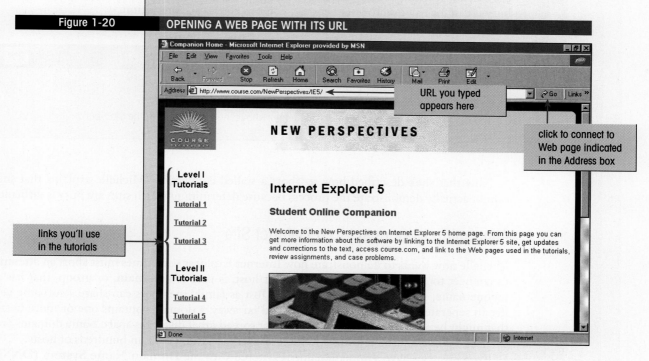

links you'll use in the tutorials

Aborting a Connection

When you enter a URL or click a link that targets a Web page, three outcomes are possible:

1. You successfully reach your target. Internet Explorer contacts the server, locates the file, transfers it from the server to your computer, and displays it on your screen.

2. The server is busy and perhaps overwhelmed with too many requests. You'll need to try again later.

3. The URL targets a file that doesn't exist or has been moved. Documents that become obsolete are often removed from Web servers or moved to new locations. The links that point to those documents are not always updated. Web hosts are also sometimes taken out of service. Some inactive sites supply an informational page that tells you the site is no longer active; others let you know that the URL has changed and provide the new URL; still others supply no forwarding information.

Like an expressway, the Internet sometimes becomes so congested that the paths cannot support the number of users at peak times. When this happens, traffic backs up and slows to a halt, in effect closing the road. **Aborting**, or interrupting, a connection is like taking the next exit ramp on the Internet. When the response time seems too slow (longer than a few minutes) or nothing seems to be happening, you have no way of knowing how long connection will take. You can tell that a link is stalled when the activity indicator is animated, but the status bar makes no progress. Rather than wait for a site that has a long queue or is so busy it cannot respond to your request, you can abort the connection.

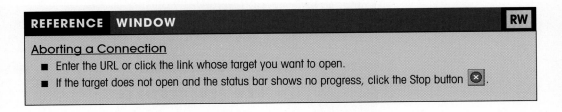

Now that she's described how to abort a stalled connection, Michelle explains that she cannot actually demonstrate the process because determining which sites are busy is difficult.

Attempting to Connect to a Defunct Site

Michelle now wants to demonstrate how Internet Explorer sometimes must abort an attempt to connect to a Web page. Every server, or host, is part of a **domain**, or group, that has a unique name, similar to a family surname. Just as family members can share a surname yet live in separate households both nearby and far away, a domain contains one or more hosts that might be at the same physical location or spread great distances apart. Some domains are small and contain just a few hosts. Others are very large and contain hundreds of hosts.

Each host can have a domain name registered with the **Domain Name System (DNS)**, a distributed database of domain names that lets computers locate each other. When you link to a site, Internet Explorer checks to see if the domain name in its URL is registered with the DNS. If Internet Explorer cannot find the necessary DNS information to locate the server indicated by the URL, it terminates the connection and informs you that it cannot find the page.

Michelle wants to demonstrate what happens when you attempt to connect to a nonexistent site.

To attempt to connect to a nonexistent site:

1. Click the **Tutorial 1** link in the left frame of the Web page to open Michelle's Teachers Workshop online Web page, which is shown in Figure 1-21.

| Figure 1-21 | MICHELLE'S TEACHERS WORKSHOP WEB PAGE |

link targets a nonexistent site

links to Web pages Michelle has prepared for the workshop

2. Click the **closed or abandoned site** link. Internet Explorer responds by opening an informational page, shown in Figure 1-22.

| Figure 1-22 | MESSAGE REGARDING TERMINATED LINK |

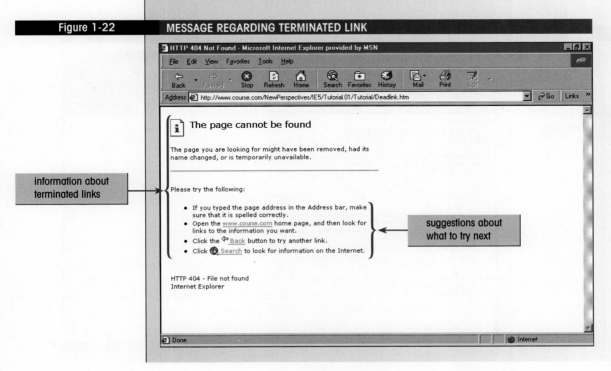

information about terminated links

suggestions about what to try next

Moving Among Web Pages

In Internet Explorer, you can flip through Web pages you've visited in a session as though they were pages in a magazine. Rather than memorizing and retyping URLs of sites you have visited, you can use toolbar buttons to move back one page at a time through the pages, move forward again one page at a time, or return to the "front cover" of your home page. Internet Explorer "remembers" which pages you've visited during your current Web session and provides navigation buttons on the Standard toolbar so that you can easily move through those pages. See Figure 1-23.

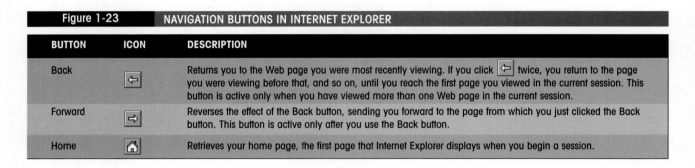

Figure 1-23		NAVIGATION BUTTONS IN INTERNET EXPLORER
BUTTON	**ICON**	**DESCRIPTION**
Back	⇐	Returns you to the Web page you were most recently viewing. If you click ⇐ twice, you return to the page you were viewing before that, and so on, until you reach the first page you viewed in the current session. This button is active only when you have viewed more than one Web page in the current session.
Forward	⇒	Reverses the effect of the Back button, sending you forward to the page from which you just clicked the Back button. This button is active only after you use the Back button.
Home	🏠	Retrieves your home page, the first page that Internet Explorer displays when you begin a session.

To visit and then move among visited Web pages:

1. Point to the **Back** button ⇐. Internet Explorer identifies the page to which you will return. See Figure 1-24.

   TROUBLE? If you click the small arrow to the right of the Back button, a list opens that shows previously visited sites. Click the arrow again to close the list, and repeat Step 5. This time be sure to click ⇐, not the arrow.

Figure 1-24	POINTING TO THE BACK BUTTON

name of the page to which you will return

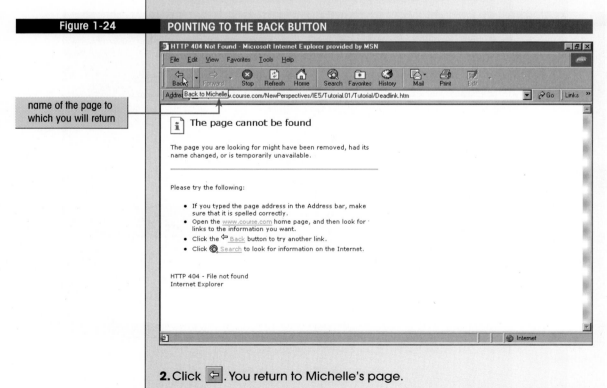

2. Click ⇐. You return to Michelle's page.

3. Art teacher Lyle Gonzales requests a look at the Gargoyle Collection, so click **The Gargoyle Collection** link. The Gargoyle Collection page opens, as shown in Figure 1-25.

Figure 1-25

LINKING TO A PAGE ON THE WEB

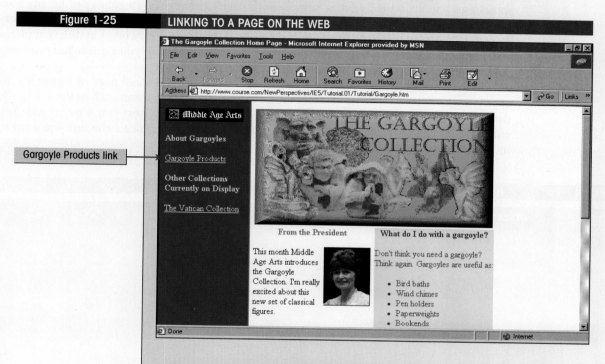

4. Click the **Gargoyle Products** link on the left side of the page. A product list appears. Notice the link to a text version of the page. Click the **text version** link. This page appears almost instantaneously, because there are no graphics to load.

5. Click ⇐ twice. You return to the Gargoyle Collection home page.

6. Click ⇐ until you return to your home page. Notice that the Back button dims, indicating that you have reached the first page you viewed since you started Internet Explorer. You can move back only as far as the home page.

7. You have moved backward through the earlier pages and now want to return to the text version of the Gargoyle Products page. Click the **Forward** button ⇒ until you reach it. Notice that the Forward button is dimmed, indicating that you are looking at the last page you visited.

8. Click the **Home** button 🏠 to return to your home page.

TROUBLE? If the Home button is dimmed, your Internet Explorer installation does not designate a home page location, and the initial page content area when you started Internet Explorer was blank. Just continue with the tutorial.

Printing a Web Page

Although reducing paper consumption is an advantage of browsing for information online, sometimes you'll find it useful to print a Web page. Although Web pages can be any size, printers tend to use 8½" × 11" paper. When you print, Internet Explorer automatically reformats the Web page text to fit the page dimensions. Because lines may break at different places or text size may change, the printed Web page may be longer than you expect. You can specify the number of pages you want to print in the Print dialog box.

You can also specify header text to appear at the top of the printed page or footer text to appear at the bottom. The header and footer can contain information such as the URL, the date, the current page number, the total pages number, and any text you want to add. You enter header and footer text in the Page Setup dialog box. You indicate the text you want to include by typing codes like those shown in Figure 1-26.

Figure 1-26	HEADER AND FOOTER CODES
CODE	**DESCRIPTION**
&w	Window title
&u	URL
&d	Date
&t	Time
&p	Current page number
&P	Total number of pages
&b	Centers text immediately following these characters.
&b&b	Centers text immediately following the first three characters, and right-justifies text following the second &b.

The Print dialog box also gives you the option to print all linked documents and a table of links, which lists all links in the document.

Lyle is interested in purchasing the Gargoyle Judge for his classroom, so he asks if you could print the text version of the Gargoyle Products page.

To print a Web page:

1. Return to the text version of the Gargoyle Products page.

2. Click **File** and then click **Page Setup**. Notice whether header and footer information appears in the Header and Footer boxes. If not, type **&w&bPage &p of &P** in the Header box and **&u&b&d** in the Footer box. This instructs Internet Explorer to print the window title, current page number, and total pages number in the header, and the URL and date in the footer. See Figure 1-27.

   TROUBLE? If different codes appear in the Header and Footer boxes, leave the entries as they are but be sure the URL code (&u) appears somewhere.

Figure 1-27	PAGE SETUP DIALOG BOX

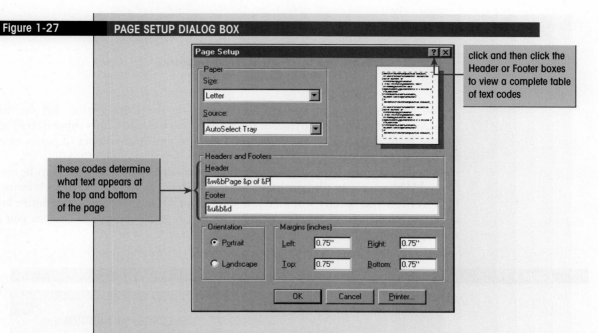

these codes determine what text appears at the top and bottom of the page

click and then click the Header or Footer boxes to view a complete table of text codes

3. Click **OK** to close the Page Setup dialog box.

4. Click **File** and then click **Print**. Notice the available printing options, especially the Print Range default setting of All. If the Web page were longer and you wanted to print only the first page, you could click the Pages option button, and enter 1 in both the from and to boxes. See Figure 1-28.

Figure 1-28	PRINT DIALOG BOX

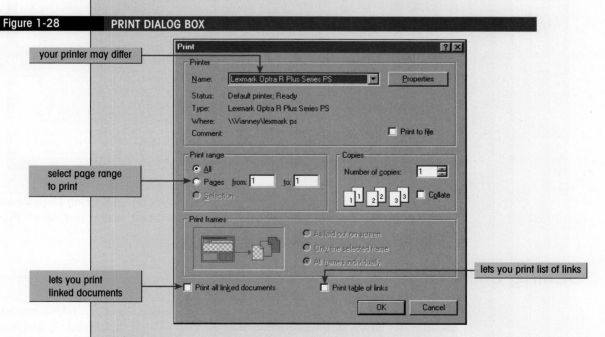

your printer may differ

select page range to print

lets you print linked documents

lets you print list of links

TROUBLE? If your Print dialog box looks somewhat different than Figure 1-28, don't worry. The Print dialog box changes to reflect the options available for the printer you are using. Continue with Step 5.

5. Be sure the **Print all linked documents** and **Print table of links** check boxes are deselected.

6. Click the **OK** button to print the Web page.

You can also print a page quickly by clicking the Print button 🖨 on the toolbar. However, the Print button bypasses the Print dialog box and prints using default settings, so use the Print button only when you don't need to limit the number of pages, choose a different printer, or change any other print settings.

When you want to print a Web page that contains frames, you need to be aware that a framed Web page actually consists of several Web pages—one page in each frame. Internet Explorer lets you specify whether you want to print all the frames (the entire layout), the selected frame, or each frame individually. Figure 1-29 shows the choices you can make when printing a page with frames.

| Figure 1-29 | PRINTING A FRAMED PAGE |

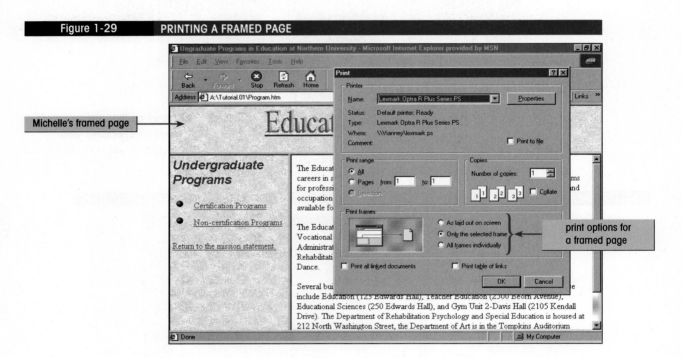

If you want to print only the text information about the Education Department, you can click within that frame's borders and then in the Print dialog box select the Only the selected frame option button.

Getting Online Help

Charlotte DuMont, another instructor at the workshop, has been taking notes on how to use Internet Explorer, but she wants to know what to do if she needs help and no one familiar with Internet Explorer is around.

Michelle explains that Internet Explorer's Help system is an online reference. You can open the Help window from the Help menu or click the Help buttons found in certain dialog boxes. The Help system provides Table of Contents, Index, and Search tabs. Similar to a book's, Internet Explorer's Table of Contents tab lists the main topics and subtopics in the

Help system, grouped by topic. The Index tab, like a book's index, lists Help topics alphabetically. You can type a topic in the Index box to jump to indexed topics on that entry. Finally, the Search tab lets you type a keyword and then locates all topics containing that keyword.

After you find the Help topic you want, it "floats" on top of the screen so you can refer to the suggested steps as you work. You can click the Hide button on the Help toolbar to reduce the Help window's size.

Charlotte has heard that you can load Web pages without images to save download time. She wants to know how to do this, because the computer and modem she will use at home for the rest of the semester are older and slower. She asks you to help her find information about this option. You suggest looking up the word "pictures" in the Index.

To get online Help:

1. Click **Help**, then click **Contents and Index**. The Help window opens.

2. If necessary, click the **Index** tab. See Figure 1-30.

Figure 1-30   HELP WINDOW INDEX

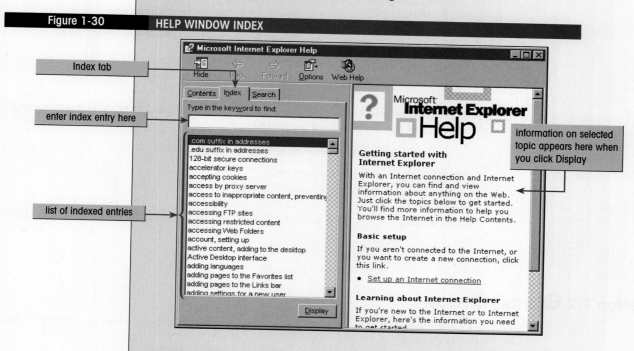

3. Type **pictures** in the box, and wait until you see the word "pictures" highlighted in the Index list. Notice that the Help system scrolls to match the letters as you type them.

   TROUBLE? If necessary, scroll down the Index list to view all pictures entries.

4. Click the entry **hiding to display pages faster**, and then click the **Display** button. The information you need appears in the Index pane on the right side of the Help window. Read the text to learn how to turn off graphics to display Web pages faster. See Figure 1-31.

Figure 1-31	HELP TOPIC

5. Click the **Options** button. Notice that a menu appears, giving you the opportunity to print the Help topic if you wish.

6. Click the **Close** button in the Help window [X] to close Help.

7. Click [X] to close Internet Explorer.

The workshop ends with a general discussion about incorporating the Internet in the schools.

Session 1.2 QUICK CHECK

1. Someone gives you the URL of an interesting Web page. How can you view that Web page?

2. What is the protocol of the URL http://www.irs.ustreas.gov/prod/cover.html? What is the server address? What is the name of the Web page file? In which folder is it located?

3. What is FTP?

4. When you see a URL containing ".edu," what do you know about that site's Web server?

5. You can easily flip through Web pages using the _____, _____, and _____ toolbar buttons.

6. True or False: You can specify how many pages of a Web page you want to print.

REVIEW ASSIGNMENTS

Michelle wants to gear her next workshop toward elementary educators. She asks if you can help by exploring the links on her page to see if any site is appropriate for use as an interesting demonstration piece.

1. If necessary, launch Internet Explorer.

Explore

2. Open the Web page at the URL http://www.course.com/NewPerspectives/IE5. (*Hint:* if you already typed this URL, click the Address bar list arrow and then click the URL.)

3. Click the Review Assignments and Case Problems link, located on the left side of the page.

4. Click The Lincoln Museum of Natural History link, and scroll through the page when it is done loading.

5. Notice the set of graphic links at the bottom of the page, shown in Figure 1-32. Explore each link and record the museum's location and its types of exhibits. Use the Back and Forward buttons as necessary.

Figure 1-32

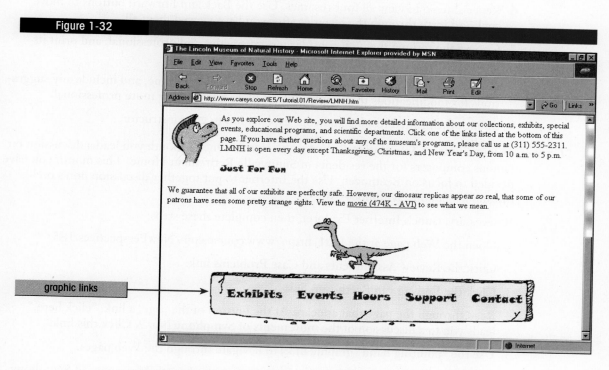

graphic links

7. Print the Contact page so Michelle can contact the museum if she has questions.

8. On your printout, circle the phone extension a teacher should use to schedule a group tour.

9. Use the Back button to return to the Review Assignments and Case Problems page.

Explore

10. Use the Help Index to find more information on using the AutoComplete feature. After you display a Help topic on the AutoComplete feature, click the Options button on the Help window toolbar and then click Print. Click OK to print the information you found.

CASE PROBLEMS

Case 1. *Mary Taylor's Resume* Your old high school friend, Mary Taylor, just graduated from Colorado State University, with a Masters Degree in International Communications. She is scheduled to interview for a job in a few weeks. She has prepared four versions of an online resume, using different background colors and layouts, and has asked you to view them to help her decide which she should use.

If necessary, start Internet Explorer, then complete these steps:

1. Open the Web page at the URL http://www.course.com/NewPerspectives/IE5.

2. Click the Review Assignments and Case Problems link.

3. Click the Online Resumes link.

4. Scroll through the first resume.

5. At the bottom of the resume is a link to the next resume. Click this link.

6. Repeat Step 6 to view all four resumes. Use the Back and Forward buttons to move back and forth through the resumes after you have viewed them all.

7. Choose the resume that you consider most attractive and professional, and print its first page.

8. On the printed copy, explain what you liked about that resume, and include any suggestions for modifications that would make it more attractive or more professional.

9. Submit the printed resume and your explanation to your instructor.

Case 2. *Music Class at Sunnyville Retirement Home* Once a month you lead a discussion on famous composers for the residents of Sunnyville Retirement Home. This month you have decided to focus on Beethoven. Use the Internet to put together discussion notes on his life and his famous Symphony No. 9.

If necessary, launch Internet Explorer, then complete these steps:

1. Open the Web page at the URL http://www.course.com/NewPerspectives/IE5.

2. Click the Review Assignments and Case Problems link.

3. Click the Ludwig van Beethoven link.

4. Read through the page that appears. At the bottom of the page, a link, "click here," leads you to a discussion of the movements of Symphony No. 9. Click this link.

5. Use the "pointing hand" graphic links to navigate through the Web pages.

6. Print the Web page that contains information on the Fourth Movement of Symphony No. 9.

7. On the back of your printout, write two key points about Beethoven's life.

8. Submit your printout and key points to your instructor.

Case 3. *Avalon Books* Avalon Books was recently sold, and its new owner, Jackie Freitag, just hired you to help orchestrate monthly promotional events at the bookstore. Jackie tells you the previous owner posted a calendar of events for the month of May on the Web. She asks you to examine the calendar and report back to her on scheduled events.

If necessary, launch Internet Explorer, then complete these steps:

1. Open the Web page at the URL http://www.course.com/NewPerspectives/IE5.

2. Click the Review Assignments and Case Problems link.

3. Click the Avalon Books link.

4. Scroll to the bottom of the Avalon Books page, and click the May Events Calendar link.

5. Print the May Events calendar, and submit it to your instructor.

Case 4. Science Club You are a freshman at Dayton University who just saw a flyer posted for the Science Club. The flyer included a URL for the Science Club Web site. Because you are interested in joining, you decide to connect to the Web site.

1. Open the Web page at the URL http://www.course.com/NewPerspectives/IE5.

2. Click the Review Assignments and Case Problems link.

3. Click the Science Club link.

4. Navigate through the special events links at the bottom of the page.

5. Decide which event you'd like to attend. Set the correct print options, and then print the first page of information on this event.

6. Submit your printout to your instructor.

LAB ASSIGNMENTS

The Internet: World Wide Web

This Lab Assignment is designed to accompany the interactive Course Lab called Internet World Wide Web. To start the Lab, click the Start button on the taskbar, point to Programs, point to Course Labs, point to New Perspectives Applications, then click Internet World Wide Web. If you do not see Course Labs on your Programs menu, see your instructor or technical support person.

The Internet World Wide Web One of the most popular services on the Internet is the World Wide Web. This lab is a Web simulator that teaches you how to use Web browser software to find information. You can use this lab whether or not your school provides you with Internet access.

1. Click the Steps button to learn how to use Web browser software. As you proceed through the steps, answer all the Quick Check questions that appear. After you complete the steps, you will see a Quick Check Summary Report. Follow the instructions on the screen to print this report.

2. Click the Explore button on the Welcome screen. Use the Web browser to locate a weather map of the Caribbean Virgin Islands. What is its URL?

3. SCUBA diver Wadson Lachouffe has been searching for the fabled treasure of Greybeard the Pirate. A link from the Adventure Travel Web site leads to Wadson's Web page called "Hidden Treasure." Click the Explore button. Locate the Hidden Treasure page, and answer these questions:

   a. What was Greybeard's ship named?
   b. What was Greybeard's favorite food?
   c. What does Wadson think happened to Greybeard's ship?

4. In the steps, you found a graphic of Jupiter from the photo archives of the Jet Propulsion Laboratory. In the Explore section of the lab, you can also find a graphic of Saturn. Suppose one of your friends wanted a picture of Saturn for an astronomy report. Make a list of the blue, underlined links your friend must click to find the Saturn graphic. Assume that your friend will begin at the Web Trainer home page.

5. Enter the URL "http://www.atour.com" to jump to the Adventure Travel Web site. Write a one-page description of this site. In your paper include a description of information at the site, the number of pages the site contains, and a diagram of the links it contains.

6. Chris Thomson, a student at UVI, has his own Web pages. In Explore, look at the information Chris included on his pages. Suppose you could create your own Web page. What would you include? Use word-processing software to design your own Web pages. Make sure you indicate the graphics and links you would use.

QUICK | CHECK ANSWERS

Session 1.1

1. an Internet Service Provider, a company that sells Internet access and other Internet services

2. False

3. the Web page that appears when you start Internet Explorer or the page that a person, organization, or business creates to give information about itself

4. in a different color

5. They let the user see different areas of information simultaneously.

Session 1.2

1. Type it in the Address box, and then press Enter.

2. protocol: http; server address: www.irs.ustreas.gov; filename: cover.html; folder: prod

3. File Transfer Protocol, used to transfer files

4. It is an educational institution.

5. Back, Forward, and Home

6. True

OBJECTIVES

In this tutorial you will:

- Use Web navigational guides

- Browse and return to sites using the Back and Forward lists, Address list, and History Explorer bar

- Create a Favorites collection to locate previously visited pages

- View external files and check file associations

- View audio and video clips with Media Player, view the Web Events page, and listen to a radio broadcast

- Search the Web for Web pages, addresses, and maps using queries and subject guides

- Save text and images in files

- Consider common file transfer concerns, including file compression, viruses, copyrights, and shareware

FINDING INFORMATION ON THE WEB

Using the Internet as a Resource at Allied Technologies Corporation

CASE

Allied Technologies Corporation

You work in the Public Relations Department at Allied Technologies Corporation, a communications solutions business on the East Coast. Allied sells and installs business phone systems, universal cabling, sound and paging systems, and security systems. Your supervisor, Miriam Ochoa, plans to develop a series of brochures that shows how ordinary people benefit from effective communications solutions. Allied has an in-house technical photographer but no archive of human-interest photographs needed for the brochure, so Miriam asked you to locate a photography company that does subcontract work.

You are fairly new to the area and unsure where to start, so over lunch you mention your assignment to a co-worker, Aaron Machotka. Aaron recommends Mayer Photography, a nearby studio, and assures you he's always been pleased with their service. Aaron remarks that they have a Web site with samples of their work. When you ask for the URL, he tells you he probably has it back at the office and promises to give it to you.

As you stroll back to the office, Aaron mentions that you also might consider exploring the medium of digital photography. Digital cameras bypass the chemical processes of film and record the image electronically. With digital photography, you can create images in a universal format that are easy to transfer between all kinds of devices and applications. For example, you can easily insert digital images into word-processing documents, e-mail them to associates, or post them on Web sites. In addition, you can use image-editing software to improve or alter images. You agree that Miriam might be especially interested in those possibilities. Aaron tells you he has found a number of interesting Web sites on the subject and suggests that you rummage around the digital photography resources on the Web.

SESSION 2.1

In this session, you will use a navigational guide, browse sites, learn efficient ways to return to sites, and add, use, and delete links to favorite pages in the Favorites folder. You will also explore your computer's file associations, listen to an audio clip, view a video clip, explore the Web events page, and listen to a radio broadcast.

Using a Navigational Guide

Aaron drops by your cubicle shortly after lunch with the URL for Mayer Photography. You decide to start your research by connecting to the Mayer Photography site.

To connect to the Mayer Photography site:

1. Start Internet Explorer and, if necessary, connect to the Internet.

2. Maximize the Internet Explorer window, replace the current entry in the Address box on the Address toolbar with the URL **http://www.course.com/NewPerspectives/IE5**, then press **Enter**.

3. Click the **Tutorial 2** link to open the Mayer Photography home page. See Figure 2-1.

Figure 2-1	MAYER PHOTOGRAPHY HOME PAGE

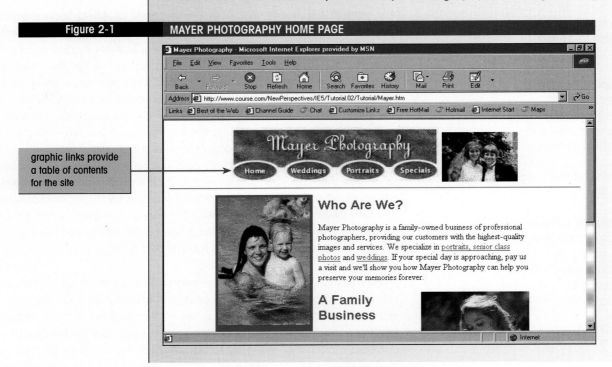

graphic links provide a table of contents for the site

Most well-developed Web sites include a table of contents on their home pages that gives overviews of the sites' contents. Some sites also include a **site map**, a graphical layout of all resources available at the site. Because Mayer Photography's site is fairly small, the graphical links at the top serve as its table of contents.

Now that you found a good resource to start with, you decide to explore other photography sites on the Web. Microsoft Corporation routinely scouts the Internet for useful or interesting sites and then places links to those URLs on pages that you can access from the Links toolbar. The Links toolbar includes buttons such as Best of the Web, which opens a page on the Microsoft Network that showcases interesting Web pages, divided into topics such as education, entertainment, health, and sports. Microsoft updates the Best of the Web page regularly. You can find similar lists on the WWW compiled by other groups or individuals. A list or index of Web pages organized around a general theme or subject is called a **navigational guide**.

You decide to explore the Best of the Web navigational guide for other photography resources.

To look at the Best of the Web page:

1. Click the **Best of the Web** button on the Links toolbar. The navigational guide appears on the left of the page. See Figure 2-2.

   TROUBLE? If the Links toolbar does not appear on your screen, click View, point to Toolbars, then click Links to display the Links toolbar. Drag the Links toolbar below the Address toolbar, if necessary.

   TROUBLE? If the Best of the Web button does not appear on the Links toolbar, connect to the Microsoft Network Web page at http://www.msn.com and then click the Web Directory button.

| Figure 2-2 | BEST OF THE WEB PAGE |

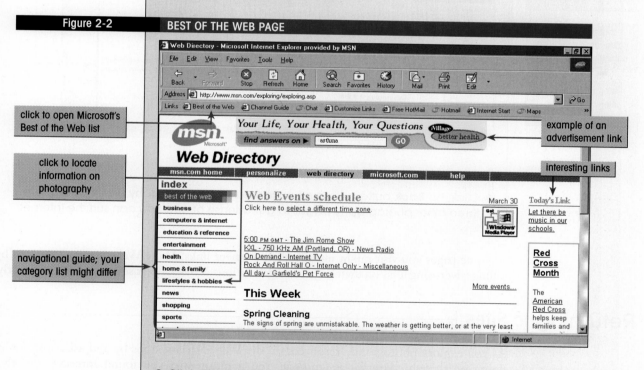

click to open Microsoft's Best of the Web list

click to locate information on photography

navigational guide; your category list might differ

example of an advertisement link

interesting links

2. Click **lifestyles & hobbies** or, if that category doesn't appear, click another category that you think might feature pages on photography.

3. Click the **Hobbies and crafts** link or, if that category doesn't appear, click another category that you think might feature pages on photography. The page is updated regularly, so your page will look different from the one shown in Figure 2-2.

   TROUBLE? If you click a link at any time during this tutorial and a dialog box opens asking if you want to install software or warning you about a potential security bug, click whatever button is appropriate to continue working on the tutorial. If you try to connect to a page and it opens in a separate Internet Explorer window, work in that window, but realize that you might need to close extra Internet Explorer windows at the end of your session. Some links are programmed to appear in a new window.

4. If necessary, scroll down the hobbies subcategory list, and click **Photography**. The Photography page lists Web sites on the subject of photography. See Figure 2-3. The Microsoft team added these sites to its Best of the Web list because the Web pages are interesting, humorous, eye-catching, or unusual in some other way.

| Figure 2-3 | PHOTOGRAPHY PAGE |

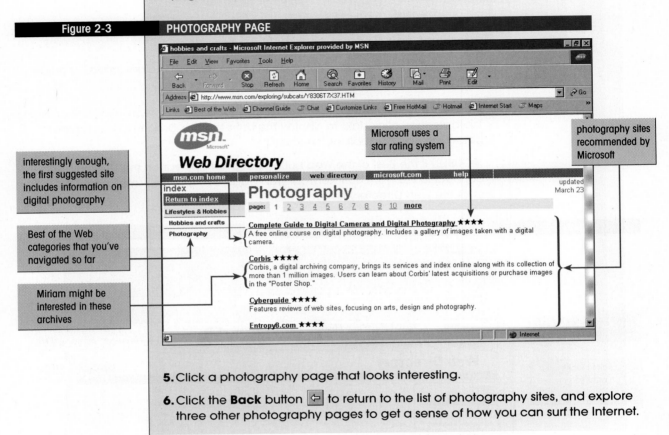

5. Click a photography page that looks interesting.

6. Click the **Back** button ⬅ to return to the list of photography sites, and explore three other photography pages to get a sense of how you can surf the Internet.

Some pages you visit might include advertisement links. Many Web sites earn revenue by selling advertising links on their pages to organizations. These advertisements change regularly.

Returning to Sites

As you explore photography resources on the Web, Miriam stops by and asks how you're doing on the photography assignment. You mention that you found Internet sites that archive thousands of photos, as well as information on digital photography. She is interested, but asks if you found information on any local photographers. You mention Mayer Photography and tell her about their Web site. She would like to see it.

You've already seen how to use the Back button to return to a previously visited site. Internet Explorer also maintains a list of the most recent sites you visited since launching Internet Explorer, so returning to the pages is easy.

Using the Back and Forward Lists

The Back and Forward buttons each contain arrows that you can click to open Back and Forward lists, which show all pages going back to a certain point and all pages going forward to a certain point. This option lets you return to a page you viewed earlier in the session with a single click. Although you can click the Back button repeatedly to return to a page, the Back or Forward list is usually quicker if you've navigated multiple Web pages. If you haven't yet navigated any pages in the current session, however, the Back and Forward buttons are gray, indicating they are unavailable.

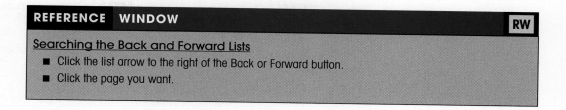

You'll use the Back list to return quickly to the Mayer Photography site.

To use the Back and Forward lists:

1. Click the list arrow to the right of the Back button. The Back list appears. See Figure 2-4. Your Back list will differ, depending on which sites you linked to using the Best of the Web pages.

Figure 2-4   **BACK LIST**

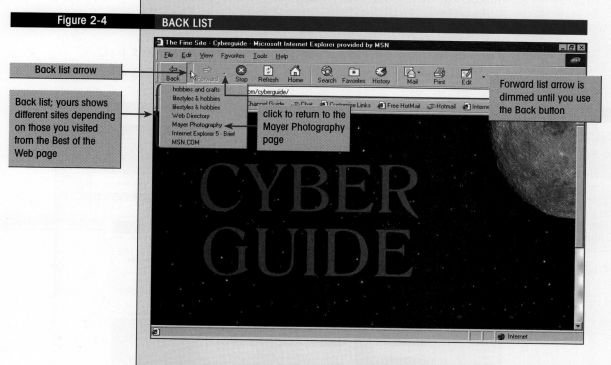

Back list arrow

Back list; yours shows different sites depending on those you visited from the Best of the Web page

hobbies and crafts
lifestyles & hobbies
lifestyles & hobbies
Web Directory
Mayer Photography
Internet Explorer 5 - Brief
MSN.COM

click to return to the Mayer Photography page

Forward list arrow is dimmed until you use the Back button

2. Click **Mayer Photography** on the Back list. Miriam likes the samples she sees on this site and asks you about some other information you've found.

TROUBLE? If you can't find the Mayer Photography home page on the Back list, you might have surfed too many sites. Internet Explorer only lists the most frequently visited sites. Enter http://www.course.com/NewPerspectives/IE5 in the Address box, then press Enter. Click the Tutorial 2 link. If the URL fills in automatically as you type, the AutoComplete feature is running on your computer. Internet Explorer's AutoComplete feature fills in a URL automatically if the URL matches one you've entered before.

3. Click the **Forward** list arrow, then click a photography site you visited.

As Miriam watches you navigate the pages you found, she pulls up a chair and sits next to you, confessing that she doesn't have much experience using the Web. Surprised by how easily you're getting around, she asks if you could show her more about navigating Web pages.

Using the Address List

Miriam has already seen how to use the Back and Forward lists, so you decide to show her the Address list. Any time you type an address in the Address box, Internet Explorer remembers it so you don't have to type it again. You can click the Address list arrow on the Address bar to view the Address list. Only sites whose addresses you typed appear on the Address list.

To return to the Course site using the Address list:

1. Click the **Address** list arrow ▼ to open the Address list. See Figure 2-5.

Figure 2-5	ADDRESS LIST

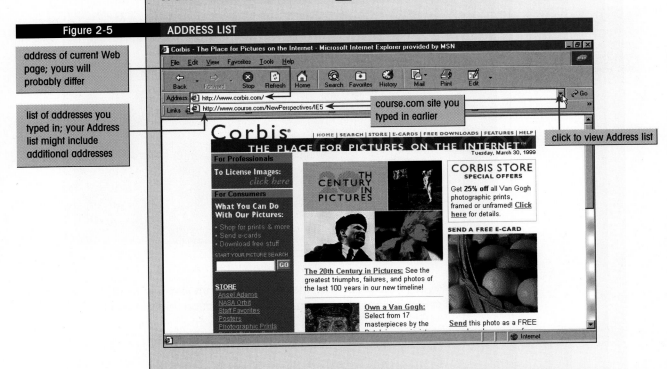

address of current Web page; yours will probably differ

list of addresses you typed in; your Address list might include additional addresses

course.com site you typed in earlier

click to view Address list

2. Click the URL for course.com in the list that appears. You return to the Course site for this tutorial.

3. Click the **Tutorial 2** link to return to the Mayer Photography site.

Using the History Explorer Bar

The Back and Forward lists only recall the sites you most recently visited in the current session (the number of sites on the menu depends on your browser's settings). To view information on all recently visited links, including those you visited in previous sessions, you can view the History Explorer bar. **Explorer bars** appear on the left of your screen and contain lists of links that help you find the pages you want. Internet Explorer offers four Explorer bars: Search, Favorites, History, and Folders, all accessible from the View menu. (Don't worry if the Folders Explorer bar doesn't appear; you won't be using it in this tutorial.) The History Explorer bar provides a list of the servers you've visited each day for the number of days specified in your browser's settings.

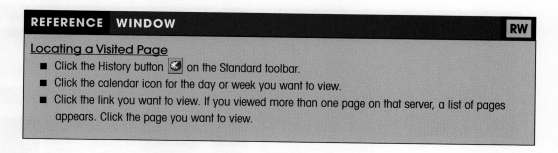

REFERENCE WINDOW **RW**

Locating a Visited Page
- Click the History button 🌐 on the Standard toolbar.
- Click the calendar icon for the day or week you want to view.
- Click the link you want to view. If you viewed more than one page on that server, a list of pages appears. Click the page you want to view.

You want to show Miriam how she can use the History Explorer bar to return to a page.

To open the History Explorer bar:

1. Click the **History** button 🌐 on the Standard toolbar. The History Explorer bar opens. See Figure 2-6.

| Figure 2-6 | HISTORY EXPLORER BAR |

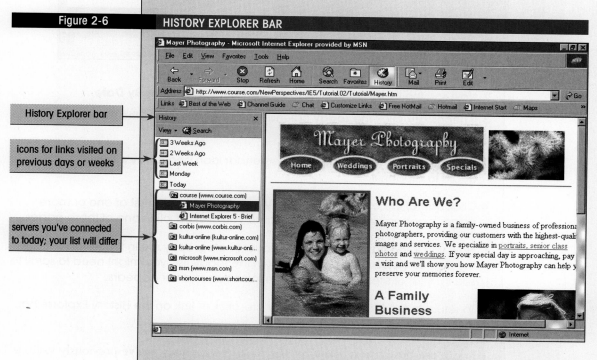

History Explorer bar

icons for links visited on previous days or weeks

servers you've connected to today; your list will differ

2. Drag the History Explorer bar border right or left, if necessary, to widen it and view more of its contents.

By default, the History list is sorted by date. You can, however, change the sort order to view the list alphabetically by site or by frequency of visit. If you know the name of the site you are looking for, you might want to sort the list by site. If, however, you only know that you visited the site within the last few days, you can view by date and then examine the list of sites visited today, yesterday, or on an earlier day or week. First you want to show Miriam the History list sorting options, and then you'll use the History list to return to previously visited sites.

To use the History list to return to a page:

1. Click the **View** button, then click **By Site** to sort the list alphabetically. See Figure 2-7.

| Figure 2-7 | HISTORY LIST SORTED BY SITE |

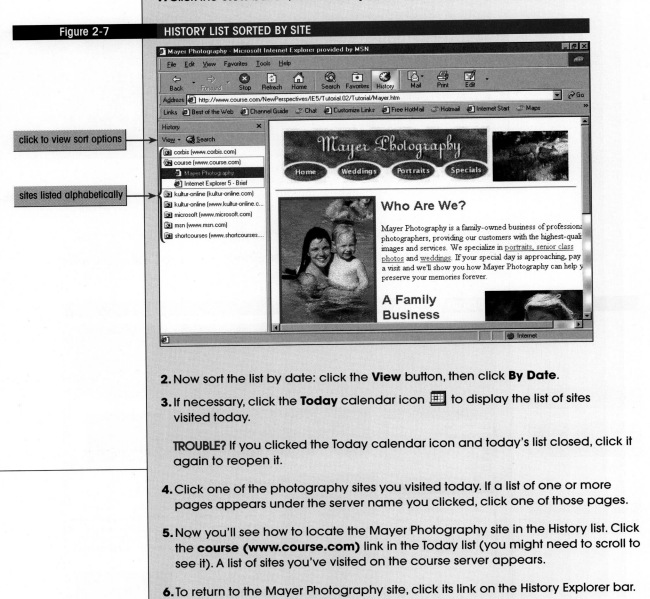

2. Now sort the list by date: click the **View** button, then click **By Date**.

3. If necessary, click the **Today** calendar icon to display the list of sites visited today.

   TROUBLE? If you clicked the Today calendar icon and today's list closed, click it again to reopen it.

4. Click one of the photography sites you visited today. If a list of one or more pages appears under the server name you clicked, click one of those pages.

5. Now you'll see how to locate the Mayer Photography site in the History list. Click the **course (www.course.com)** link in the Today list (you might need to scroll to see it). A list of sites you've visited on the course server appears.

6. To return to the Mayer Photography site, click its link on the History Explorer bar.

You can use the History Explorer bar to search for sites you've previously visited. Try searching for pages on photography.

To search for a specific page in the History Explorer bar:

1. Click the **Search** button [icon] on the History Explorer bar.

2. Type **photography** in the Search for box.

3. Click the **Search Now** button. Pages that include the word "photography" appear on the History Explorer bar. See Figure 2-8.

Figure 2-8	SEARCHING THE HISTORY LIST

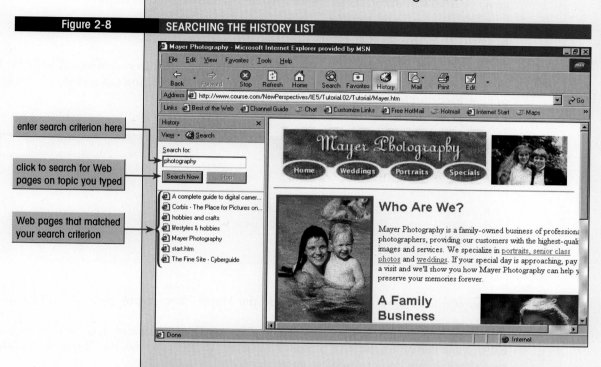

enter search criterion here

click to search for Web
pages on topic you typed

Web pages that matched
your search criterion

4. You could click a photography link to connect to its site, but for now just click the **Close** button [X] on the History Explorer bar to close it.

You've now shown Miriam several methods of returning to sites. She asks under what circumstances you use the various methods. You suggest these guidelines:

- When you want to return to one of the pages you just viewed, use the Back and Forward lists.

- When you want to return to a page that you viewed quite some time ago, or in a different session, such as yesterday or last week, use the History Explorer bar.

- If you want to return to a page whose URL you typed, use the Address bar's list arrow. If you want to type a URL that you've typed before, you can also type just the site's name and then press Ctrl+Enter to use the AutoComplete feature, which attempts to fill in a URL based on a list of previously visited sites. For example, if you entered the Microsoft site at one time and want to return to it, you could type "microsoft" and AutoComplete would fill in http://www.microsoft.com for you.

Miriam asks if you can mark the Mayer Photography site so you can return to it later.

Organizing **Favorite Pages in Folders**

While surfing the Web, you might find an interesting or unusual site to which you want to return. Rather than trying to remember the site's URL, you can add it to your list of favorite pages, stored in the Favorites folder on your hard drive (usually C:\Windows\Favorites). You can access the pages in your Favorites folder from the Favorites menu on the Start menu or from within Internet Explorer, via the Favorites button or menu.

Adding a Page to the Favorites Folder

Adding a page to the Favorites folder is helpful when you want to return to a specific Web site, try other links on that page, or show someone a certain site. You can add any Web page to your Favorites folder by using the Add to Favorites option.

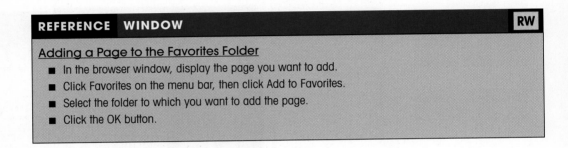

REFERENCE WINDOW | RW

Adding a Page to the Favorites Folder
- In the browser window, display the page you want to add.
- Click Favorites on the menu bar, then click Add to Favorites.
- Select the folder to which you want to add the page.
- Click the OK button.

You decide to show Miriam how to add the Mayer Photography page to the Favorites folder.

In some labs you might not be able to modify your Favorites folder, because your technical support person might have prohibited changes to the Favorites list. If this is the case, read through, but do not complete, these steps.

To add the Mayer Photography page to your Favorites folder:

1. Make sure the Mayer Photography page is the active page, then click **Favorites** on the menu bar.

   TROUBLE? Make sure you click Favorites on the menu bar, not the toolbar. Clicking Favorites on the toolbar opens the Favorites Explorer bar; you don't want to do that yet.

2. Click **Add to Favorites**. The Add Favorite dialog box opens. See Figure 2-9.

   TROUBLE? If the Create in folders list doesn't appear, click the Create in button.

Figure 2-9   **ADDING A PAGE TO THE FAVORITES FOLDER**

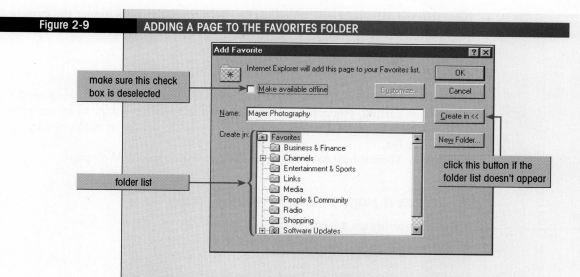

make sure this check box is deselected

folder list

click this button if the folder list doesn't appear

3. Make sure the **Make available offline** check box is deselected.

4. Click the **OK** button to add the current Web page, the Mayer Photography page, to your list of favorites.

5. Click **Favorites** again, if necessary, to open the Favorites menu and display the Favorites list, which now includes Mayer Photography, probably at the end of the list. If your list is quite long, you might need to click the down arrow at the bottom of the Favorites menu to view the Mayer Photography page. Notice that the page is listed by its title, which is more descriptive than its URL. See Figure 2-10.

Figure 2-10   **FAVORITES MENU**

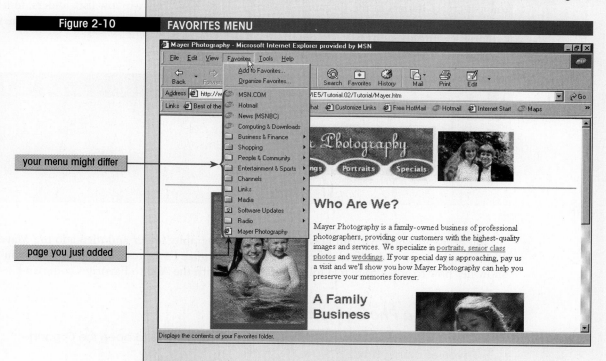

your menu might differ

page you just added

6. Click a blank area of the Internet Explorer window to close the Favorites menu, then click the **Back** button ⇦ several times to move to a different Web page.

Now that the Web page you added to the Favorites folder is no longer the current page, you can show Miriam how to refer back to it.

Accessing a Page in the Favorites Folder

Because the menu bar is available no matter what Web page you are viewing or how long you have been surfing, you can click any page in the Favorites folder to return directly to that Web page. The pages you placed in the Favorites folder are available until you delete them from the list.

You'll show Miriam how to return to the Mayer Photography Web page.

To access a page in the Favorites folder:

1. Click **Favorites** on the menu bar.

2. Click **Mayer Photography**.

Miriam is glad to see that the Favorites folder is so easy to use. She notices, however, that the Favorites folder includes folders in addition to individual pages. She asks you to explain.

Managing Favorites Folders

Most browser users organize their favorite pages into folders grouped by category so finding a certain page is easier. The Favorites collection included with Internet Explorer comes with several folders that contain a variety of interesting links, but you can add your own folders. You can create folders in the Organize Favorites dialog box. This window lists folders, indicated by 🗀, and favorite Web pages, indicated by 📄 or 📄, depending on how Internet Explorer was installed on your computer.

REFERENCE   WINDOW   **RW**

Creating a Folder for Favorite Pages

- Click Favorites on the menu bar, then click Organize Favorites.
- Open the folder in which you want to create the new folder.
- Click the Create Folder button.
- Type the folder name, then press Enter.

You decide to show Miriam how to create a Photography folder and then add the Mayer Photography page to that folder from within the Organize Favorites dialog box. Then you'll show her how to add a page to a folder "on the fly" with the Add to Favorites command.

To create a Photography folder:

1. Click the **Favorites** menu, then click **Organize Favorites** to open the Organize Favorites dialog box.

   TROUBLE? If your Favorites list is too long and you had to scroll down to see the page you added, you might now need to click the up arrow at the top of the menu. Then click Organize Favorites.

2. Click the **Create Folder** button.

3. Type **Photography** in the box, then press **Enter**.

TROUBLE? If nothing happens when you type, right-click New Folder, click Rename, and then type Photography.

4. In the Organize Favorites dialog box, locate and click the **Mayer Photography** page you added to the Favorites folder earlier. (It is probably at the bottom of the list.)

5. Click the **Move to Folder** button. The Browse for Folder dialog box opens. Locate and click the **Photography** folder. See Figure 2-11.

Figure 2-11	ADDING A PAGE TO A FOLDER

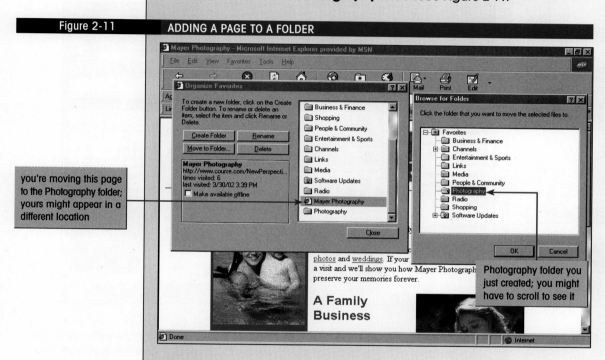

you're moving this page to the Photography folder; yours might appear in a different location

Photography folder you just created; you might have to scroll to see it

6. Click the **OK** button. Internet Explorer moves the Mayer Photography page into the Photography folder.

7. In the Organize Favorites dialog box, click the **Photography** folder you just created to open it. The Mayer Photography page appears, indicating that it is now stored in that folder.

8. Close the Organize Favorites dialog box.

After you add a page to a folder, you access it by opening the Favorites menu and then navigating to the folder you want. The pages in that folder appear in a menu that cascades off to the side of or below the Favorites menu.

You can also access favorite pages from the Favorites Explorer bar. You decide to show Miriam this method.

To access a page stored in a folder using the Favorites Explorer bar:

1. Click the **Back** button ⬅ to go to a different page.

2. Click the **Favorites** button ⊡. The Favorites Explorer bar appears on the left side of the Internet Explorer window.

3. Click **Photography** on the Favorites Explorer bar. The page you stored in the Photography folder appears. See Figure 2-12.

Figure 2-12	FAVORITES EXPLORER BAR

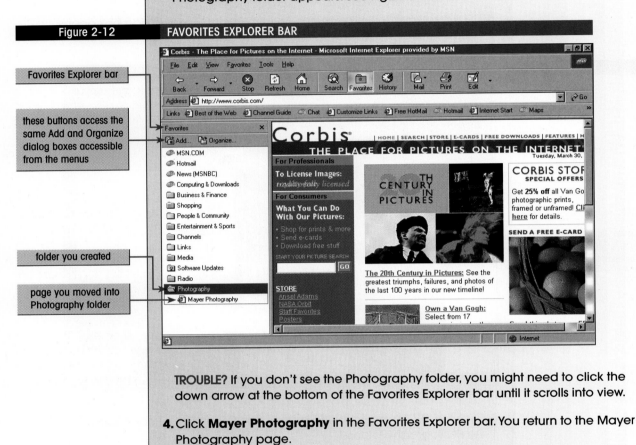

Favorites Explorer bar

these buttons access the same Add and Organize dialog boxes accessible from the menus

folder you created

page you moved into Photography folder

TROUBLE? If you don't see the Photography folder, you might need to click the down arrow at the bottom of the Favorites Explorer bar until it scrolls into view.

4. Click **Mayer Photography** in the Favorites Explorer bar. You return to the Mayer Photography page.

5. Click the Explorer bar **Close** button ✖ to close the Favorites Explorer bar.

You are back at the Mayer Photography page. You've already moved a page to a specific Favorites folder using the Organize Favorites dialog box. Now, you're going to add a page to a specific folder right from the Add Favorite dialog box instead of from the Organize Favorites dialog box. You'll first open a different photography page.

To add a page to a folder from the Add Favorite dialog box:

1. Click the **Back** list arrow, then click one of the photography pages you visited earlier.

TROUBLE? If the photography pages you visited earlier no longer appear, try using the History Explorer bar to locate one. If necessary, you can return to the Best of the Web page and locate a new photography page.

2. Click the **Favorites** menu, then click **Add to Favorites**.

3. Click the **Photography** folder in the Add Favorite dialog box. See Figure 2-13.

| Figure 2-13 | ADDING A PAGE TO THE PHOTOGRAPHY FOLDER |

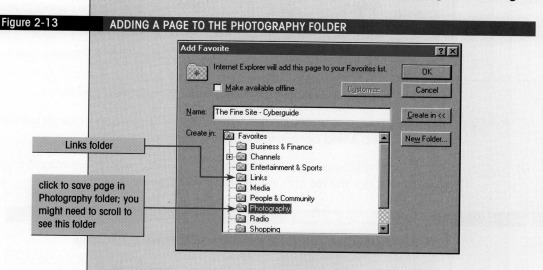

Links folder

click to save page in Photography folder; you might need to scroll to see this folder

4. Click the **OK** button in the Add Favorite dialog box.

5. Test the page you just added. Click the **Back** button several times. Now click the **Favorites** menu, point to **Photography**, and then click the page you just added. You return to that page.

TROUBLE? If your Favorites list is too long, you might need to click the down arrow to locate the Photography folder.

In Figure 2-13, you might have noticed the Links folder in the Organize Folders dialog box. The Links folder contains the sites that appear on the Links toolbar. If you save a URL in the Links folder, you make it available on the Links toolbar. You might want to add sites that you visit most frequently to the Links folder. You'll have an opportunity to try this in the Case Problems.

Adding a Page for Offline Viewing

Miriam comments that you could spend all day reading through interesting sites, but you tell her about an easy way to save sites temporarily on your computer during the day to view later when you are no longer connected to the Internet. Commuters, for example, might find it handy to save their favorite news pages for offline viewing on the train. You can use the Favorites folder as a temporary storage place. When you add a Web page to the Favorites folder for offline viewing, the Offline Favorite Wizard starts.

The Wizard asks if you want to include just the page you are viewing or also the pages targeted by links on the page, including those on other Web sites. You can indicate the number of links deep from the current page that you want to include. For example, if you enter the number 2, Internet Explorer includes the page, all pages targeted by links on the page, and all pages targeted by links on those pages. If you have limited hard disk space or time, you might want to limit the number of linked pages you store.

To show Miriam this feature, you'll start and then cancel the Wizard to save time and space.

To view the Offline Favorite Wizard:

1. Activate the page whose content you want to save for offline viewing. Because you're just practicing using this feature, you can stay on the current page.

2. Click **Favorites** on the menu bar, then click **Add to Favorites**.

3. Click the **Make available offline** check box, then click the **Customize** button. The Offline Favorite Wizard starts.

4. Click the **Next** button to acknowledge the introduction screen.

   TROUBLE? If the first introduction screen doesn't appear, a previous user disabled it. Skip Step 4 and continue to Step 5.

5. Now the Wizard asks you to indicate whether you want to download targeted pages. Click the **No** option button, shown in Figure 2-14.

Figure 2-14	OFFLINE FAVORITE WIZARD

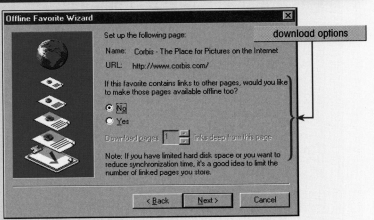

6. Click **Next**. Make sure the **Only when I choose Synchronize** option button is selected.

7. Click **Next**. You are asked if you need to supply a password. Make sure the **No** option button is selected.

8. Click **Cancel**. If you really wanted to include this page for offline viewing, you would click Finish and then click Synchronize from the Tools menu, but you won't do that now.

9. Click **Cancel** again to close the Add Favorite dialog box.

10. Return to the Mayer Photography page.

Miriam asks what you do when you want to tidy up your Favorites folder.

Deleting a Page from the Favorites Folder

Deleting pages from the Favorites folder is almost as easy as adding them. Deleting unused or outdated Web pages is a good idea. This helps keep your list of favorite pages manageable and organized. In the Organize Favorites dialog box, you can delete individual pages or entire folders. If you delete a folder, you also delete all the pages it contains.

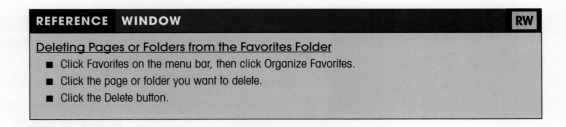

REFERENCE   WINDOW   **RW**

<u>Deleting Pages or Folders from the Favorites Folder</u>
- Click Favorites on the menu bar, then click Organize Favorites.
- Click the page or folder you want to delete.
- Click the Delete button.

You decide to show Miriam how to delete the entire Photography folder.

To delete the Photography folder:

1. Click **Favorites** on the menu bar, then click **Organize Favorites** to open the Organize Favorites dialog box.
2. Click the **Photography** folder.
3. Click the **Delete** button.
4. Click the **Yes** button when asked if you are sure.
5. Close the Organize Favorites dialog box.

Viewing External Files

Miriam now suggests that you look more closely at the services Mayer Photography offers. The page should be active in your browser.

To examine the Mayer Photography page:

1. Scroll down the Mayer Photography page. Notice the Welcome logo at the bottom of the page.
2. Point to the **Welcome** logo, and notice its filename appears at the end of the URL in the status bar as Welcome.wav. See Figure 2-15.

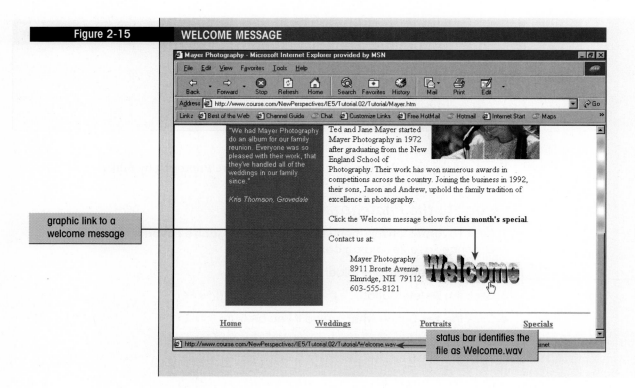

Figure 2-15   WELCOME MESSAGE

graphic link to a
welcome message

status bar identifies the
file as Welcome.wav

You tell Miriam that with the Web you can access many types of files on the Internet, not just Web pages. Internet Explorer can display files such as HTML Web page files and certain types of graphic images. When Internet Explorer encounters an **external file**—a file it cannot display on its own—it searches your computer for other software that can display the file. Internet Explorer uses a three-step process to determine what to do when you click a link that targets an external file:

1. First, Internet Explorer checks the file extension of the link's target. A filename usually has two parts, separated by a dot: the first part is the name itself and the second part is the **file extension**, which is usually 2 to 4 letters long and identifies the file type. A Web page named Index.htm, for example, has the extension .HTM. The file Welcome.wav contains a welcome message, with the extension .WAV.

2. Next, Internet Explorer checks the file extension against a list of file extensions and their corresponding programs that your computer's operating system maintains, called **file associations**.

3. Finally, Internet Explorer checks which program is associated with that file extension and starts that program if it finds it.

For example, if you click a link targeting a DOC file, Internet Explorer might discover that your computer associates DOC files with Microsoft Word word-processing software. Internet Explorer then automatically starts Word. Figure 2-16 illustrates this process.

Figure 2-16   **LINKING TO AN EXTERNAL FILE**

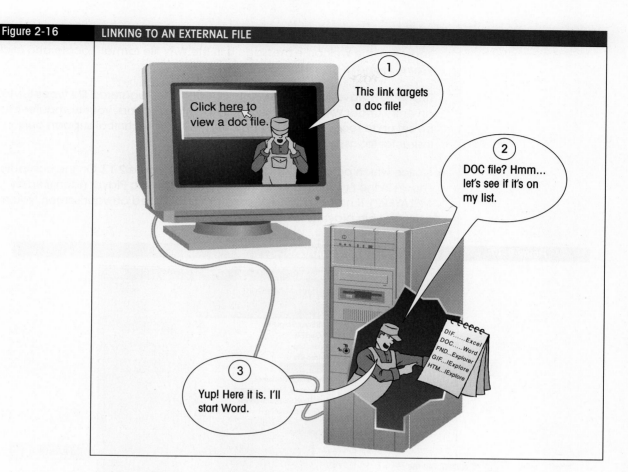

Checking File Associations

You decide to show Miriam the file association list on your computer so she can see which programs are associated with which files. Every computer has a different list, depending on the software it contains. You especially want to show her how sound files with the .WAV extension are handled, because the Welcome link you pointed to targets a WAV sound file.

To check your computer's file associations:

1. Minimize Internet Explorer, then from your computer's desktop, start **My Computer**.

   TROUBLE? How you open My Computer depends on your mouse settings. Try clicking the My Computer icon on the desktop once. If the My Computer window opens, proceed to Step 2. Otherwise, press Enter. The My Computer window should now open.

2. Click **View** on the My Computer menu bar, then click **Folder Options**.

   TROUBLE? If you are using Windows 95, click View and then click Options.

3. Click the **File Types** tab. A list of registered file types appears.

4. Click any file type in the Registered file types list. The File type details area identifies the program that handles that file type.

5. Now you're going to check how WAV sound files are handled, because you know that the Welcome message is in the WAV file format. Locate and click **Wave Sound** in the Registered file types list.

TROUBLE? If Wave Sound does not appear in the Registered file types list, look for an entry under WAV or Sound Clip. If no entry appears, your computer may not be set up to recognize WAV sound files. Ask your technical support person or instructor for assistance.

6. Notice which program handles WAV files. See Figure 2-17. On the computer shown in the figure, WAV files are handled by Media Player (identified by MPLAYER2). If no command or program is identified on your screen, you might have trouble playing WAV files.

| Figure 2-17 | CHECKING FILE ASSOCIATIONS |

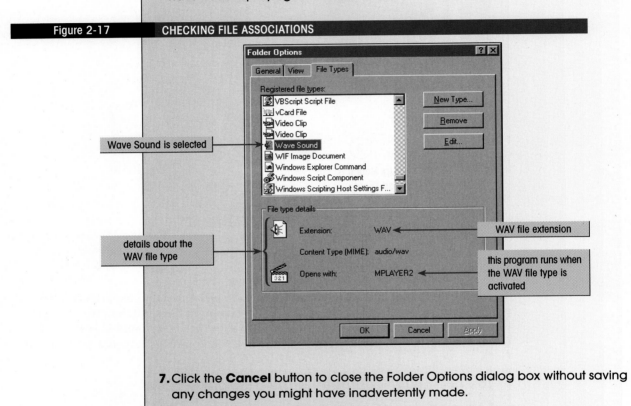

7. Click the **Cancel** button to close the Folder Options dialog box without saving any changes you might have inadvertently made.

8. Close the My Computer window.

You tell Miriam that when you click a link targeting a WAV file, Internet Explorer uses the program indicated in the File type details section to open the file.

Playing **Audio and Video Files**

The most common types of external files you'll probably want to open on the Web (beyond Web pages themselves) are sound and video files. These files let you hear the roar of a lion, the beat of a healthy heart, a promotional movie clip for the next big feature, or a cut from a recently released CD. Any sound or movie on a Web page is actually a file, called an **audio clip** or a **video clip**, respectively. You can store audio and video clips in different formats. Some formats provide better quality but create a larger clip.

Each type of audio or video file needs to be interpreted by a **playback device**, software that identifies the file and its format and then uses the appropriate hardware, such as a sound card, to play it through your computer. The Internet Explorer suite includes an accessory, **Media Player**, that plays audio, video, and mixed-media files in the most popular formats, shown in Figure 2-18.

Figure 2-18	COMMON AUDIO AND VIDEO FILE TYPES

FILE TYPE	FILE EXTENSIONS
Microsoft Windows Media formats	.avi, .asf, .asx, .rmi, .wav
RealNetworks ReadAudio and RealVideo	.ra, .ram, .rm, .rmm
Moving Pictures Experts Group (MPEG)	.mpg, .mpeg, .m1v, .mp2, .mpa, .mpe
Musical Instrument Digital Interface (MIDI)	.mid, .rmi
Apple QuickTime, Macintosh, AIFF Resource	.qt, .aif, .aifc, .aiff, .mov
UNIX formats	.au, .snd

In the past, you had to acquire separate software for each media type. Media Player, however, handles all these file types on request. Moreover, using a technology called **streaming media**, Media Player can begin playing a clip without first transferring the entire file. As the file begins to "stream" onto your computer, Media Player stores the first part in memory and immediately begins to play it. Media Player then stores the rest of the file in memory and plays each part as it becomes available. Often the clip plays so smoothly that you don't even notice a delay. However, if your Internet connection is slow or if Internet traffic is heavy, the clip might play in "fits and starts" as you wait for the next piece to appear. In this case, wait until the entire clip plays so that it is all stored in memory and then replay it.

Your computer might be configured with one or more playback devices other than Media Player. If this is the case and file associations are properly set, when you click an audio or video clip link, the playback device starts automatically and plays the clip. (For some devices, you might need to click the Play button.) However, if your computer does not have the correct playback device for a clip that you click, Internet Explorer warns you and sometimes suggests a source for the necessary software. If your computer isn't equipped to handle audio or video clips, you might receive such a message when working on the next set of steps.

To open the Mayer Photography home page and listen to an audio clip:

1. Maximize the Internet Explorer window, and then click the **Welcome** graphic on the Mayer Photography page. Media Player starts. You might need to wait a minute or two as your playback device starts and loads the audio clip. Figure 2-19 shows the Microsoft playback device. Be patient; it might take a minute.

   TROUBLE? If a playback device opens but you don't hear a sound, try clicking the Play button ▶ . If you still don't hear a sound, your computer might not have audio capabilities or the sound might be turned down (a common practice in computer labs to reduce noise). Check with your instructor or technical support person.

TROUBLE? If a message warns you that the file cannot be accessed, your computer does not recognize this type of audio file and you cannot hear the audio clip. For now, close the dialog box and continue with the tutorial. You might need to acquire a playback device, or you might need to check your computer's file type associations. Use the instructions in the previous section to check the Sound Clip file association.

TROUBLE? If the File Download dialog box opens, click the Open this file from its current location option button.

TROUBLE? If the clip sounds choppy, let it play through once, and then click the Play button to hear it again. It plays as it transfers, and, if your Internet connection is slow, you won't hear it all at once. After it's stored on your computer, however, it will play smoothly.

| Figure 2-19 | MEDIA PLAYER PLAYBACK DEVICE PLAYING AUDIO CLIP |

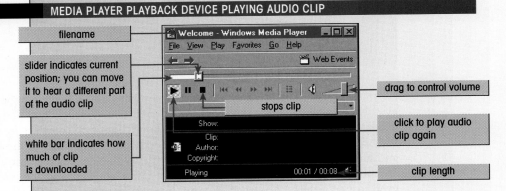

filename

slider indicates current position; you can move it to hear a different part of the audio clip

white bar indicates how much of clip is downloaded

drag to control volume

stops clip

click to play audio clip again

clip length

2. Close Media Player or your playback device.

Media Player also plays a variety of movie file formats.

To view a movie:

1. Click the **Weddings** link on the Mayer Photography page.

2. Scroll down the Weddings page, then click the **video clip** link at the bottom of the page. Media Player starts and plays the video clip. See Figure 2-20.

TROUBLE? If the clip takes a minute to start, don't worry. Watch its transfer status. When the status reaches 100%, the clip plays. Transferring video clips over the Internet takes longer than audio clips because the video clips are usually much bigger. Moreover, the video clip on the Mayer Photography Web site does not employ streaming video technology, so it doesn't start until it's completely downloaded.

TROUBLE? If the video clip doesn't play continuously, wait until it is completely saved in the temporary file and then press the Play button.

Figure 2-20 | VIDEO ON MEDIA PLAYER

3. Close Media Player.

Viewing Web Events

You tell Miriam that if she's interested in streaming media and its possibilities for Allied Technologies Corporation, she can use the Channel Guide button on the Links toolbar to connect to Microsoft's Web Events page. This page, a "Best of the Web" page for online audio and video, provides access to the best streaming media on the Internet. Content providers include companies such as Warner Brothers, TV Guide Entertainment Network, and CNN. Miriam expresses interest in the page.

To view the Web Events page:

1. Click the **Channel Guide** button on the Links toolbar. The Web Events page opens. This page is regularly updated, so your page might differ from the one shown in Figure 2-21.

TROUBLE? If the Channel Guide button does not appear, connect to the Microsoft Network Web page at http://www.msn.com and locate and click the Web Events link.

Figure 2-21	WEB EVENTS PAGE

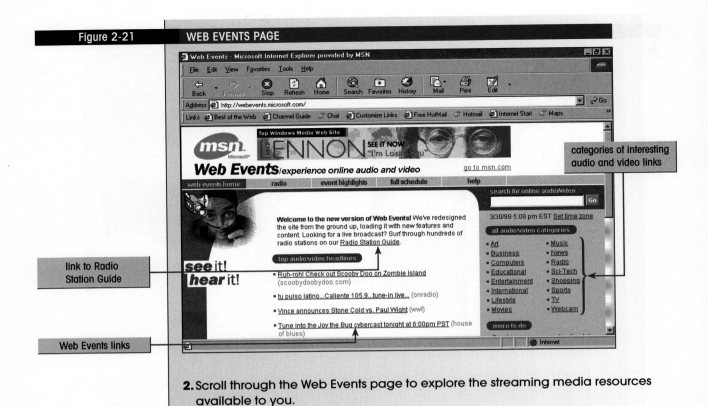

2. Scroll through the Web Events page to explore the streaming media resources available to you.

Listening to Internet Radio

Miriam notices the Radio Station Guide link at the top of the Web Events page, shown in Figure 2-21 (though you might not see it on your page), and asks you about it. You explain that radio stations around the world take advantage of streaming media technology to send their broadcasts, called **webcasts**, directly to subscribers' computers. The Radio Station Guide helps you locate radio stations. The Radio Station Guide lets you view stations by format (such as Classical, Jazz, or Modern Rock), zip code (for local radio stations), state, or country. Internet Explorer provides the Radio toolbar to help you access Internet radio and the Radio Station Guide. Miriam asks you to demonstrate.

To listen to a radio station:

1. Click **View**, point to **Toolbars**, and then click **Radio** if it is not already checked. The Radio toolbar appears.

2. Click the **Radio Stations** button.

3. Click **Radio Station Guide**. The Radio Station Guide appears. See Figure 2-22.

Figure 2-22	LISTENING TO WEB RADIO

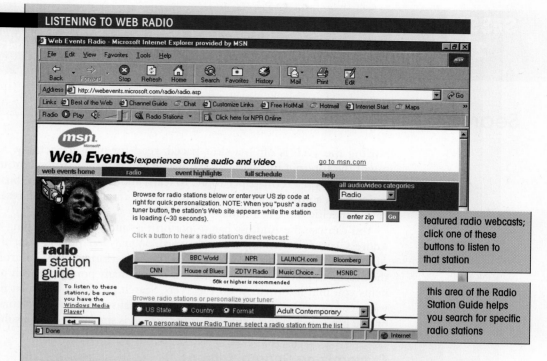

featured radio webcasts; click one of these buttons to listen to that station

this area of the Radio Station Guide helps you search for specific radio stations

4. Click a button for the radio station you want to listen to, such as NPR. Internet Explorer connects to the radio station and begins to play the broadcast.

TROUBLE? If requested to choose an audio format, do so.

5. Click the **Stop** button ⊙ to stop playing the radio broadcast.

6. If the Radio toolbar was hidden when you started these steps, click **View**, point to **Toolbars**, and then click **Radio** to return the toolbar area to its original state.

7. Close Internet Explorer.

You tell Miriam she could add a station to the Radio toolbar or Favorites menu using the Add Station to Favorites option (available by clicking the Radio Stations button on the Radio toolbar), but you won't do that now.

Miriam thanks you for your instruction and suggests you contact Mayer Photography to see whether they would be interested in collaborating on Allied's public relations campaign. She also encourages you to keep hunting for information, especially on digital photography, which Miriam agrees could be an efficient medium for Allied to use.

Session 2.1 QUICK CHECK

1. What is a site map?

2. True or False: You can click the Address list arrow to view a list of URLs you typed.

3. True or False: The History Explorer bar contains a list of previously visited Web sites.

4. You can store a Web page you might want to visit again in the _____ folder.

5. True or False: Internet Explorer uses its own software to interpret every type of file format.

6. What software does the Internet Explorer suite provide to view audio and video clips?

SESSION 2.2

In this session, you will search for information on the Web using queries and subject guides. You'll also learn how to look for addresses and maps. Finally, you'll save text and images you find on the Web in files and learn about useful utilities that will help you with file transfer.

Searching the Web

Surfing the Web is often a slow-paced, read-for-pleasure activity. Another, more focused use of the Internet involves fact-gathering and research. You might use the Internet to find information on a term-paper topic, to learn about opening a new business, or to obtain statistics from a government agency. A common thread in all these research goals is that they have a specific topic or theme.

You can use the Address bar to perform a quick search by typing the word "find" in the Address bar, followed by a search word. When you press Enter, the Microsoft Network AutoSearch feature lists links you might try. To perform a more controlled search, you can use the Search Explorer bar, which makes available many popular **search providers**, software that helps you find information on the Web. Search providers help you find information in two ways: you can either search by **query**, which means you request information on a specific topic, or you can search using a **subject guide**, which is similar to using a subject catalog in a library.

Customizing Search Settings

The Search Explorer bar displays a predetermined set of search categories, such as Web pages, personal or business addresses, maps, newsgroups, or encyclopedia information. When you perform a search, you first select the category you want to use. The Search Explorer bar displays options appropriate to that category. You then enter a subject and click a button such as Search, Find, Go, or "?". The appearance of the button that starts the search depends on the search provider Internet Explorer is using.

You can control the categories and the providers that appear on the Search Explorer bar using the Search Assistant. Each category has its own list of providers. Internet Explorer automatically starts with the first provider in that list. If you don't find the information you want with the first search provider, you can continue to search using the next provider on the list. You can also control the order in which the providers in a category are used so that Internet Explorer searches with your favorite providers first.

To customize your search settings:

1. Start Internet Explorer, maximize the Internet Explorer window, and then click the **Search** button 🔍 . The Search Explorer bar appears.

2. Click the **Customize** button.

3. Make sure the **Use the Search Assistant for smart searching** option button is selected at the top of the Customize Search Settings dialog box.

4. Make sure that the **Find a Web page**, **Find a person's address**, and **Find a map** check boxes are all selected. You'll need to scroll through the Customize Search Settings dialog box. If additional check boxes are selected, leave them selected. Now you'll check your Web page search provider order.

5. If necessary, scroll to the top of the Customize Search Settings dialog box. See Figure 2-23. Make sure that at least the **Yahoo!** and **InfoSeek** check boxes are selected. If Yahoo! isn't first on the list, click Yahoo!, then click the **Move Up** button repeatedly to move Yahoo! to the top of the list. If InfoSeek isn't second on the list, click it, then click the **Move Up** button to move InfoSeek to second place.

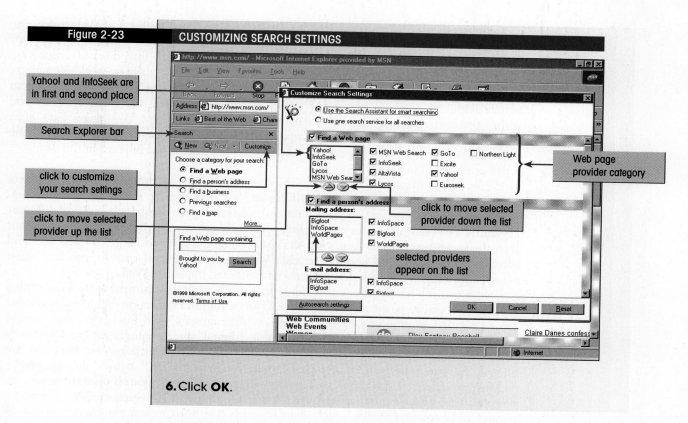

Figure 2-23   CUSTOMIZING SEARCH SETTINGS

Yahoo! and InfoSeek are in first and second place

Search Explorer bar

click to customize your search settings

click to move selected provider up the list

Web page provider category

click to move selected provider down the list

selected providers appear on the list

6. Click **OK**.

Now any searches you perform will use the same settings as those in this tutorial.

Searching by Query

To manage the growing number of files and documents on the Internet, search providers collect information and store it in databases. A **database** is a collection of related information that you can search by topic. The database software contains a **search engine**, which retrieves information from the database based upon a person's query. A **query** is a request for information. You enter a specified word or phrase, called a **keyword**, into a box and then click a button, such as Search or Find, to send your request to the search engine. For example, you might want to search for information that matches the keyword "photography." The search engine generates a list of sites on the Internet that contain that word.

How is the database created? Most search providers employ a **spider**, indexing software that compiles a large index of existing Web pages on a database that you can search to find references to a specific subject. The term "spider" is perhaps the most popular name for indexing software because it extends the Web analogy. However, the software is sometimes also called a robot, harvester, or worm.

To understand how the spider creates a database, imagine a library that arranges its books randomly on its shelves and has no catalog index. The only way to locate information about a topic is to pick up a book and start reading and indexing it, jotting down keywords and references to other books. You follow these references and links until you reach a dead end; then you repeat this process for all other books in the library. The resulting list, in effect, is a database of the keywords and bibliography in each reference—a valuable way to locate all reference materials related to a keyword, such as Mozart. Now imagine adding to your list all the books in all the libraries in your state, the country, and even the world. The resulting database, although time-consuming and tedious to compile, would yield even more information about a topic.

A spider creates this type of database by circulating through millions of Web pages, one at a time, reading and storing keywords and links, until the links dead-end. The spider's helper programs organize the database by connecting some of the linked servers, removing duplicate entries, and categorizing results. A spider periodically (daily or weekly) connects to servers throughout the Internet to update its database. When you submit a query to search a spider's database, the query results include only those references available and within the spider's range when it last updated its database. If new Web pages have been added since the last update or the spider couldn't access a Web page during an update, the index contains no current references to them. If a Web page is not indexed in the database, it will not turn up in a search.

Relatively few organizations perform the enormous task of indexing the Internet. Spiders on these organizations' servers travel different, but overlapping, routes on the Internet. Each independently creates and maintains a database, so each database is built on different keywords. For example, a query performed with InfoSeek usually provides a different result than the same query performed with AltaVista. To obtain a broad range of references and increase your chances of finding the data you need, use several search providers when researching a topic. No provider claims to have indexed the entire Web.

Before you use a new search provider, you need to determine how to write a query that produces the results you want. For example, if you want information on digital photography, some providers assume you mean "digital" *or* "photography" and find pages that contain either word. Other providers assume you mean "digital" *and* "photography" and find only pages with both words. These searches take longer and offer fewer pages, but the pages are likely to be more useful. Other providers assume you mean "digital" *and/or* "photography."

Most providers let you refine your query with symbols called **search operators**, such as the plus sign, which requires a term or phrase; the minus sign, which excludes a term or phrase; and quotation marks, which identify words that must appear together. Figure 2-24 provides examples of how these operators work in Yahoo! and InfoSeek; other providers' search operators might work differently. When using a provider, you can check its online Help to learn how to structure your search query.

Figure 2-24	REFINING A KEYWORD SEARCH
KEYWORD	**RETURNED PAGES**
digital photography	*digital* and/or *photography*
"digital photography"	the word *digital* next to the word *photography*
+digital +photography	*digital* and *photography* but not necessarily next to each other
+digital photography	*digital* but not necessarily *photography*
+photography –digital	*photography* but not *digital*

When you perform a search, most search providers return a list of links to sites that contain your keyword. If it finds more than 10 sites, the search provider usually displays only the first 10 links. At the bottom of the list, a "Next 10" link usually appears. You can click it to view the next 10 links (links 11-20). At the bottom of that list, two links appear, one to the previous 10 sites (links 1-10) and one to the next 10 (links 21-30). Some search providers also group links that match your keyword into categories so you can focus only on those links likely to be most useful.

To conduct a query:

1. Click the query box, then type **"digital photography"** to indicate the keywords you want to search for. Make sure you include the quotation marks. The list of references returned will include any documents that contain the phrase "digital photography."

2. Click the **Search** button to initiate the query and compile a list of relevant sites. The first search provider, in this case Yahoo!, indicates the number of categories or sites that match your keyword and displays the first 10.

   TROUBLE? If a Security Alert dialog box warns you that sending information over the Internet might not be secure, click the Yes button. You can click the check box if you want to disable this warning in the future. Security is important because sending or receiving information over the Internet always exposes you to a security risk. Internet Explorer lets you specify the level of security you want to maintain, and, depending on your configuration, this message might or might not appear.

3. Scroll through the list of links on the Search Explorer bar to determine which links are relevant.

4. Click one or more relevant links to request that the pages appear in the Internet Explorer window. You can click additional links in the Search Explorer bar until you find one containing the information you need. Your results will differ from Figure 2-25 because the database is constantly updated.

Figure 2-25	QUERY RESULTS

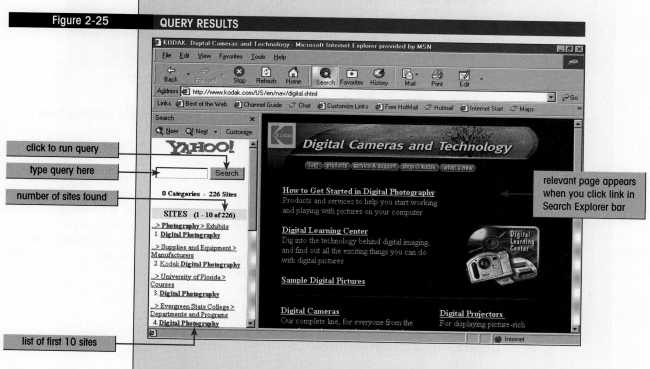

click to run query

type query here

number of sites found

relevant page appears when you click link in Search Explorer bar

list of first 10 sites

5. Scroll to the bottom of the Search Explorer bar list, then click the **Next 10 Matches** link to see the next 10 links.

Sometimes one search provider might not locate the information you need. Internet Explorer makes it easy to try another.

To search using a different provider:

1. Click the **Next** list arrow on the Search Explorer bar, then click **InfoSeek**. Notice the providers are listed in the order you specified in the Customize Search Settings dialog box. See Figure 2-26.

| Figure 2-26 | SEARCHING THE NEXT PROVIDER |

if you click the Next button without clicking the list arrow, Internet Explorer shows search results for the next provider

list of providers; yours might be different

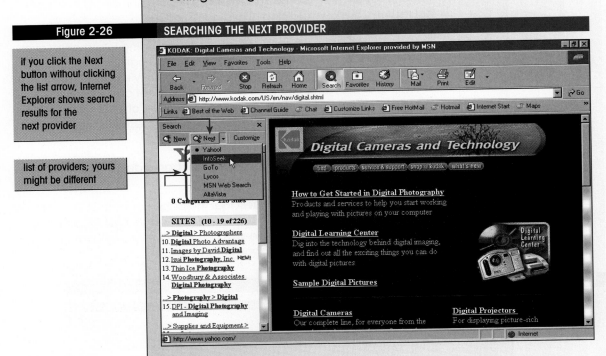

2. Click **InfoSeek**. The sites that InfoSeek finds are probably very different from those that Yahoo! found. Surf some sites found by InfoSeek.

Sometimes a very general query may result in a large list of references that includes unrelated data. At other times, a very specific query results in few references or none. In either case, you'll need to revise the query so that it is more or less inclusive. Try adding adjectives or nouns to help focus the search, or try choosing synonyms more specific to your needs. Using the root of words can also help. Sometimes queries are case-sensitive, so capitalize any word that might be capitalized in references. Using capital letters for proper names can exclude, for example, pages on the color green when you search for information on Green Acres.

You have now used two search providers, Yahoo! and InfoSeek, to locate information by performing queries. Now try a different kind of search: a subject search.

Searching a Subject Guide

When you search by query, you are asking the search engine to locate information on the topic you specify. In a subject search, however, you search for information by browsing through a hierarchy of topics called a **subject guide**. The search service creates and maintains subject guides, organizing them first by general, and then successively more specific, subjects.

Most search services let you search by query or subject. When you aren't sure where to begin, a subject search is a good starting point.

To use a subject search it's usually most efficient when you connect directly to a search provider's Web site. You can access search provider Web sites right from the Search Explorer bar. Some providers open their pages in the main Internet Explorer window; others list their subject guides in the Search Explorer bar.

To search by subject:

1. Click the **Next** list arrow and then click **Yahoo!**. Click the **Yahoo!** logo. The subject guide appears in the Internet Explorer window.

2. Click **Photography** in the Arts and Humanities category. **Yahoo!** displays the photography categories in the Internet Explorer window.

   TROUBLE? If you can't locate the Photography category in Arts and Humanities, click other probable locations until you locate Photography. Then click Photography.

3. Click **Digital**. Digital photography links appear. Scroll down to see them if necessary. See Figure 2-27.

| Figure 2-27 | SUBJECT GUIDE |

URL indicates your current position in the Yahoo! subject guide heirarchy

Yahoo! logo

digital photography links in Yahoo! subject guide

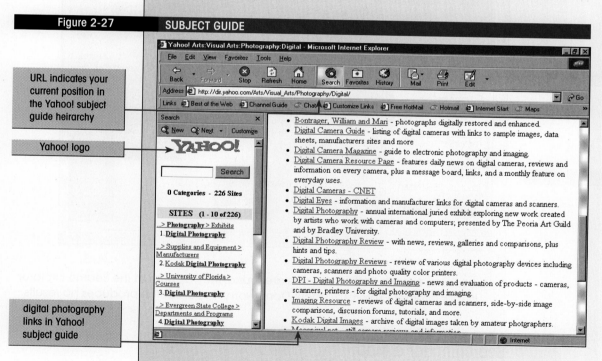

4. Scroll through the links, then click one that interests you.

In your search you notice that numerous sites provide images for royalty-free use. You buzz Miriam on the intercom and ask her to come to your cubicle. As she examines your findings, she notices the other search features and asks you about them.

Searching for an Address

You can use Internet Explorer to search for information about specific people. Similar to a telephone book, Internet Explorer locates information such as a person's mailing or e-mail address. You enter a name, and the search service returns a list of addresses with that name. For common names the list is very long; for some names no information is available. Try finding your own name.

To search for an address:

1. Click the **New** button in the Search Explorer bar.

2. Click the **Find a person's address** option button.

3. Enter your name, city, and state in the boxes, as shown in Figure 2-28.

| Figure 2-28 | SEARCHING FOR AN ADDRESS |

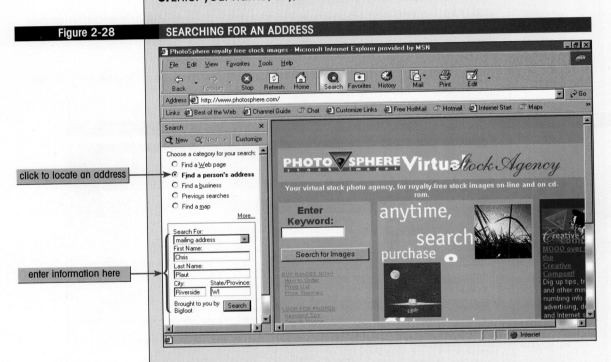

click to locate an address

enter information here

4. Click the **Search** button. If results are found, they appear in the Search Explorer bar or Internet Explorer window. Don't worry if your search produces no results.

Searching for a Map

Map services on the Internet provide street maps for addresses you enter. Try searching for your own address. After you locate the map, you can "zoom in" or "zoom out" on the map to view more local detail or more of the surrounding area. Try finding a map of your home or other location.

To locate a map:

1. Click the **New** button on the Search Explorer bar.

2. Click the **Find a map** option button.

3. Enter your address, city, state, and zip code in the appropriate boxes.

4. Click the **Search** button. The map appears in the Internet Explorer window. See Figure 2-29.

   TROUBLE? If the address you used yields no map, try a different address, or try the one shown in Figure 2-29.

Figure 2-29	SEARCHING FOR A MAP

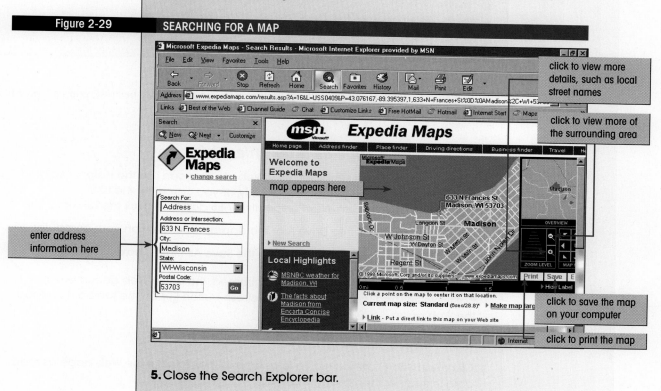

5. Close the Search Explorer bar.

Miriam comments on the wealth of material available on the Internet and asks what you do when you want to keep information you find. You suggest that she take a seat, and you demonstrate how to save information found on the Web on a disk.

Saving **Text and Images in a File**

You've already told Miriam about how to use offline viewing to reduce time spent online. However, pages designated for offline viewing are only saved temporarily. If you want to save a Web page permanently, you can save it in a file in several different formats. For example, when you save a Web page as text, Internet Explorer saves only the text. When you open such a file, formatting, color, and special fonts do not appear.

Alternatively, you can save a Web page as an HTML file, complete with graphics or other files it contains. If you open the saved HTML file in Internet Explorer or word processors such as Microsoft Word, it looks the same as when you viewed it on the Web.

Saving a Web Page as a Text File

You tell Miriam you'll demonstrate the save features by returning to the Mayer Photography page.

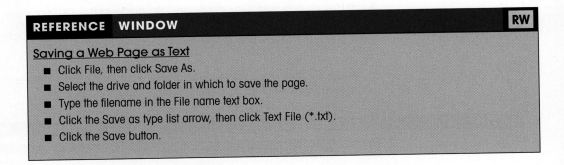

> **REFERENCE WINDOW**   **RW**
>
> **Saving a Web Page as Text**
> - Click File, then click Save As.
> - Select the drive and folder in which to save the page.
> - Type the filename in the File name text box.
> - Click the Save as type list arrow, then click Text File (*.txt).
> - Click the Save button.

You decide to save the Mayer Photography page as a text file, because you can save text files very quickly.

To save a Web page as a text file:

1. Connect to the Mayer Photography Web site. You can use the History Explorer bar or the Address list to connect quickly, or you can enter the URL http://www.course.com/NewPerspectives/IE5 and then click the Tutorial 2 link.

2. Insert your Data Disk into Drive A or the appropriate drive on your computer.

3. Click **File**, then click **Save As** to open the Save As dialog box.

   TROUBLE? If the Save As command is dimmed, the entire Web document may not have finished loading. Click the Refresh button 🔄 on the toolbar to reload the Web page.

4. Click the **Save as type** list arrow.

5. Click **Text File (*.txt)** in the Save as type list box to save the Web page as readable text rather than as HTML coding.

6. Click the **Save in** list arrow, then choose the drive containing your Data Disk.

7. Make sure **Mayer Photography** appears in the File name box as shown in Figure 2-30.

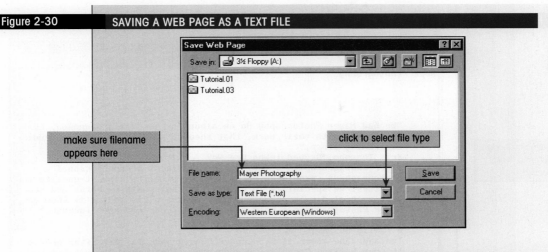

Figure 2-30   SAVING A WEB PAGE AS A TEXT FILE

make sure filename appears here

click to select file type

8. Click the **Save** button to close the dialog box and save the file on your disk.

Before you save more pages, you'll show Miriam that you saved the page properly.

Opening a Text File

Because you saved the document as a text file, you can open and edit it with any word-processing program. When you open it with Internet Explorer, Notepad automatically starts.

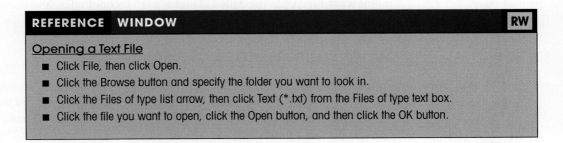

REFERENCE WINDOW   **RW**

Opening a Text File
- Click File, then click Open.
- Click the Browse button and specify the folder you want to look in.
- Click the Files of type list arrow, then click Text (*.txt) from the Files of type text box.
- Click the file you want to open, click the Open button, and then click the OK button.

You'll open the Mayer Photography file from within Internet Explorer to verify that it was properly saved.

To open a file:

1. Click **File**, then click **Open**. The Open dialog box opens.

2. Click the **Browse** button, click the **Look in** list arrow, and then select the drive containing your Data Disk.

3. Click the **Files of type** list arrow, then click **Text Files**.

4. Click the **Mayer Photography** file, then click the **Open** button.

5. Click the **OK** button in the Open dialog box. Internet Explorer starts Notepad and displays the text file's contents. Notice that no color, special fonts, links, or graphics were saved. See Figure 2-31.

Figure 2-31   VIEWING A TEXT FILE

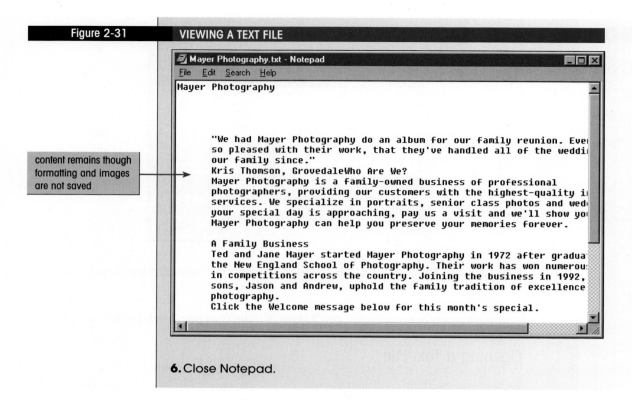

content remains though formatting and images are not saved

6. Close Notepad.

Miriam mentions that a photo similar to the photo on Mayer Photography's home page might work nicely for the Allied sound system technologies. You decide to show her how to save images.

Saving an Image from a Web Page

You can save images you see on Web pages as separate files in a variety of file formats. As with audio files, image file types differ in quality and size. You need software that can interpret these different image file types if you want to view and use them.

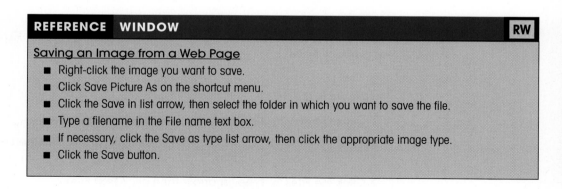

REFERENCE WINDOW   **RW**

<u>Saving an Image from a Web Page</u>
- Right-click the image you want to save.
- Click Save Picture As on the shortcut menu.
- Click the Save in list arrow, then select the folder in which you want to save the file.
- Type a filename in the File name text box.
- If necessary, click the Save as type list arrow, then click the appropriate image type.
- Click the Save button.

To save an image from a Web page:

1. Right-click the image of the woman singing into the microphone on the right side of the Mayer Photography page. You might have to scroll down slightly to see it. The shortcut menu opens.

2. Click **Save Picture As** to open the Save Picture dialog box. See Figure 2-32.

Figure 2-32   SAVING AN IMAGE ON A WEB PAGE

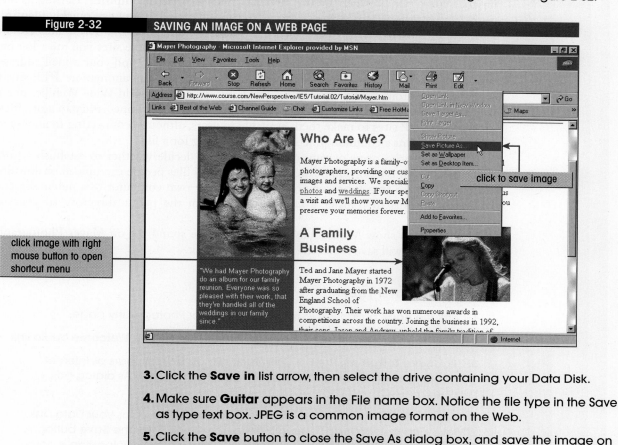

click image with right
mouse button to open
shortcut menu

click to save image

3. Click the **Save in** list arrow, then select the drive containing your Data Disk.

4. Make sure **Guitar** appears in the File name box. Notice the file type in the Save as type text box. JPEG is a common image format on the Web.

5. Click the **Save** button to close the Save As dialog box, and save the image on your disk. Now you'll open the file in Internet Explorer and view the image to verify that you saved it properly.

6. Click **File**, then click **Open**. The Open dialog box opens.

7. Click the **Browse** button, click the Look in list arrow, and then click the drive containing your Data Disk.

8. Click the **Files of type** list arrow, then click **JPEG Files**.

9. Select the **Guitar** image, click **Open**, and then click **OK**. The image appears in the Internet Explorer window.

Downloading External Files

You can save external files referenced in the Web pages you browse without first opening them. You can transfer many files on the Internet to your hard drive so you can use them later. For example, a financial company might place its fund prospectus on its Web site for potential investors to examine. Software developers often post trial versions of their software on the Web for potential buyers to preview.

You can transfer a file over the Internet from a Web server onto your hard drive with relative ease. File transfer over the Internet is so easy, in fact, that it has revolutionized the way people share information. For years, the common way to retrieve files from the Internet was with the File Transfer Protocol (FTP). **FTP** provides a means of logging on to, or connecting to, a computer elsewhere on the Internet, called a **remote computer**, viewing its directories, and transferring files to and from your local computer. You can quickly identify an FTP site by its URL, which begins with "ftp://" instead of "http://". These sites are often called **anonymous FTP sites** because to access the files on these sites you must log on to the remote computer, entering "anonymous" as your username and your e-mail address as the password. When you use Internet Explorer to connect to an anonymous FTP site, the logon occurs automatically. In recent years, however, as the World Wide Web became the primary means of accessing data from the Internet, it became unnecessary to store files in anonymous FTP sites to make them available to users, although connecting to anonymous FTP sites remains a common practice when searching for a file.

The person who owns or runs a Web server can decide whether to establish a **public directory**, which is a portion of the server that stores files people can upload or download. **Upload** means to transfer a copy of a file from your own computer to a public directory. **Download** means to transfer a copy of a file from the public directory to your own computer.

You decide to show Miriam how to download the sound file on Mayer Photography's home page. You will save it directly on your Data Disk.

To transfer a file:

1. Click the **Back** button ⬅ to return to the Mayer Photography page.

2. Scroll down to the welcome message, then right-click the **Welcome** audio link.

3. Click **Save Target As**. The File Download dialog box appears as Internet Explorer gathers information on the target. Then the Save As dialog box appears.

4. Click the **Save in** list arrow, then click the drive that contains your Data Disk. Make sure Welcome appears in the File name box. Click the **Save** button. A progress bar tells you the download status, and when downloading is complete, the saved file is on your Data Disk. The File Download dialog box displays the file's size, expected download time, and transfer rate. See Figure 2-33. The dialog box informs you when the download is complete.

| Figure 2-33 | DOWNLOADING A FILE |

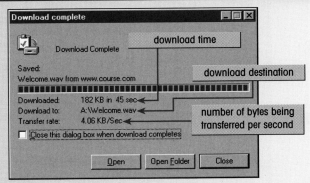

5. Click the **Close** button to acknowledge the Download complete message.

Now that the Welcome audio file is on your Data Disk, you can run it using Media Player or any other audio software.

You have successfully downloaded text, audio, and graphic files from the Web. Miriam asks if she should know anything special when downloading files from the Internet. After a moment's thought, you mention that she should learn about file compression, as she is likely to encounter compressed files if she spends much time downloading files over the Internet. She should also check any files she downloads for viruses, and she should ascertain whether the files are in the public domain before she does anything with them. You agree to go over these subject areas with her, assuring her that the software she needs to accomplish these tasks is readily available on the Internet, often in the format of shareware or freeware.

Trying and Buying Shareware

A program that you can try before buying is called **shareware**. People who write these programs enjoy sharing their ideas and creations, hence the name "shareware." Shareware authors are not necessarily employees of software companies; some are college students, professionals, or hobbyists who had an idea for a program or an interest in programming. The Internet provides a convenient and inexpensive way to market a program and get feedback on its features.

Authors make their programs available for a free trial period; if you decide to keep the program, you must send the author a fee, as outlined in the text file attached to the program. To help ensure that people send the appropriate fee after a trial period, many authors distribute a demonstration version, which might have disabled features. When you register and purchase the program, you'll receive a full working version and information about updates, or revisions, to the program. Registering and sending payment for any shareware you plan to keep and use encourages shareware authors to continue to write new versions and create new programs. Other programs called **freeware** are made available to the public free of charge.

Working with Compressed Files

The length of time taken to transfer a file over the Internet depends largely on the computer modem's speed and the file's size. To conserve space on a network server and decrease time spent transferring a file, many files are compressed. **Compression** compacts data into a smaller size by scanning a file, eliminating duplicate words or phrases, replacing them with reference codes, and storing the codes in a small internal chart that accompanies the compressed file. For example, compression might replace the words "Internet Explorer" with a code such as #1 every time the words appear in the file for these tutorials, decreasing the space they occupy by 15 characters. Applying this same coding to every repeated word in a lengthy document results in a much smaller file. Often, several related files are compiled in a single compressed file. The most common compression program on the Internet today creates files called **zip files**, compressed files with the file extension .ZIP. Zip files are created with the popular PKZIP for DOS or WinZip for Windows compression programs, both available as shareware on the Web.

For example, say Mayer Photography wants to place a collection of photos on their Web site for prospective clients to examine. They might save the collection in a PowerPoint presentation file named Photos.ppt. Then they might use the WinZip program to compress the PowerPoint file. The compressed file, much smaller in size, is named Photos.zip. Mayer Photography places Photos.zip on their Web server. Figure 2-34 illustrates this process.

| Figure 2-34 | COMPRESSING A FILE AND PLACING IT ON A WEB SERVER |

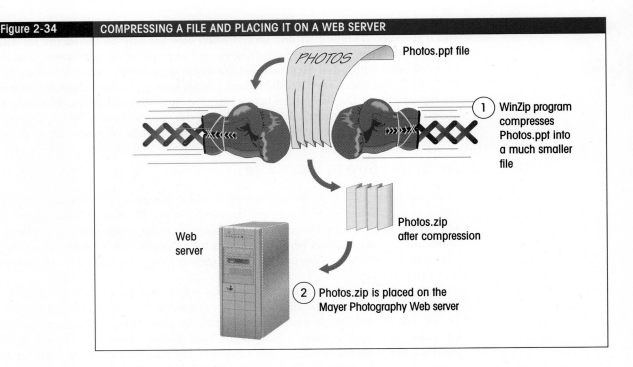

A compressed file placed on a server can be downloaded much more quickly. If you download a compressed file, however, you must use a **decompression program** that interprets the reference codes and restores the file's original structure and size. Your compression program might also include an extraction feature that lets you extract, or decompress, one file at a time. Some compressed files are self-extracting. A **self-extracting file**, which usually has the .EXE extension, extracts its compressed files without a separate decompression program.

If you don't have a compression program, you can download one from a Web site that makes software utilities available, following the general steps in the next section on viruses. Ask your instructor for recommendations on a suitable compression and decompression program and a URL where you might find it. If you spend much time downloading files on the Internet you will almost certainly encounter compressed files, so learning how to handle them is time well spent.

Protecting Against Viruses

Files stored in public directories are highly subject to viruses. You warn Miriam that she should routinely check any file that she downloads from an unknown source. A **virus** is a destructive program code embedded, or hidden, in an executable file. When you run an infected program, the virus can affect your computer's performance, display messages or images on your screen, or even damage your data.

To protect your computer, you should run an anti-virus program on every file you download and on every disk someone gives you. An **anti-virus program** looks for suspicious series of commands or codes within an executable file and compares them to a list of known virus codes. If the program finds a match, it removes the virus from your disk. If you haven't opened an infected file, then it doesn't infect your computer. Anti-virus programs are frequently updated because new viruses appear constantly.

You can download some current anti-virus programs from the Internet and then run them on the files you download. You probably would not be able to download and install an anti-virus program on a school lab computer, but you might find these steps useful if you have your own computer at home. Skip these steps if you are in a school lab. These steps are necessarily general because they do not recommend one particular product, and the download and installation procedure differs from product to product. Your instructor might be able to recommend a favorite brand of anti-virus software.

To download an anti-virus program:

1. Perform a Web page search for the words **virus protection** or **virus program** until you find a site that supplies anti-virus utilities. Make sure the Search Explorer bar is set to search for Web pages. You can use any search provider on the Search Explorer bar. Figure 2-35 shows some virus protection links located by the Yahoo! search provider.

Figure 2-35	SEARCHING FOR A VIRUS PROTECTION PROGRAM

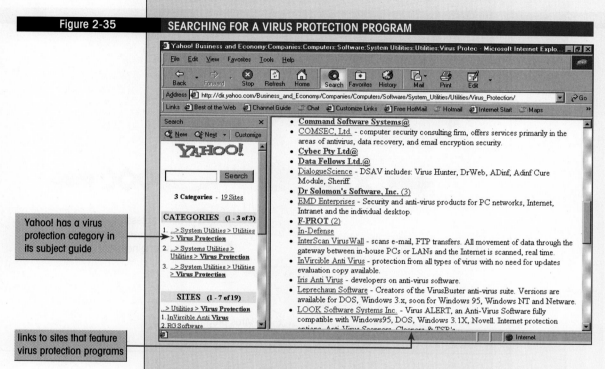

Yahoo! has a virus protection category in its subject guide

links to sites that feature virus protection programs

2. Link to an anti-virus site, and continue to search through the links until you find the virus product you want.

3. Locate a download link. Most vendors have a "try" link and a "buy" link; for now, use the "try" link. If you like the software, you can buy it later. You might need to select the correct version of the program for your operating system. You might also be required to provide your address and other information about how you plan to use the product.

4. After you click the download link, you will be asked where you want to store the file. Choose a location on your hard disk, such as a special folder you create for the virus software or a Program Files folder. Many programs are too big to save easily on floppy disks. Wait until the software downloads; this could take some time, depending on the speed of your Internet connection.

5. After the program is installed, locate it on your computer. Most likely it is an executable setup file, so to run it, click or double-click the file, depending on your computer's settings. After you run the setup file, an installation program starts automatically and installs the product on your system. Use the product's Help system to learn how to use the product.

6. Close the Search Explorer bar.

After you have a decompression program and an anti-virus program, you are ready to download and use many files from the Web. Suppose you want to download the zipped photos from the Mayer Photography server. First, you download the file. Then you use a program to unzip, or decompress the file and place it in a folder. Next, you check the downloaded file for viruses. Open the file only after it passes the virus check. Figure 2-36 illustrates the process.

Figure 2-36	DOWNLOADING, DECOMPRESSING, AND CHECKING A FILE FOR VIRUSES

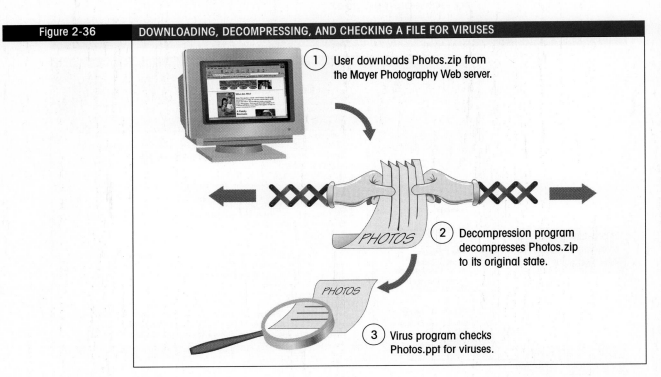

1. User downloads Photos.zip from the Mayer Photography Web server.
2. Decompression program decompresses Photos.zip to its original state.
3. Virus program checks Photos.ppt for viruses.

Internet Explorer also lets you change the security settings on your computer so that you can exclude content that could damage your computer or receive warnings about potentially damaging content, so you can check for viruses before you transfer it to your computer. You aren't, however, likely to be able to do that in a lab.

Respecting Copyrighted Material

As you've seen, saving text and images on your own computer from Internet sites around the world is easy to do, perhaps even easier than photocopying. The quality of the copied material is the same as the original; colors, shading, and graphics do not darken or distort, as they might in a photocopy. This makes copying an image or text from the Internet and reproducing it for personal, academic, or commercial use simple. Restrictions similar to those for printed material apply to the use of these files.

Copyright law protects all printed material, such as books and magazines, and all audio material, such as music CDs or books on tape, from unlimited reproduction. Under federal law, a **copyright** lets an author (or the copyright holder) to control how his or her work is used, including how the material is reproduced, sold, distributed, adapted, performed, or displayed. You might need to obtain permission from the Web page owner (the copyright holder), depending on how much material you want to reproduce from the Internet and your purpose in reproducing it. In some cases, you might pay a fee. Figure 2-37 outlines some guidelines for determining when you need to request permission before reusing material from the Internet. Remember that people, authors and artists, make their works available over an electronic medium for increased distribution, not for increased duplication.

Figure 2-37	COPYRIGHT NOTICES	
COPYRIGHT NOTICE	**ACADEMIC USE**	**COMMERCIAL USE**
Copyrighted	Can quote a certain amount without permission. Include proper citation. Request permission to reuse large amounts.	Request permission
No copyright information appears	Assume copyrighted	Assume copyrighted
Source states "Use freely, no restrictions"	Can reuse without permission	Can reuse without permission

If you find a graphic you like on the Internet, you could use it with its citation for a research paper. To use the graphic in a commercial setting for profit, however, you need to request its distributor's permission.

Session 2.2 QUICK CHECK

1. What is the difference between saving a page as text and saving it in HTML format?

2. What is an external file?

3. What is the difference between uploading and downloading?

4. True or False: You can insert one JPEG image, copied from the Internet, into a college term paper without requesting permission from the Web page owner, as long as you cite the reference.

5. True or False: Shareware is free, regardless of how long you use it.

REVIEW ASSIGNMENTS

Miriam comes by your cubicle a few days later and asks if you could do some research for her. She is intrigued by the idea of digital photography and wants more information. She asks if you could locate information on digital cameras for her.

If necessary, launch Internet Explorer, and then complete these steps:

1. Open the Search Explorer bar, and search for pages on digital cameras. (*Hint:* Use the keywords "digital camera" and include quotation marks.)

2. Connect to one or more of the pages located by the search provider.

3. After you find a page you like, print the first page. On your printout, write the name of the search provider you used (the one currently selected in the Search Explorer bar). Also write the names of three companies you find that provide information on digital cameras.

4. Click the Next button on the Search Explorer bar to look for the same information using a different search provider. Write this second search provider's name on your printout.

5. Examine the first 10 links the second search provider found, and then write the name of at least one link in the first 10 found by the second provider, but not by the first.

6. Read through the information you found, and try to locate price information for different types and styles of digital cameras. Also locate information on how digital cameras are usually powered. Write a paragraph that summarizes your findings.

7. Open the History Explorer bar.

8. Use the History Explorer bar Search button to locate only pages on digital cameras. How many pages appear?

9. Locate a page that includes basic information about digital cameras. Save a copy of the page as a text file on your Data Disk with the name "Digital Camera."

10. Create a folder in your Favorites folder named Digital Cameras.

11. Use the Back list to return to a page on digital cameras.

12. Use the Add to Favorites command to add the page to the Digital Cameras folder you just created.

Explore ▷ 13. Save an image from one of the digital camera pages you found on your Data Disk with the name "Camera." Open the image in Internet Explorer, then print the image.

Explore ▷ 14. Check your file associations list, and try to find the name of the program associated with the file type of the image you just printed. (*Hint:* Open My Computer, click View, then click Folder Options, click the File Types tab, and then scroll down the Registered file types list for the file type of the image. The image file type might be listed by its file extension.)

15. Remove the Digital Cameras folder from the Favorites folder.

CASE PROBLEMS

Case 1. Japanese Restaurant   Yoko Muramoto wants to open a take-out restaurant serving Japanese food, and she regularly checks the Web for new sites that might help her. She is interested in any page that deals with Michigan, small businesses, the restaurant business, or Japanese culture. Right now Yoko is looking for information on insurance for her business. She learned from other small business owners that the Michigan Insurance Bureau provides information specially geared to small businesses. She asks you to find the Web page for the Michigan Insurance Bureau, and, while you are looking, any Web pages dealing with Japanese food, recipes, or restaurants.

If necessary, launch Internet Explorer, then complete these steps:

1. Open the Search Explorer bar, and start a new search.

2. Search for "Michigan Insurance Bureau" using the first search provider on the list.

3. Do you see a link to the Michigan Insurance Bureau? If so, click that link. If not, locate and connect to a link for the state or government of Michigan, and continue searching for the Michigan Insurance Bureau site.

4. Save a copy of the Michigan Insurance Bureau page as a text file named "MIB" on your Data Disk.

5. Print the first page of the text file you saved.

6. Choose a different search provider on the Search Explorer bar, and try the "Michigan Insurance Bureau" query again. How do the results differ? Write your answer on the back of your printout.

7. Use the Yahoo! subject guide to search for information on entertainment and food subjects. Locate a list of Web pages related to Japanese food by clicking appropriate links.

8. Open a Web page related to Japanese food.

9. Add this page to your Favorites folder.

10. Create a folder called Japanese Food, and move the page you just saved to that folder.

11. Open three additional Japanese food Web pages, and add each to your Japanese Food folder.

Explore ▷ 12. Save an image from one of the Japanese food Web pages you see on your Data Disk. Name the image "Japanese Food."

Explore ▷ 13. Return to your favorite Japanese food Web page so you can add it as a button on your Links toolbar. Click Favorites, click Add to Favorites, click the Create in button, then click Links.

Explore ▷ 14. Test the button you just added. You might need to click the scroll arrow on the Links toolbar to view the button you added.

Explore ▷ 15. Open the Organize Favorites dialog box, open the Links folder, then delete the link you just placed on the Links toolbar. Also delete the Japanese Food folder you created in the Favorites folder and its contents.

Case 2. LaFrancois Travel   Danielle LaFrancois, owner and chief agent at the LaFrancois Travel Agency, uses the Web to keep tabs on various festivals and activities taking place at tourist sites around the country. She recently learned of an inexpensive airfare to Edinburgh, the capital of Scotland. The tickets will be available at the discounted price for only a short time, so she wants to find some current information on Edinburgh and Glasgow, a nearby city, to help encourage people to purchase the tickets. She asks you to use the Web to find the following information for both cities: a list of upcoming activities, a list of museums and galleries, and a list of other places of interest in or near these cities.

If necessary, launch Internet Explorer, then complete these steps:

1. Use the Search Explorer bar to perform a query search for information on the city of Edinburgh.

2. Surf through the links until you find a page that interests you.

3. Print the first page of your favorite Edinburgh Web page.

4. Save the information on the Edinburgh page as a text file named "Edinburgh" on your Data Disk.

5. Now use a subject guide such as the Yahoo! subject guide to locate a map of Edinburgh.

6. Print the page that shows the map and, on the back, write the subject guide categories you navigated through to locate the map.

7. Use the History Explorer bar to return to one of the Edinburgh pages. Follow the appropriate links to locate information on Edinburgh tourist attractions. Write the name of at least two attractions on the map printout.

8. Investigate Glasgow using the Search Explorer bar. Surf the Glasgow links to get a feel for how a Glasgow vacation might compare to an Edinburgh vacation.

9. Write a short note on the back of the map stating whether you think Glasgow or Edinburgh offers better tourist attractions at this time.

Case 3. Reading the News from Halifax   In Halifax, a city in Nova Scotia, Canada, situated along the Atlantic Ocean, fishing is a major industry. In recent years, Halifax has also flourished as a tourist town, thanks to the area's natural beauty. David Wu wants to spend his summer working at one of the fishing resorts in the area. Before packing his bags, he wants to learn a little more about daily life in Halifax. He asks you to use the Web to get headlines from a Halifax newspaper, find out about the climate, and determine popular sporting events in Halifax.

If necessary, launch Internet Explorer, then complete these steps:

1. Use Yahoo!'s subject guide to reach a listing of newspapers published on the Internet. Start with a category such as News and Media. What subject guide links did you click to locate Halifax newspapers?

2. Now locate a Halifax newspaper using one of the search providers on the Search Explorer bar. (*Hint:* Search for Halifax newspaper.)

3. Connect to the newspaper and add it to your Favorites folder.

4. Navigate through the pages to obtain the information about today's weather and about popular local sporting events.

5. When you have all the information, print the page containing the headlines of a Halifax newspaper for your instructor.

6. On the back of the page, briefly summarize the facts you gathered. Submit this page to your instructor.

7. Save one image from the newspaper on your Data Disk with the name "Halifax."

8. Open the image file in the Internet Explorer window, then print the image file and submit it to your instructor.

9. Remove the newspaper link you added to your Favorites folder.

Case 4. *Job Searching on the Web*   Keisha Williams, a senior at MidWest University, is actively searching for employment in marketing, her major field of study. She'd like to move to Texas. She asks you to help her use the Web to locate resources for job searches and to find some tips on writing résumés. One popular site to find job listings is the CareerMosaic home page. CareerMosaic contains the JOBS database, which you can use to search for specific jobs in different parts of the country. Unfortunately, you don't know the address of the site, so you'll have to find the Web page before you can search for job listings. The JOBS database page contains several fields in which you can enter information specific to the job you're seeking.

If necessary, launch Internet Explorer, then complete these steps:

1. Try using one of the search tips in this tutorial: type "careermosaic" in the Address bar, then click Go. What URL does Internet Explorer find?

2. Using the search criteria given by Keisha, look for available positions. In Keisha's case, you should search for jobs related to marketing and limit the search to jobs in Texas. If you don't find any in Texas, expand your search to nearby states.

3. Connect to a link that describes a job you think is appropriate for Keisha.

4. Save a job description as a text file with the name "Job" on your Data Disk. Print the first page of the job description for your instructor.

5. Use the Search Explorer bar to search for pages that contain résumé writing tips. What keywords did you use for your search?

6. Investigate the pages that seem the most helpful. Select the one that looks like the best resource, and save it on your disk as a text file named "Resume" on your Data Disk. Then print the text file for your instructor.

Case 5. Scavenger Hunt on the World Wide Web   Now that you've had some experience using search tools on the WWW, you should be able to locate almost any type of information on the Web. Complete the following scavenger hunt, using any search tool available. When you find an answer, write it down. Submit the answers to your instructor, and indicate the URL of the page you used to find the answer.

If necessary, launch Internet Explorer, then answer these questions:

1. In what Shakespearean play does a character say, "There's no trust, no faith, no honesty in men; all perjured, all forsworn, all naught, all dissemblers" (specify the act and the scene)? *Hint:* Look for a Shakespeare page that contains a tool for searching the contents of all Shakespeare's plays and poems.

2. In the movie "Three Little Words," who played the part of Harry Ruby? *Hint:* Look for an Internet movie database page, and then use a search tool to find a movie titled "Three Little Words."

Explore

3. While you explore movie pages, try to locate a video clip from a movie. Many movie pages include previews of upcoming movies. When you click the video clip link, does the movie play automatically? If so, what software starts? How could you save the clip on your Data Disk? Write the steps.

4. What are the current temperature, humidity, wind, and barometric pressure in Caribou, Maine? *Hint:* Look for a page that deals with news or weather.

5. What are the address, phone number, and e-mail address of your congressional representative in the U.S. House of Representatives? *Hint:* Use the Yahoo! subject guide to search for government resources.

6. What is the zip code for Nome, Alaska (abbreviated AK)?

7. What is the URL for the Smithsonian Institution's home page?

8. When you find the answers to these questions and have a list of the URLs from which you obtained them, write a report including all the information and submit it to your instructor.

QUICK CHECK ANSWERS

Session 2.1

1. a graphical layout of all resources available on a site

2. True

3. True

4. Favorites

5. False

6. Media Player

Session 2.2

1. When you save a page as a text file, only the text is saved, not the formatting.

2. a file that doesn't appear in the browser window but must be viewed in a separate program

3. Uploading is the transfer of a copy of a file from your computer to a public directory; downloading is the transfer of a copy of a file from a public directory to your computer.

4. True

5. False

OBJECTIVES

In this tutorial you will:

- Customize the Outlook Express window and check your account information

- Send, receive, reply to, print, forward, and save e-mail messages

- Explore mail security, stationery, and mail rules

- Organize addresses in the Address Book

- Manage messages in folders and send and receive e-mail attachments

- Send a Web link by e-mail

- Delete e-mail messages and Address Book entries.

- Explore identities in a multi-user environment

- Subscribe to and unsubscribe from a newsgroup

- Work with newsgroup messages

- Search newsgroup messages for information

LABS

E-mail

CORRESPONDING WITH OUTLOOK EXPRESS

Communicating over the Internet at Carey Outerwear

CASE

Carey Outerwear

Carey Outerwear is a corporation specializing in high-quality outerwear for campers, hikers, and climbers. The company has outlet stores in several western states and recently opened outlets in Madison, Wisconsin, and Boston, Massachusetts. The main branch in Seattle, Washington, is hosting the Spring Conference sales meeting next June 11–15. Employees will spend the first part of the week in sales meetings, but during the weekend following the conference, Carey Outerwear is offering its employees various opportunities to field-test Carey merchandise on organized outings throughout Washington state.

You just started working as a summer intern in the Seattle sales department, and your job is to help organize a guided tour of Mt. Rainier National Park for the conference. Your supervisor, John Kruse, told you that the regional supervisor, Katie Herrera, wants you to e-mail her as soon as you get settled, so she can add your name to her conference mailing list. He gives you Katie's e-mail address and tells you that with **e-mail**, the electronic transfer of messages between hosts on the Internet, you can correspond with people around the world without worrying about time zones, expensive long-distance charges, or answering machines.

You've heard about e-mail before, as well as newsgroups, another great source of information on the Internet. A **newsgroup** is a discussion group on the Internet that focuses on a single topic. Newsgroups exist on just about every conceivable topic. By subscribing to a newsgroup, you can see what others have to say about the topic and can take part in the conversation. You hope that when you have some free time, you can explore newsgroups and see how they work.

SESSION 3.1

In this session, you will learn how to start Outlook Express, customize the display, and examine your mail account. You will also use Outlook Express to send and receive e-mail messages and learn how to reply to a message and print and secure messages.

Getting Started with Outlook Express

Outlook Express, one of the tools that comes with the Internet Explorer suite, lets you send, receive, and manage electronic mail. As more people connect to the Internet, communicating by e-mail is becoming more common. When you need to send information to someone, an e-mail message can save time and money: you don't need to wait for expensive postal delivery, nor do you need to make expensive long-distance phone calls. You can send e-mail to and receive e-mail from anyone in the world who has an e-mail address, regardless of the operating system or type of computer they use.

Just as you need an Internet account to use the Internet Explorer browser, you also need an account with a mail, news, or directory server, to use the available Outlook Express features. For example, to use Outlook Express to manage your e-mail, you need an account with a mail server.

John informs you that the company's systems administrator just finished installing the Internet Explorer suite on the computer you will use. He hands you a slip of paper with your account information, including your user ID, password, and e-mail address. A **user ID**, also called a **user name**, is the name that identifies you on the mail server. A **password** is a personal code that verifies you have the right to read incoming mail and also provides security for your e-mail account. An **e-mail address** consists of the user ID, the @ symbol, and a host name (the domain address of your incoming mail server). For example, John's e-mail address is:

jkruse@carey.com

userID@host name

Like URLs, every e-mail address is unique. Many people might use the same host, but a user ID distinguishes one e-mail address from another.

Customizing the Outlook Express Window

The Outlook Express window offers a number of components that you can choose to display or hide, depending on your needs. These components include:

- **Contacts list:** lists people whose e-mail addresses or other contact information you have saved
- **Folder bar:** identifies the current folder (and, when applicable, the current identity, as discussed in Session 3.2)
- **Folder list:** displays the hierarchy of Outlook Express folders that you can use to store and organize messages

- **Outlook bar**: contains icons for the folders in the Folder list (because this duplicates the information in the Folder list, you don't really need to view it unless you find it easier to use than the Folder list)
- **Status bar**: displays messages about the current folder
- **Toolbar**: displays the toolbar buttons used to accomplish most tasks
- **Views bar**: lets you quickly change the message list view so you can switch from showing all messages to hiding read or ignored messages
- **Info pane**: an informational window at the bottom of the Outlook Express window, which may be an available option, depending on how Outlook Express is installed on your computer

Before you start using Outlook Express, first ensure that your Outlook Express window matches the one shown in the figures. You start Outlook Express by clicking the Outlook Express button 🖳 from the Quick Launch toolbar, clicking the Outlook Express icon on the desktop, or using the Start menu.

To control the Outlook Express display:

1. To open Outlook Express, click the **Start** button 🏁Start , point to **Programs**, then click **Outlook Express**.

TROUBLE? If more than one e-mail program is installed on your computer, and Outlook Express is not your current default mail client, a dialog box appears asking if you want Outlook Express to be your default mail client. If you are using your own computer and want to use Outlook Express as your mail client, click the Yes button. If you are using a school or institutional computer, click the No button or ask your technical support person for assistance.

TROUBLE? If the Identity Logon dialog box opens, you are using a version of Outlook Express configured for multiple users. If your name appears, click it, and then enter the password as requested. Otherwise, ask your technical support person for assistance.

TROUBLE? If a connection dialog box appears, you are probably not connected to the Internet. Click the Connect button and follow the directions on your screen. If the dialog box prompts you to enter your user name and password and you do not know them, consult your technical support person.

2. If necessary, click the Outlook Express **Maximize** button 🔲. Figure 3-1 shows the maximized Outlook Express window.

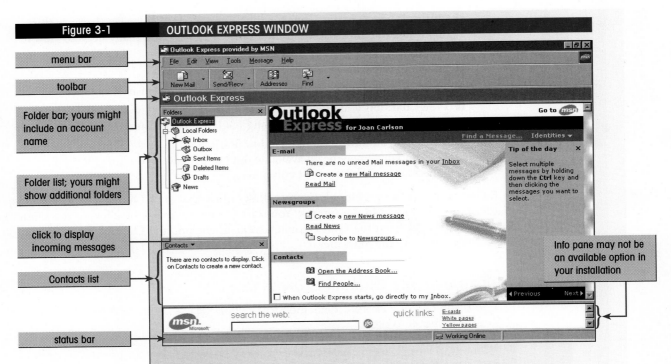

| Figure 3-1 | OUTLOOK EXPRESS WINDOW |

menu bar

toolbar

Folder bar; yours might include an account name

Folder list; yours might show additional folders

click to display incoming messages

Contacts list

status bar

Info pane may not be an available option in your installation

3. Click **Inbox** in the Folder list.

TROUBLE? If you see more than one Inbox on the Folder list, you might have more than one mail account. Click Inbox under Local Folders.

4. Click **View**, point to **Current View**, then click **Show All Messages** so you can view all messages.

5. Click **View**, point to **Sort By**, click **Received**, then click **View** again, point to **Sort By**, and click **Sort Ascending**. You want to sort your messages in the order of their receipt, newest first.

TROUBLE? If the Sort By list already contains bulleted Received and Sort Ascending options, don't worry. Clicking a bulleted menu option does *not* dese-lect it. However, clicking a checked menu option *does* deselect the option.

6. To work with the Outlook Express components layout, click **View** and then click **Layout**.

7. In the Basic area, make sure all check boxes *except* the Outlook Bar, Views Bar, and Info Pane are checked.

TROUBLE? If the Info Pane check box doesn't appear in your Layout dialog box, don't worry. Some installations of Outlook Express do not include this option. Just make sure that the check boxes for Outlook Bar and Views Bar are *not* checked.

8. In the Preview Pane area, make sure the Show preview pane and Show preview pane header check boxes are both selected and that the Below messages option button is selected. See Figure 3-2.

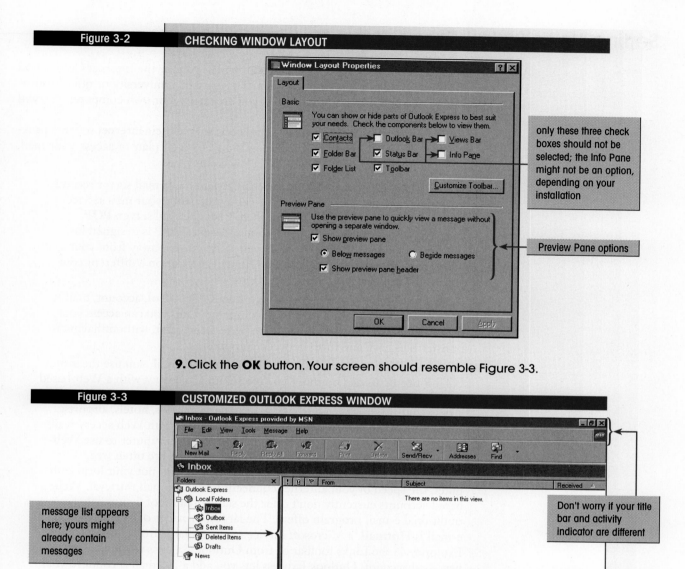

Figure 3-2   CHECKING WINDOW LAYOUT

only these three check boxes should not be selected; the Info Pane might not be an option, depending on your installation

Preview Pane options

9. Click the **OK** button. Your screen should resemble Figure 3-3.

Figure 3-3   CUSTOMIZED OUTLOOK EXPRESS WINDOW

message list appears here; yours might already contain messages

Don't worry if your title bar and activity indicator are different

preview pane displays contents of selected message; it is empty now because the message list contains no messages

Now that you have ensured that your display matches the one shown in the figures, you are ready to check the status of your Outlook Express account using the information John Kruse gave you.

Setting Up an Outlook Express Account

After you establish an account with a mail service provider, you use the Internet Connection Wizard to add your account to Outlook Express. If you are in a university or other institution, this has probably been done for you, but if you are using your own computer, you will probably need to add it yourself.

Many ISPs currently include mail and news service as part of their Internet services package. The type of mail account you choose depends on how you plan to access your mail. Outlook Express supports POP, IMAP, and HTTP account types:

- With a **POP**, or **Post Office Protocol**, account, your mail server receives incoming mail and delivers it to your computer. After your mail service delivers messages, it usually deletes them from the mail server. POP accounts work best for a single computer, because POP is designed for offline mail access. To receive POP mail while you are away from your computer, you must be able to set up a POP mail account on a different computer, an impossibility in many situations.

- With an **IMAP**, or **Internet Message Access Protocol**, account, mail is stored on a mail server, not on your computer. Thus you can access your mail from any computer on which you have an account, without having to transfer files back and forth between computers.

- With an HTTP account, known as **Web-based e-mail**, you use the same HTTP protocol used on the Web. You set up an account with a Web-based e-mail provider, and that provider's mail server stores your mail. You can access your messages from any Web browser. Libraries, hotels, airports, banks, and other sites increasingly make computers with Web access available to the public, so you don't even need to own a computer to use Web-based e-mail. Moreover, Web-based e-mail accounts are often free. However, because messages are stored on a server and not your local computer, the speed of your Internet connection limits e-mail retrieval. Web-based accounts currently don't offer the same breadth of features that a traditional e-mail program offers. The largest provider of free Web-based e-mail is **Hotmail**, a Microsoft service made available from Internet Explorer via the Links toolbar or from Outlook Express when you set up a new mail account. Outlook Express lets you add a Hotmail account to your Folder list, and treats incoming mail just like a POP account does. Hotmail even lets you check POP mail.

You might find having several mail accounts handy, for example, one at work or school, and a Web-based account that you can use when traveling.

REFERENCE   WINDOW   `RW`

Setting Up an E-Mail Account
- In the Outlook Express window, click Tools and then click Accounts.
- Click Add.
- Click Mail. Follow the steps in the Internet Connection Wizard.

The following steps help you determine whether or not you have a mail account. If you don't, you need to set one up before continuing with this tutorial. Outlook Express can help with this task. You can set up a Hotmail account almost instantaneously, but setting up a POP or IMAP account requires you to provide account information, such as your incoming and outgoing mail server address and type, your user name and password, and your e-mail address.

To examine your mail account:

1. Click **Tools**, then click **Accounts** to open the Internet Accounts dialog box.

2. Click the **Mail** tab, if necessary. Figure 3-4 shows one mail account already set up.

Figure 3-4   MAIL ACCOUNTS

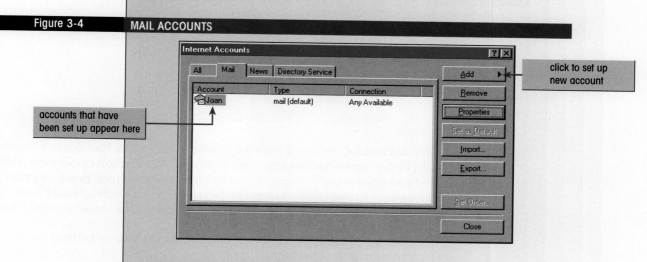

3. Click the account you want to use.

TROUBLE? If no account appears with your name, no account has been set up for you. To set up an account yourself, click the Add button and then click Mail. The Internet Connection Wizard starts. This wizard steps you through setting up a mail account. If you cannot answer all the questions the wizard asks, seek further assistance from your technical support person or your Internet Service Provider.

4. Click the **Properties** button. Your name and e-mail address should appear in the account Properties dialog box; Outlook Express uses this information when you send and receive e-mail. See Figure 3-5.

TROUBLE? If the name and e-mail address boxes are blank, ask your instructor or technical support person what to enter in these boxes.

Figure 3-5   CONFIGURING E-MAIL PROPERTIES

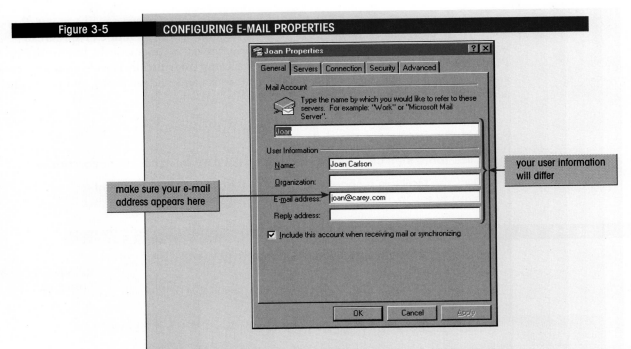

make sure your e-mail
address appears here

your user information
will differ

5. Click the **Servers** tab to check your mail server information. Your account name
(user ID) and password should appear, along with information about your mail
server. If you have an HTTP account, you see the URL of the mail provider's Web
page. However, Carey Outerwear uses POP accounts, so each account must
identify the incoming and outgoing mail server address, as shown in Figure 3-6.

TROUBLE? If any of these boxes are blank, ask your instructor or technical support person what to enter in them.

Figure 3-6   CHECKING MAIL SERVER INFORMATION

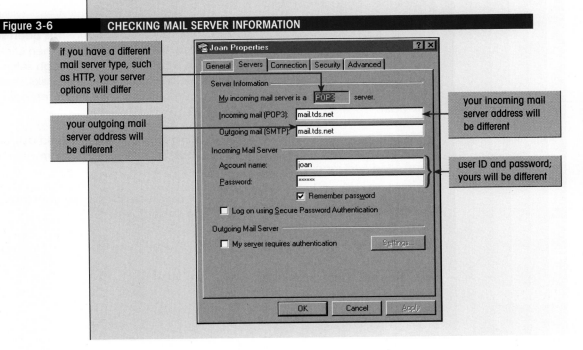

if you have a different
mail server type, such
as HTTP, your server
options will differ

your outgoing mail
server address will
be different

your incoming mail
server address will
be different

user ID and password;
yours will be different

6. Click the **OK** button to close the account Properties dialog box, then close the Internet Accounts dialog box.

Now that you have ensured that Outlook Express can handle your e-mail, you're ready to send e-mail messages.

Sending E-mail

An e-mail message uses the same format as a standard memo: it typically includes From, Date, To, and Subject lines, followed by the content of the message. The To line indicates who will receive the message. Outlook Express automatically supplies your name or e-mail address in the From line and the date you send the message in the Date line. The optional Subject line tells the recipient the topic of the message. Finally, the message area contains your message text. You can also include additional information, such as a Cc line, which indicates who will receive a copy of the message, or a Priority setting, which indicates the importance of the message.

When you prepare an e-mail message, remember some commonsense guidelines:

- Think before you type; read before you send. Your name and your institution's name appear on everything you send.
- Type in both uppercase and lowercase letters. Using all uppercase letters in e-mail messages is considered shouting, and messages in all lowercase letters are difficult to read and decipher.
- Edit your message. Keep your messages concise so the reader can understand your meaning quickly and clearly.
- Send appropriate amounts of useful information. Like junk mail, e-mail messages can pile up quickly. If you must send a long message, attach it as a file.
- Determine whether an employee may receive personal e-mail messages on a work account. E-mail is not free. (Businesses pay to subscribe to a server.)
- E-mail at your workplace is not confidential. Your employer, for example, might be able to access your e-mail.

Using Stationery

When you send an e-mail message, you can choose to create it on special "electronic stationery." Outlook Express features several **stationery templates**—HTML files with pre-designed backgrounds and text, including a party invitation, a birthday greeting, and a holiday letter. You can create your own stationery template by designing and saving an HTML file and using it for the messages you compose. To use stationery in an e-mail message, click the New Mail list arrow. You can then choose the stationery template you want, or you can click Select Stationery to view more templates or create new ones. Remember that the recipient of a mail message on stationery must be able to read HTML e-mail, in order to view the formatting you use. Figure 3-7 shows a message that uses one of the stationery templates on the New Mail list.

Figure 3-7   STATIONERY TEMPLATE

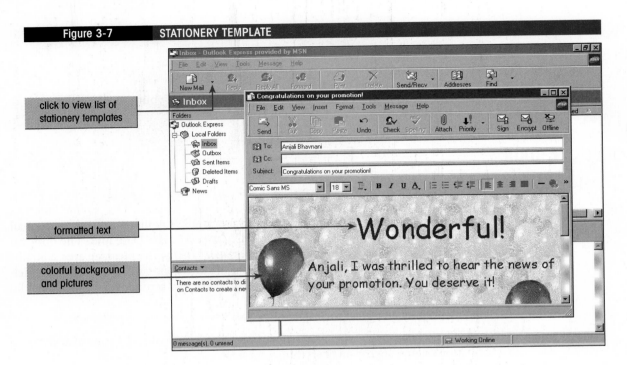

click to view list of stationery templates

formatted text

colorful background and pictures

Although you won't use stationery in this tutorial, you'll have a chance to experiment with it in the Review Assignments.

Viewing Outlook Express Folders

Outlook Express organizes all the messages it handles, outgoing and incoming, into **folders**, or compartments that let you sort your messages. The folders' names appear on the Folder list in the Outlook Express window. You'll learn later that you can also create **subfolders** within the folders that let you file and store your messages in groups. Figure 3-8 describes the Outlook Express folders that you can use to store mail.

Figure 3-8   OUTLOOK EXPRESS FOLDERS

FOLDER	DESCRIPTION
Inbox	Stores messages that have just been delivered and messages that you've read but haven't discarded or filed
Outbox	Stores messages that you've finished composing and plan to send as soon as you connect to the Internet
Sent Items	Stores a copy of every message you've sent
Deleted Items	Stores the messages you've discarded. They remain in this folder until you delete them from here, and then they are permanently gone.
Drafts	Stores messages that you have drafted but not yet sent

When a folder contains one or more messages that you have not sent or read, the folder name appears in boldface, and Outlook Express places the number of new or pending messages in that folder within parentheses.

Any folder that contains subfolders is preceded by a plus box ⊞ or minus box ⊟ in the Folder list. When ⊞ appears before a folder's name, its subfolders are hidden. When ⊟ appears, its subfolders are visible. Outlook Express automatically starts with Local Folders open. To see a folder's contents, you click its name in the Folder list.

To work with Outlook Express folders:

1. Click **Outbox** on the Folder list. It's probably empty, unless you have other outgoing mail. See Figure 3-9.

Figure 3-9 | VIEWING THE OUTBOX FOLDER

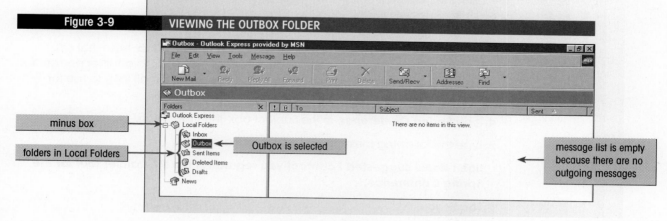

minus box

folders in Local Folders

Outbox is selected

message list is empty because there are no outgoing messages

Now you're ready to compose and send your first message.

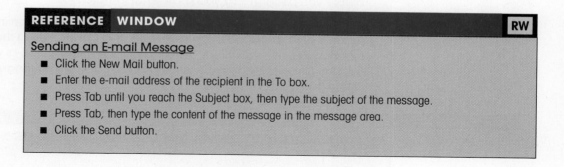

REFERENCE WINDOW   RW

Sending an E-mail Message
- Click the New Mail button.
- Enter the e-mail address of the recipient in the To box.
- Press Tab until you reach the Subject box, then type the subject of the message.
- Press Tab, then type the content of the message in the message area.
- Click the Send button.

When you click the Send button, Outlook Express places the message in the Outbox and immediately sends it. Because you opened the Outbox, you can watch this happen. Remembering that John wanted you to contact Katie Herrera as soon as you got settled, you decide to compose your first message to her. Her e-mail address is kherrera@carey.com.

To send an e-mail message:

1. Click the **New Mail** button ⬜. The New Message window opens, which lets you compose a new message.

TROUBLE? If you receive an error message at any point during these steps, check your mail server properties using the procedure you learned in the previous section. Record your settings and ask your instructor or technical support person for help.

TROUBLE? If you have more than one account or are using an account such as Hotmail, be aware that in the outgoing message, Outlook Express identifies the sender for the currently selected account. For example, if you want to send a message from your Hotmail account, click Hotmail in the Folder list before you click the New Mail button.

2. Type **kherrera@carey.com**, then press **Tab**.

3. Type your own e-mail address in the Cc box, then press **Tab**. Note that you would not normally copy yourself on an e-mail you send to another person. You are sending yourself a copy to ensure that you receive mail later to use for practice in other sections of this tutorial.

4. Type **Spring Conference** in the Subject box, then press **Tab**.

5. Type the following message in the content area:

   John Kruse suggested I contact you regarding the Mt. Rainier tour for the Spring Conference.

   Thank you,

   (your name)

6. Before sending the message, make sure to watch the Outbox. Read all of Step 7 before you perform it so you know what to watch for.

7. Click the **Send** button. Outlook Express moves your message into the Outbox, which is briefly boldfaced and followed by a (1), indicating there is one outgoing message. Then, Outlook Express sends the message on its way. The message and the (1) disappear, and the Outbox is empty and no longer boldfaced. See Figure 3-10.

Figure 3-10	SENDING A MESSAGE

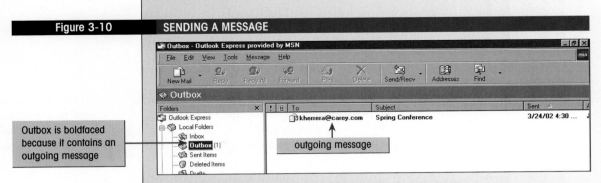

Outbox is boldfaced because it contains an outgoing message

outgoing message

TROUBLE? If Outlook Express does not send the message immediately and the (1) does not disappear, Outlook Express might be configured to send messages only when you click the Send/Recv button. Click the Send/Recv button 🖳 and watch Outlook Express send the message. If you want to change this setting, click Tools, click Options, click the Send tab, click the Send messages immediately check box, and then click OK to indicate that you want outgoing mail sent immediately.

TROUBLE? If Outlook Express requests a password, you might need to enter a password before you can send and receive your mail messages.

The time it takes to send an e-mail message depends on the size of the message, the speed of your Internet connection, and the quantity of Internet traffic at that time. When you send e-mail, your outgoing mail server examines the host name in the e-mail address, locates the host, and delivers the message to that host. Because your mail server is not connected to every other host, e-mail rarely travels a direct path to the recipient. Instead, one host hands the message to another until the e-mail reaches its destination. Figure 3-11 shows how the Internet routes a message from a student at the University of Alaska to a student at the University of the Virgin Islands.

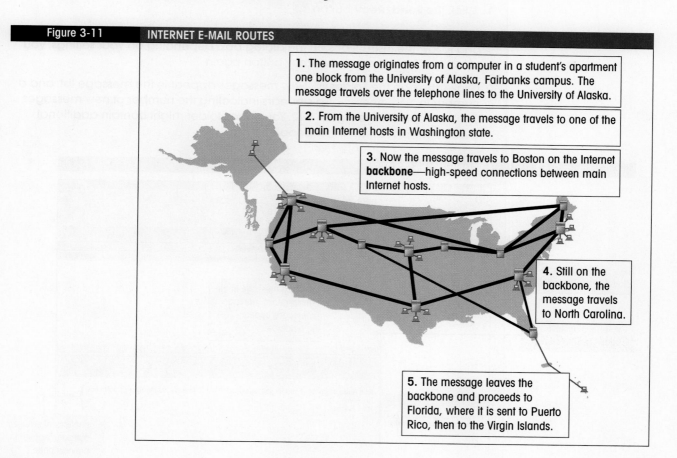

Figure 3-11   INTERNET E-MAIL ROUTES

1. The message originates from a computer in a student's apartment one block from the University of Alaska, Fairbanks campus. The message travels over the telephone lines to the University of Alaska.

2. From the University of Alaska, the message travels to one of the main Internet hosts in Washington state.

3. Now the message travels to Boston on the Internet **backbone**—high-speed connections between main Internet hosts.

4. Still on the backbone, the message travels to North Carolina.

5. The message leaves the backbone and proceeds to Florida, where it is sent to Puerto Rico, then to the Virgin Islands.

Receiving E-mail

How you receive e-mail depends on your account. For example, if you use a Web-based account, you connect to your provider's Web page where you view your messages. If you use a POP account, your mail server collects and holds your mail until your mail software contacts the mail server and requests any mail addressed to your user ID. Your mail software then downloads any waiting messages to your computer. (Remember that the Outlook Express mail software lets you set up a Hotmail account so that it too can receive local mail delivery.)

You can check your e-mail at any time by clicking the Send/Recv button ![]. Your mail server delivers any e-mail messages that have arrived since you last checked. Some people check for new e-mail messages sporadically during the day, while others check at regular intervals, such as every hour or every morning and evening. If you are connected to the Internet, Outlook Express automatically checks for messages at a specified interval. You can set this interval on the General tab of the Options dialog box, available on the Tools menu, but you won't do that now.

Remember that you sent a copy of your e-mail to yourself for the purpose of completing this tutorial. Now you'll check to see whether the copy arrived.

To check for incoming mail:

1. Click the **Send/Recv** button ![].

TROUBLE? If a dialog box opens requesting your password, enter your password and follow the instructions on the dialog box. Depending on your settings, you may have to click the Send/Recv button again.

2. Click **Inbox** on the Folder list. New messages appear in the message list, and a number in parentheses also appears indicating the number of new messages you've received. See Figure 3-12. Your Inbox folder might contain additional e-mail messages from other people.

Figure 3-12	RECEIVING MESSAGES

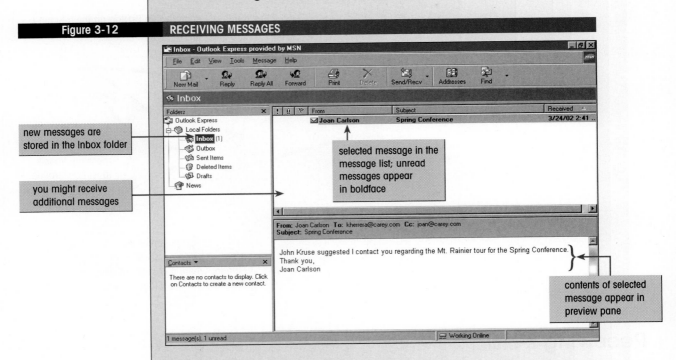

new messages are stored in the Inbox folder

you might receive additional messages

selected message in the message list; unread messages appear in boldface

contents of selected message appear in preview pane

TROUBLE? If you receive a Returned Mail message in addition to the copy of your message to Katie, don't worry. This happens because the e-mail address you are using for Katie Herrera is fictional. You'll soon learn more about returned mail.

TROUBLE? If enough time has elapsed since you sent the message, Outlook Express might have checked for incoming mail already. If that's the case, the copy should already appear. If no messages appear, your mail server might not have received or sent the messages yet. Occasionally, some mail servers cause mail to be delayed. Come back later to see if your mail has arrived, or consult your technical support person.

Unread messages appear in boldface, preceded by the unread mail icon ✉. You can view a message in its own window or in the preview pane. The message list displays a **message header** for each message that identifies the sender, subject (truncated if it's too long), and date received. Your window might list additional columns. You can change the width of the columns in the message list by dragging the column header border in the appropriate direction. You can also click a column button to sort columns by that button. For example, if you click the From button, Outlook Express sorts messages in the current folder alphabetically by name. The default sort order is by date and time received, with newest messages on top.

The message list displays a variety of icons that help you determine the status of the message. For example, ✉ tells you the message has been read; ✉ tells you the message has not been read; ✉ tells you the message is in progress in the Drafts folder.

When you select an e-mail message from the message list, the contents of that message appear in the preview pane. After a predetermined number of seconds, the message header no longer appears in boldface, indicating that you've displayed the message. You already saw how you can hide the preview pane if you want to view only the message list. You can also resize the preview pane by dragging its upper border up or down. For example, to enlarge the preview so you can see more of a message, drag the top border of the pane up.

Your Inbox should contain the copy of the message you sent yourself. Try reading it now.

To read an e-mail message:

1. If necessary, click the message you sent yourself. (Its subject is "Spring Conference" in the message list.) The contents of that message appear in the preview pane. After a few seconds (five is the default), the unread icon ✉ changes to read ✉ and the message no longer appears in boldface.

2. Now try adjusting the column widths. Point at the vertical line between one of the column borders, shown in Figure 3-13, until your pointer turns to ↔.

3. Drag the pointer slightly to the right to see more of the column or to the left to see less.

TROUBLE? If your window shows additional columns, don't worry. You can specify what information appears by clicking View, clicking Columns, and then removing the check from the box of the column display you wish to suppress.

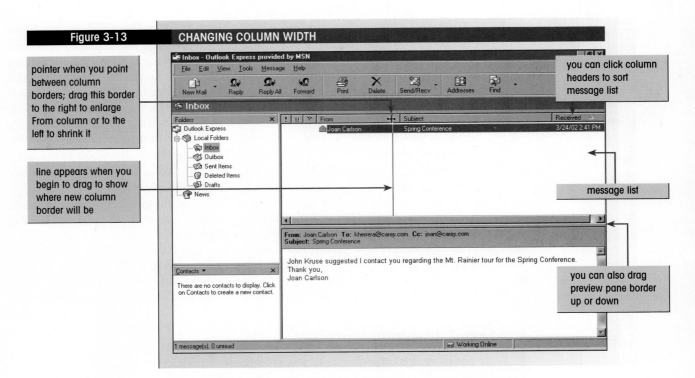

Figure 3-13 — CHANGING COLUMN WIDTH

By successfully viewing the copy of the message you sent to yourself, you verify that Outlook Express is configured properly on your computer.

Receiving Undelivered Messages

Sometimes you send an e-mail message to an Internet address that is no longer active; for example, the intended recipient may have switched to another ISP. When your outgoing mail server cannot locate a recipient's address, it sends you an undeliverable mail message. This is similar to the postal service returning a letter with an incorrect street address.

Because Katie's e-mail address is fictional, the mail delivery subsystem of your outgoing mail server will probably send you a returned mail message, telling you that it did not find the host. Check for this message now.

To read a returned mail message:

1. Click the **Send/Recv** button.

2. Click a message with "Returned mail" or something similar in the Subject column.

   TROUBLE? If no such message appears, don't worry. It might appear later. Normally you just delete returned mail messages; you'll learn how to do so later. It's also possible that your mail server is not configured to return undeliverable mail messages, so don't worry if you never receive such a message.

3. Read the message. It should inform you that the e-mail address had an unknown host.

If e-mail messages you send are returned undelivered, you should verify the e-mail addresses that you used. Make sure that you typed everything correctly and the person still uses that e-mail address.

Replying **to a message**

Often, you'll want to respond to an e-mail message. Although you could create and send a new message, using the Reply feature is easier. It automatically inserts the sender's e-mail address and the subject into the proper lines in the message window. The reply feature also "quotes" the sender's text to remind the sender of the message to which you are responding. When you reply to an e-mail message, you can respond to the original sender of the message, or to the sender and everyone else who received the message.

First you will view the message you sent yourself, this time in its own window, and then you'll practice replying to it. To open a message in its own window, double-click the message in the message list. This lets you see more of the message at once.

Note that this is a *practice* reply. Normally, you would not reply to yourself! Rather, you would reply to someone who sent you a real message.

To open a message in its own window and then reply to it:

1. Double-click the **Spring Conference** message in the message list. The message opens in its own window. Maximize this window if necessary.

2. Click the **Reply** button [icon]. The message window opens, with your name in the To box (because you're replying to your own message) and the original message's subject in the Subject box, preceded by "Re:", which is short for "regarding." The message quotes your original message.

3. Type the following reply in the message area (the cursor automatically blinks at the beginning of a blank line):

   Thanks for the information.

   (your name)

4. If necessary, scroll down to see how the original message text is quoted after the reply you just typed. See Figure 3-14.

   TROUBLE? If your mail format is plain text rather than HTML, the original message will appear with a > symbol before each line.

| Figure 3-14 | REPLYING TO A MESSAGE |

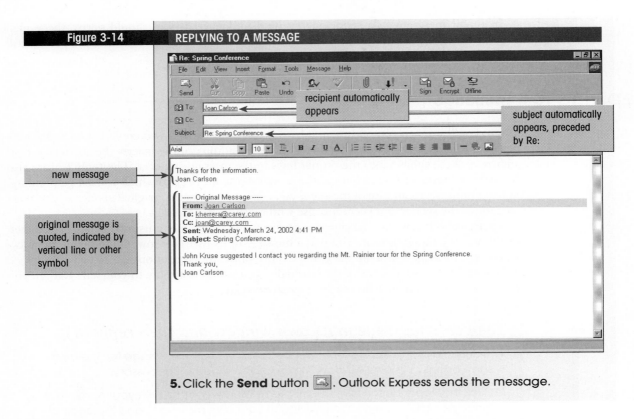

new message

original message is quoted, indicated by vertical line or other symbol

recipient automatically appears

subject automatically appears, preceded by Re:

5. Click the **Send** button. Outlook Express sends the message.

Deciding whether to quote the sender's original message when you reply to a message depends on several factors. If the recipient might need to be reminded of the message content, quoting is appropriate. However, long messages take longer to download, so whenever possible you should delete quoted material from your messages.

Printing a Message

You can print an e-mail message using the File menu's Print command. You decide to print the message you received from yourself.

To print an e-mail message:

1. Make sure the message you received is either open in its own window or selected in the message list.

2. Click **File**, then click **Print**.

3. Check the print settings in the Print dialog box, then click the **OK** button.

4. If necessary, click the **Close** button to close the message.

By default, Outlook Express formats messages using HTML. When you print a message formatted in HTML, it includes lines and boldfaced headings. However, if the message you are printing uses plain text instead of HTML, the printout contains no formatting, and some lines might be uneven. You can change this setting by clicking Tools, clicking Options, and then specifying HTML on the Send tab. Your messages will then be sent formatted. If you need a high quality printout of a plain text message, you can save the message as a text file, open it in a word processor, and edit it so that it looks professional.

Securing E-mail

When you send confidential information in an e-mail message or an attachment, you need to be concerned about who might access your message. Several Outlook Express security features give you more control over your e-mail. You can obtain a **digital ID**, a secret code from a certification authority, which is attached to the e-mail you send. This ID proves your identity to others and lets you send and receive **encrypted**, or coded, messages to ensure their privacy. Special icons in Outlook Express mark e-mail that uses digital signatures and encryption: ✉ tells you the message is digitally signed and unopened, and ✉ tells you the message is either encrypted and unopened, or encrypted, digitally signed, and unopened. If you search the Outlook Express Help system for information on obtaining a digital ID, you will find a link to the Microsoft Web site that includes links to certification authorities on the Internet.

Incoming e-mail can also be a concern. E-mail from certain sources can contain **active content**, or code that automatically installs and runs on your computer, such as scripts or ActiveX controls. (Don't worry if you haven't heard these terms; all you really need to know is that, like viruses, they have the potential to damage your system.) You can control the access these codes have to your computer by assigning a given source to a security zone, and you can then assign that zone a certain level of security. For example, you might place Web sites that you trust in a restricted zone and then assign low level security to that zone. For all other sites, you can assign medium or high level security so that active content from those sites cannot run at all or cannot run without your intervention.

All security settings are controlled on the Security tab of the Options dialog box, available on the Tools menu. You won't work with security settings in this tutorial, but you should be aware that they exist, in case you need to configure security for your e-mail in the future.

Session 3.1 QUICK CHECK

1. Identify the user ID portion and the host name portion of the e-mail address: pcsmith@icom.net.

2. How can you view your mail account properties?

3. Where can you find a copy of a message you sent?

4. Why shouldn't you type your messages in all uppercase letters?

5. A high-speed connection between main Internet hosts is called a(n) _____.

6. Name two advantages the Reply feature has over the New Mail feature when you respond to an e-mail message.

SESSION 3.2

In this session you will learn how to organize addresses in the Address Book, attach files to messages, organize messages in folders, save and forward messages, and set mail rules. You'll learn to delete Outlook Express information, send a Web page link by e-mail, and configure Outlook Express for multiple users.

Organizing Addresses in an Address Book

Every message sent across the Internet requires an e-mail address, but like the wrong zip code on a letter, any misspelled words or incorrect punctuation in an e-mail address makes a message undeliverable. Outlook Express helps you use accurate addresses by providing the **Address Book** feature, in which you can store a list of your contacts, including their e-mail addresses and personal, home, business, and other contact information. You can also specify a nickname that you can type instead of the e-mail address, and Outlook Express replaces the nickname you type with its assigned address.

You can open the Address Book by clicking the Addresses button [icon] on the toolbar or using the Contacts list, which lists all contacts in your Address Book.

You can add a contact from scratch or from messages you receive.

REFERENCE WINDOW	RW

Adding a New Contact to the Address Book
- Click Contacts on the Contacts bar.
- Click New Contact.
- Enter a name and an e-mail address in the appropriate boxes, as well as any other information you want to include.
- Click the OK button.

You can build an accurate Contacts list from the e-mail messages you receive. Outlook Express automatically adds to your Address Book the addresses of people to whose messages you reply, unless your Outlook Express settings have been modified. (You can check this setting by clicking Tools, clicking Options, and then clicking the Send tab.)

REFERENCE WINDOW	RW

Adding a Contact from a Received Message
- Display the message in its own window.
- Right-click the sender's name in the From column.
- Click Add to Address Book.

John stops by to give you his e-mail address. He suggests that you add his address, along with Katie Herrera's, to your Address Book.

Because you have not received e-mail from John, you must use the New Contact method. John's e-mail address is jkruse@carey.com. You can add Katie's address from the message you sent her, stored in the Sent Items folder.

To add an address to the Address Book:

1. Click **Contacts** on the Contacts bar, then click **New Contact**. See Figure 3-15.

Figure 3-15	CREATING A NEW CONTACT

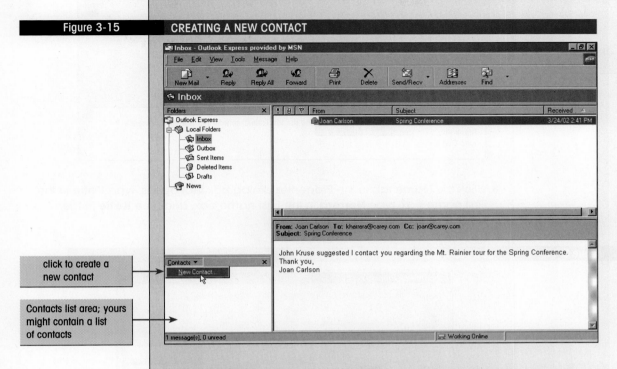

click to create a
new contact

Contacts list area; yours
might contain a list
of contacts

2. Type **John** in the First box, press **Tab** twice, then type **Kruse** in the Last box.

3. Type **John** in the Nickname box so you can simply type "John" next time you
   want to send him e-mail.

4. Press **Tab**, then type **jkruse@carey.com** in the E-Mail Addresses box.

5. Click the **Add** button to add the address, then click **OK**. After a moment, John's
   address appears along with any other addresses already in the Contacts list.

6. To add Katie's address, click the **Sent Items** folder, and then double-click the
   message you sent to Katie to open it.

   TROUBLE? If your message to Katie no longer appears, your computer might not
   save messages. You'll need to add Katie's contact information the same way
   you added John's.

7. Right-click Katie's e-mail address, then click **Add to Address Book**, as shown in
   Figure 3-16.

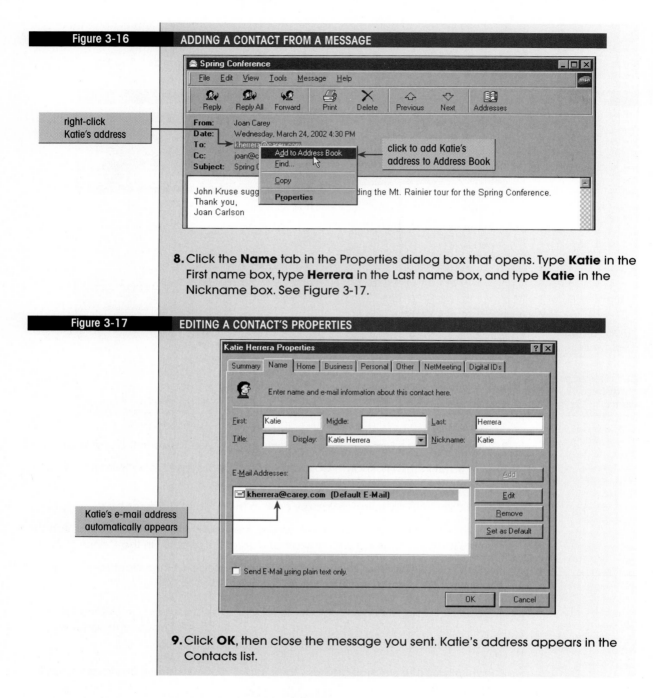

Figure 3-16 ADDING A CONTACT FROM A MESSAGE

right-click Katie's address

click to add Katie's address to Address Book

8. Click the **Name** tab in the Properties dialog box that opens. Type **Katie** in the First name box, type **Herrera** in the Last name box, and type **Katie** in the Nickname box. See Figure 3-17.

Figure 3-17 EDITING A CONTACT'S PROPERTIES

Katie's e-mail address automatically appears

9. Click **OK**, then close the message you sent. Katie's address appears in the Contacts list.

Grouping Address Book Entries

When you regularly send e-mail messages to the same people, you can create a **group**, a specified list of contacts that can be referenced by a single name. You can place a single contact in as many groups as you need. When you want to send e-mail to everyone in the group, you enter the group name in the To box. When you change a contact's information, Outlook Express automatically references the updated address when you use any group that includes it.

You decide to create a group called "Conference" that will contain John's and Katie's addresses, as you frequently send them both the same message. To create a group, you open the Address Book, which lists all your contacts and provides the commands needed to organize them.

To create a group:

1. Click the **Addresses** button 📖 on the toolbar. The Address Book opens.

   TROUBLE? If the Addresses button is not visible on the toolbar, click the double arrow ▶▶ to view additional toolbar buttons.

2. Click the **New** button 🖼, then click **New Group** on the menu that appears. The Properties dialog box opens. Type **Conference** in the Group Name box.

3. Click the **Select Members** button. The Select Group Members dialog box opens.

4. Scroll through the entries until you locate John Kruse's entry. Click John's entry, then click the **Select** button. A copy of John's entry appears in the Members list.

5. Locate and click Katie Herrera's entry, then click the **Select** button. See Figure 3-18.

Figure 3-18	ADDING CONTACTS TO A GROUP

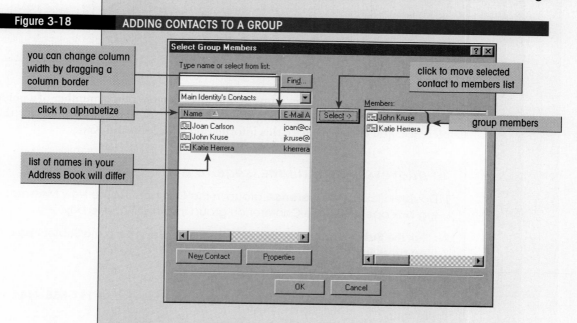

6. Click **OK** in the Select Group Members dialog box, then click **OK** again in the Conference Properties dialog box.

7. Close the Address Book. The Conference group's name now appears in the Contacts list.

   TROUBLE? If the Outlook Express informs you that a group with the name Conference already exists, click **OK**, change the group name so it is unique, and then substitute the group name you specified throughout the remainder of this tutorial.

You can easily add or remove contacts from a group now by right-clicking the group's name in the Contacts list and then clicking Properties.

Sending a Message Using the Address Book

After you enter an address or group name in the Address Book, you can address a message to that person or group by selecting it from the Contacts list.

REFERENCE WINDOW   **RW**

<u>Selecting Contacts from the Address Book</u>

- Double-click the contact in the Contacts list. Outlook Express opens the New Message dialog box with the contact's name and e-mail address already filled in.

  or

- Click the New Mail button to open the New Message dialog box. If you assigned a nickname to the contact, type the nickname in the To box and Outlook Express replaces the nickname with the corresponding e-mail address.

  or

- In the To box, type as much of the contact's e-mail address as you remember. Outlook Express attempts to match it. Stop typing when you see the correct name. If your entry has several possible matches, Outlook Express opens a dialog box from which you can choose the correct recipient.

  or

- If you can't remember anything about the address, click the To button in the New Message box. The Select Recipients dialog box opens, from which you can select the contact or contacts you want.

A co-worker, Pat LaFrancois, stops by and gives you the phone number of a guide service you might want to contact regarding the Mt. Rainier tour you're planning for the Spring Conference. You decide to share this information with John and Katie.

To address an e-mail message to a group:

1. Double-click the **Conference** group in the Contacts list. The New Message dialog box opens with the Conference group inserted in the To box.

2. Click the **Subject** box, type **Mt. Rainier Guide Service** in the Subject box, and then press **Tab**.

3. Type the following message:

   Pat suggested we contact the Rainier Guide Service at 111-555-4444 for the tour.

   (your name)

4. Click the **Send** button 📧. Outlook Express sends the message.

Sending and Receiving Attached Files

When two people work in the same office or use the same local area network (LAN), sharing files is relatively easy because they share a common server and can open each other's files. When people who do not share the same network work in different states or even different countries, however, they must use other means. Attaching a file to an e-mail message is an easy and effective way to send files, if both people use the same or compatible e-mail programs. Note however, that some mail servers limit the size of file attachments. For really large files, you should use another file transfer method, such as FTP.

REFERENCE WINDOW   **RW**

Attaching a File to an E-mail Message
- Click the New Mail button, and fill in the New Message window with the recipient and subject information and any message you want to include.
- Click the Attach button.
- Locate and select the file, then click the Attach button.
- Click the Send button.

John called the Mt. Rainier Guide Service and received confirmation of their services. He would like you to e-mail a copy of the confirmation file, Confirmation.doc, to Katie. This file is in the Tutorial.03\Tutorial folder on your Data Disk. You decide also to mail a copy to yourself so you can practice opening an attached file.

To attach a file to an e-mail message:

1. Double-click **Katie Herrera** in the Contacts list. The New Message opens with Katie's address automatically inserted.

   TROUBLE? If Katie's name is no longer in your Contacts list, click the New Mail button, type kherrera@carey.com in the To box, and then continue with Step 2.

2. Type your own e-mail address in the Cc box, then press **Tab**.

3. Type **Confirmation** in the Subject box, then press **Tab**.

4. In the message area, type:

   Attached is a copy of the confirmation letter.

   (your name)

5. Click the **Attach** button [📎]. The Insert Attachment dialog box opens.

6. Click the **Look in** list arrow, then click the drive containing your Data Disk.

7. Open the **Tutorial.03** folder, then open the **Tutorial** folder. Click the **Confirmation** file.

8. Click the **Attach** button. An Attach box appears beneath the Subject box in the New Message window, displaying the name and size of the file you just attached. See Figure 3-19.

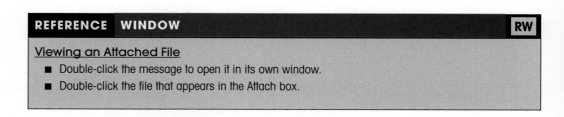

Figure 3-19   FILE ATTACHMENT

filename of file you just attached; don't worry if your file size is slightly different

9. Click the **Send** button.

With a file attached, the message is bigger than usual and takes a little longer to send. Outlook Express sends it to both you and Katie.

Messages that contain attached files appear with a paper clip icon in the message list. If you have the appropriate software for the attached file type, you can view attached files right from the message. However, until you save the attachment as a separate file, you can't access it from a software program without first opening the e-mail message to which it is attached. You can easily save an attached file by right-clicking it, clicking Save As, choosing a name and location, and clicking the Save button. Whether or not recipients can open and view an attached file depends on their software.

When you reply to a message containing an attached file, the reply does not include the attached file. However, when you forward a message containing an attached file, the attached file is included.

REFERENCE WINDOW	RW

Viewing an Attached File
- Double-click the message to open it in its own window.
- Double-click the file that appears in the Attach box.

You decide to check your messages to verify that the attached file arrived.

To receive the Confirmation.doc file you just sent:

1. Click the **Send/Recv** button 🖳. Because the message you sent to yourself has an attached file, it takes a little longer than usual to receive your messages.

   TROUBLE? If you received no messages, you might need to allow time for your mail server to process the message. Try again later.

   TROUBLE? If you receive the reply to the Spring Conference message you sent earlier, just leave it in your Inbox for now.

2. Click the **Inbox** folder.

3. After the Confirmation message appears in your Inbox, double-click it to open it in its own window and then maximize the message window.

4. Double-click **Confirmation.doc** in the Attach box. Depending on which program DOC files are associated with on your computer, either WordPad or Word may open to display it.

   TROUBLE? If you are asked whether you want to open or save the file, click the Open it button and then click OK.

   TROUBLE? If the file does not open in WordPad or Word, your computer might not associate DOC files with one of these programs. If a different program starts, continue with Step 5. If a message warns you that the file type is not recognized, click the Cancel button and skip Step 5.

5. View the document, then click the **Close** button for the program that displays the attachment.

6. Close the Confirmation message.

Managing Messages

You already know that Outlook Express uses folders to organize messages passing through your computer. You can further organize your mail by creating subfolders. For example, a student might create a subfolder to file all correspondence with her Latin professor, or an architect might create one folder for each project.

Creating a Folder

The Folder list displays folders and subfolders in a hierarchy. When you create a new folder, you need to specify its location in this hierarchy. The top level of this hierarchy is Outlook Express itself. The next level contains the Local Folders folder, other mail accounts, and your news accounts (you'll learn more about these in Session 3.3). Within the Local Folders folder are the default folders, which include the Inbox, Outbox, and Sent Items folders that you've already used. You can also create subfolders within any of these folders.

   Figure 3-20 shows the subfolders a student created within the Inbox folder: Homework and Student Government. Within the Homework folder are three subfolders: Calculus, History, and Physics. Within the Student Government folder are two subfolders: Budget and Homecoming.

Figure 3-20   MESSAGE FOLDER STRUCTURE

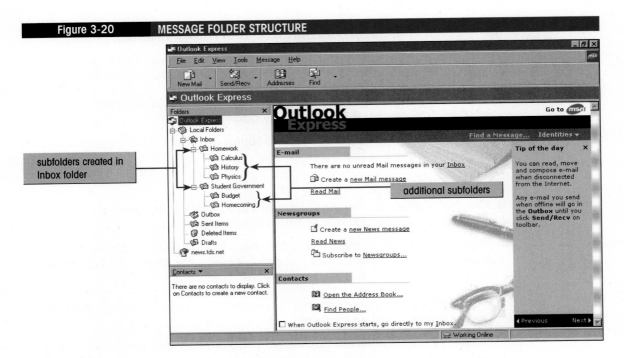

subfolders created in Inbox folder

additional subfolders

You can show all folders in the hierarchy or only those at the levels you choose. The plus ⊞ and minus ⊟ boxes indicate whether the folders in that level are visible or hidden.

REFERENCE   WINDOW   RW

Creating a Message Folder
- Click File, point to Folder, and then click New.
- Type a folder name.
- Click the folder in which you want to place the new folder.
- Click the OK button.

You are going to create a folder called Rainier where you will file the correspondence you have regarding the Spring Conference ascent of Mt. Rainier. You'll create that folder within the Inbox folder.

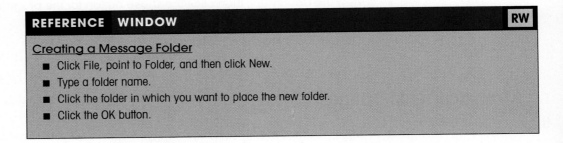

To create a folder within the Inbox folder:

1. Click **File**, point to **Folder**, and then click **New**.

2. Type **Rainier** in the Folder name box.

3. Click **Inbox**. See Figure 3-21.

Figure 3-21   CREATING A NEW FOLDER

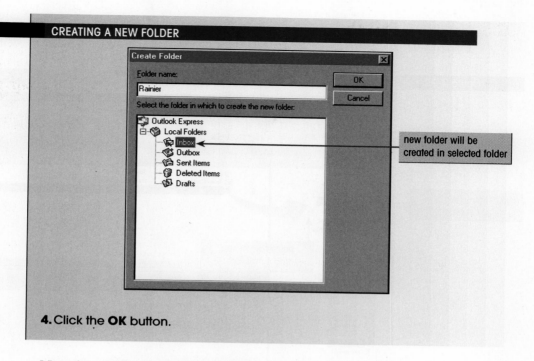

new folder will be
created in selected folder

4. Click the **OK** button.

Now that you have created the folder, you are ready to save messages in it.

Filing Messages

When a message comes into the Inbox, you can file it immediately or file it later.

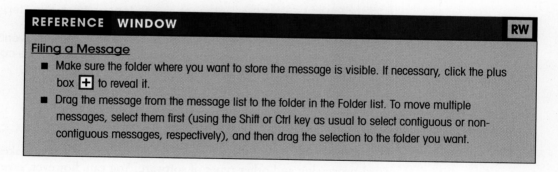

REFERENCE   WINDOW   **RW**

Filing a Message

■ Make sure the folder where you want to store the message is visible. If necessary, click the plus
box ⊞ to reveal it.

■ Drag the message from the message list to the folder in the Folder list. To move multiple
messages, select them first (using the Shift or Ctrl key as usual to select contiguous or noncontiguous messages, respectively), and then drag the selection to the folder you want.

You decide to file the copy of the message you sent Katie in the Rainier folder. Then
you'll examine the contents of the Rainier folder.

To file a message:

1. If necessary, click the **plus box** ⊞ next to Inbox so that the Rainier folder is
visible.

2. Make sure that the Confirmation message is visible in the Message list.

3. Drag the **Confirmation** message from the Message list into the Rainier folder.
The pointer changes from ⬚ to ⬚. See Figure 3-22.

TROUBLE? If the Confirmation message is no longer there, use any message in the Inbox.

| Figure 3-22 | FILING A MESSAGE |

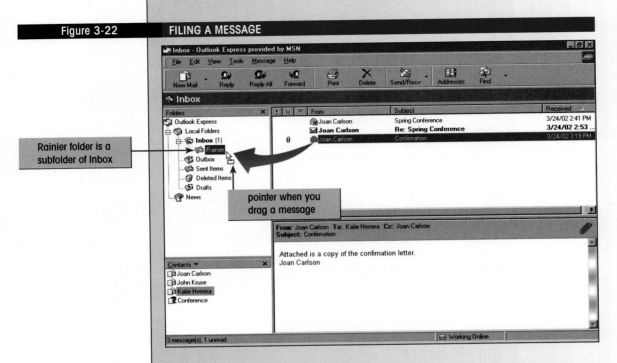

4. Repeat Steps 2 and 3 to move the two **Spring Conference** messages (the original and the reply) to the Rainier folder.

TROUBLE? Again, if the messages are no longer there, skip Step 4.

5. Click **Rainier** in the Folder list to open the Rainier folder to verify that it contains the messages you just filed. The Message list now shows the contents of the Rainier folder.

Saving a Message in a File

Messages exist in the Outlook Express folders in a format that makes them inaccessible to word-processing and other types of software. You can, however, save a message as a file so that you can store it on a disk or open it with a different program.

You decide to practice saving a message as a text file, because, at some point, you will probably need to incorporate information from an e-mail into other documents.

To save an e-mail message to a disk:

1. In the Rainier folder, click the **Spring Conference** message.

TROUBLE? If you moved another message to the Rainier folder in previous steps because the Spring Conference message was not available, substitute that file now.

2. Click **File**, then click **Save As**.

3. Click the **Save in** list arrow, then, if necessary, click the drive containing your Data Disk. Open the **Tutorial.03** folder, then open the **Tutorial** folder. Spring Conference automatically appears in the File name box.

4. Click the **Save as type** list arrow, then click **Text Files (*.txt)**.

5. Click the **Save** button.

6. Now view the file you just saved by clicking the **Start** button on the Windows taskbar: point to **Programs**, point to **Accessories**, then click **WordPad**.

7. In WordPad, click the **Open** button 📂, click the **Files of type** list arrow, then click **Text Documents (*.txt)**.

8. Locate and select the **Spring Conference** file you saved on your Data Disk, then click the **Open** button. The message appears as a text file in WordPad. Notice that when you save an e-mail message as a text file, it contains no formatting, such as boldface or lines.

9. Close **WordPad**.

You have stored your message as a text file on your Data Disk.

Forwarding a Message

Forwarding a message is similar to replying to an e-mail message. When you forward an e-mail message, you send another person a copy of the entire message. Outlook Express inserts Fw: [subject] into the Subject box and includes any attached files in the Attach box. When forwarding a message, you can add new comments to the original message text in the outgoing message area.

John asks you to forward the confirmation letter to Chris Lopez, an administrative assistant at Carey Outerwear. Her e-mail address is clopez@carey.com. Because you have a copy of the confirmation message in your Rainier folder, you decide it will be simplest just to forward it to her.

To forward mail:

1. If necessary, open the Rainier folder.

2. Click the **Confirmation** message (the one with Confirmation.doc attached).

3. Click the **Forward** button 🔁.

4. Type **clopez@carey.com** in the To box. Leave the subject as it appears. Notice Outlook Express inserted Fw: to indicate the message is a forwarded message.

5. Click the top of the message area, then type:

    Attached is the confirmation letter you requested for the Rainier project.

    (your name)

6. Click the **Send** button 📤.

Outlook Express forwards the message to Chris Lopez, who will receive both the message and the attachment.

Sending a Web Link by E-mail

Sending Web links or pages by e-mail is a quick, easy way to get information to other Internet users. The Internet Explorer browser contains an e-mail option that lets you send the current Web page or a link to the current Web page. John asked you to find a Web site on Mt. Rainier. You locate a site that contains a Mt. Rainier newsletter, so you decide to e-mail the link to John.

To send a Web link by e-mail:

1. Start Internet Explorer.

   TROUBLE? Click the Internet Explorer icon 🅔 or click the Start button, point to Programs, and then click Internet Explorer.

2. Enter **http://www.course.com/NewPerspectives/IE5** in the Address box, then click the **Go** button 🔁.

3. After the page opens, click the **Tutorial 3** link. The Rainier page opens.

4. Click the **Mail** button 🖃. Notice you can choose to send just the link or the entire page by e-mail. See Figure 3-23.

| Figure 3-23 | E-MAIL OPTIONS FROM INTERNET EXPLORER |

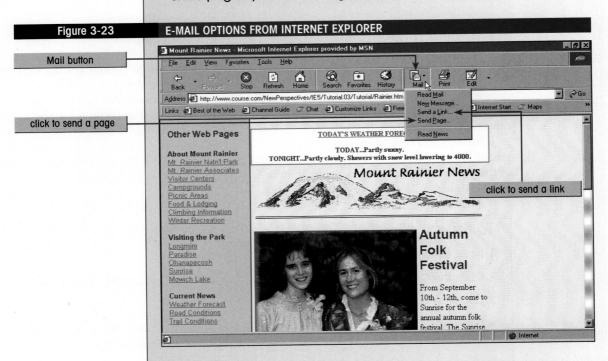

5. Click **Send a Link**. A message dialog box opens with the name of the Web page that you are mailing in the Attach box and the link in the message area. You can type your own message above or below the link, and you can change the subject. See Figure 3-24.

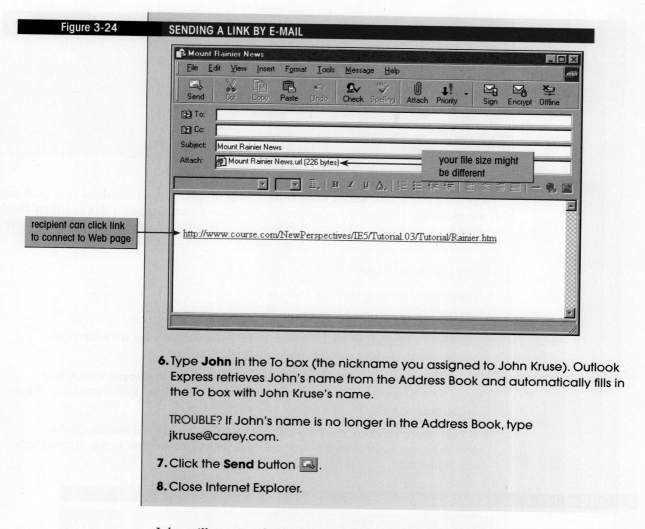

Figure 3-24   SENDING A LINK BY E-MAIL

recipient can click link to connect to Web page

your file size might be different

6. Type **John** in the To box (the nickname you assigned to John Kruse). Outlook Express retrieves John's name from the Address Book and automatically fills in the To box with John Kruse's name.

   TROUBLE? If John's name is no longer in the Address Book, type jkruse@carey.com.

7. Click the **Send** button 🖃.

8. Close Internet Explorer.

John will receive the message and see a link in it that he can click to connect to the Rainier Web page. If you had chosen Send Page instead of Send a Link, Outlook Express would have inserted a copy of the page, graphics and all, into the message area. John then would have been able to view the page without connecting to it.

Setting Mail Rules

You can set mail rules to process your mail more efficiently. A **mail rule** is an action Outlook Express takes if it encounters a mail message that meets a defined condition. For example, you can set a rule that automatically saves any message from a given address in a specified folder or deletes any message whose subject line contains a specified word or words. You can block messages from certain senders and domains, automatically reply to or forward certain messages, and highlight certain messages in color.

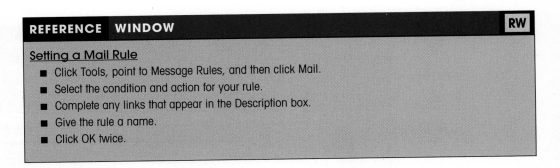

REFERENCE   WINDOW   RW

Setting a Mail Rule
- Click Tools, point to Message Rules, and then click Mail.
- Select the condition and action for your rule.
- Complete any links that appear in the Description box.
- Give the rule a name.
- Click OK twice.

Next week you will be out of town visiting your brother, so you decide to set a mail rule that automatically forwards messages to your brother's e-mail account. He can then check your mail for you. Because this rule is fictional, you'll cancel it without actually creating it.

To set a mail rule:

1. If necessary, reopen Outlook Express.

2. Click **Tools**, point to **Message Rules**, and then click **Mail**.

3. Scroll to the bottom of the Conditions box, then click the **For all messages** check box to select it as a condition for your new rule.

4. Scroll down the Actions box, then click the **Forward it to people** check box to select it as the action for your new rule. Notice the Description box contains a link so you can select the contact you want to use.

5. In the Description box, click the **people** link. The Select People dialog box opens. Type your brother's e-mail address, **jack@home.com**, in the Address box. See Figure 3-25.

Figure 3-25	CREATING A MAIL RULE

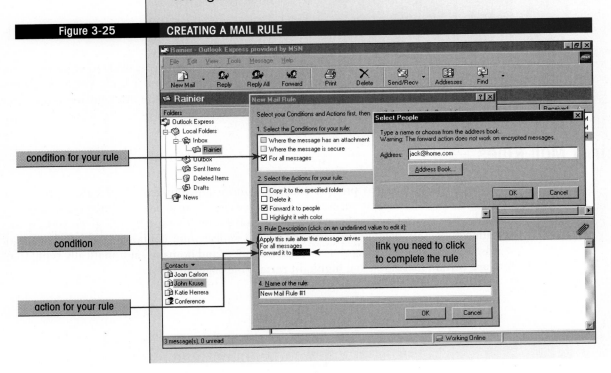

condition for your rule

condition

action for your rule

link you need to click to complete the rule

6. Click **OK**. Now you can add another condition, such as designating that a saved message be sent as a reply, informing people that you are on vacation, but you won't do that now.

7. In the Name box, select the default name and then type **Forward Messages** as the name of your rule. Figure 3-26 shows the completed rule.

Figure 3-26	COMPLETED MAIL RULE

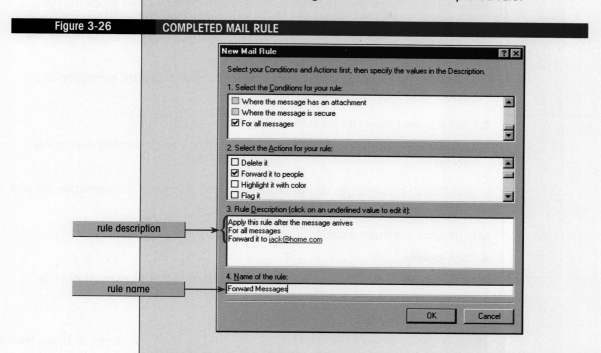

rule description

rule name

8. Click **Cancel** because this e-mail rule is fictional. Click **OK** to close the Message Rules dialog box.

Deleting Outlook Express Information

Your folders and Address Book can easily become cluttered with information you no longer need. You should periodically clear unwanted messages and remove obsolete entries from your Address Book. After the Mt. Rainier tour plan is complete, you can delete information associated with it.

Deleting Messages and Folders

After you read a message and reply to or forward it as necessary, you can delete it, file it in a folder, or leave it where it is. Outlook Express automatically transfers any message you delete to the Deleted Items folder. You'll first delete the returned mail messages and then the entire Rainier folder.

To delete unwanted e-mail and folders:

1. If necessary, click the **Inbox** folder in the Folder list.

2. Right-click the returned mail message, then click **Delete**. If you didn't receive a returned mail message, right-click one of the other messages you received during this tutorial. Repeat this step for any other e-mail in the Inbox that you generated during this tutorial. If you want to delete several messages, press and hold down the **Ctrl** key while you click multiple messages. Then right-click the selection and click **Delete**.

   TROUBLE? If no messages you generated in this tutorial are still available, skip Step 2.

3. Click the **Sent Items** folder in the Folder List.

4. Delete any messages in the Sent Items folder that you generated during this tutorial.

   TROUBLE? If no messages you generated in this tutorial are still available, just skip Step 4.

5. Right-click the **Rainier** folder.

6. Click **Delete**.

7. Click the **Yes** button if you are asked to confirm that you want to delete the folder, and move it to the "Deleted Items folder."

Deleted messages remain in the Deleted Items folder until you empty it. If you want to retrieve a deleted message, you can do so by moving it out of the Deleted Items folder.

To empty the Deleted Items folder:

1. In the Folder List, right-click the **Deleted Items** folder.

2. Click **Empty 'Deleted Items' Folder**. Click the **Yes** button to confirm.

By deleting unwanted messages regularly, you save space on your hard drive.

Deleting Address Book Entries

Ensuring that the Address Book contains only relevant entries is also important. Periodically, you should remove outdated or unneeded entries from your Address Book. You no longer need addresses you entered in this tutorial, so delete them all from the Address Book.

To delete entries from the Address Book:

1. Click the **Addresses** button to open the Address Book window.

2. Right-click **Conference**, click **Delete**, and then click **Yes** to confirm deleting the Conference group.

3. Click **John Kruse**, then press and hold down the **Ctrl** key and Click **Katie Herrera**.

4. Right-click the selection, click **Delete**, and then click **Yes** to confirm the deletion.

5. Click the **Close** button to close the Address Book window.

You deleted all unwanted information from Outlook Express, and you're ready to start your next project.

Configuring Outlook Express for Multiple Users

When more than one person uses the same version of Outlook Express, you can create an **identity** that lets you store mail and contacts separately for each person who uses your computer. At Carey Outerwear, for example, several interns might share the same computer, so each intern can create a separate identity. Because you are unlikely to be able to work with identities in a lab environment, you won't create an identity now, but you can read the Reference Window steps to learn how to do so.

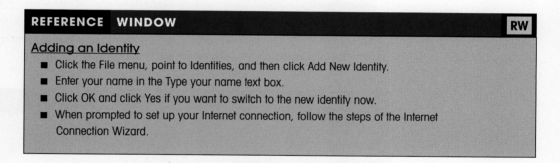

REFERENCE WINDOW   **RW**

Adding an Identity
- Click the File menu, point to Identities, and then click Add New Identity.
- Enter your name in the Type your name text box.
- Click OK and click Yes if you want to switch to the new identity now.
- When prompted to set up your Internet connection, follow the steps of the Internet Connection Wizard.

You can also switch identities "on the fly" when Outlook Express is running.

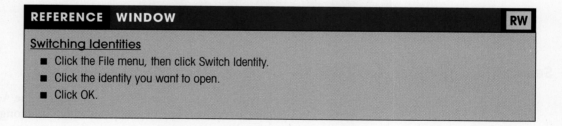

REFERENCE WINDOW   **RW**

Switching Identities
- Click the File menu, then click Switch Identity.
- Click the identity you want to open.
- Click OK.

After you create identities, you can switch between them without closing Outlook Express. The folder bar identifies the name of the current identity. See Figure 3-27.

| Figure 3-27 | USING AN IDENTITY |

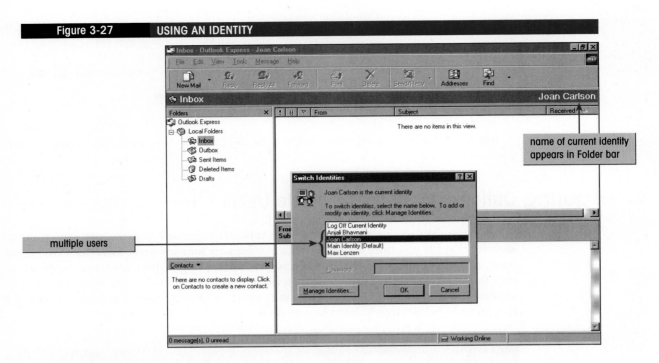

To remove an identity, you must first switch to the default identity. You cannot remove an identity under which you are currently working.

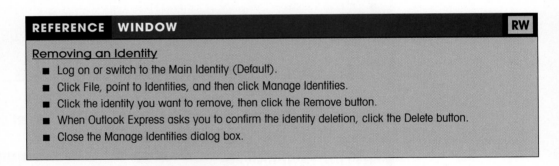

REFERENCE   WINDOW   RW

Removing an Identity

- Log on or switch to the Main Identity (Default).
- Click File, point to Identities, and then click Manage Identities.
- Click the identity you want to remove, then click the Remove button.
- When Outlook Express asks you to confirm the identity deletion, click the Delete button.
- Close the Manage Identities dialog box.

Session 3.2 QUICK CHECK

1. True or false: If you change someone's e-mail address in the Address Book, you must also update that address in any groups to which it belongs.

2. How do you know when you've received an e-mail message with an attached file?

3. How can you view the subfolders of a folder in the Folder List?

4. What usually happens to e-mail messages that have incorrect or obsolete e-mail addresses?

5. True or False: Deleting an Inbox message permanently removes the e-mail message from your hard disk.

6. What key should you press to select noncontiguous multiple messages?

SESSION 3.3

In this session you will learn to set up a newsgroup account, subscribe to a newsgroup, follow the threads in and post a message to a newsgroup, sort and search newsgroup posts, and unsubscribe from a newsgroup.

Newsgroups

So far in this tutorial you've learned how you can use e-mail to communicate with others and gather information on a topic. Now you'll look at a means of bringing people with a common interest together—**discussion groups**, most commonly called **newsgroups**. There are thousands of newsgroups on the Internet. Interested users subscribe to a newsgroup and then exchange messages with other subscribers on that topic using regular e-mail. The act of sending an e-mail message to a newsgroup is called **posting**; a message sent to a newsgroup is often called a **post**. Newsgroups can be open to everyone or restricted to a private group. A private newsgroup might be created, for example, for scholars who want to limit membership to their peers.

When a newsgroup member posts a message to a newsgroup, the message is sent to a special server called a **news server**, which stores and manages messages posted to various newsgroups. To retrieve messages posted to a newsgroup, you need special software called a **newsreader**. Outlook Express can function as a newsreader. When you subscribe to and then open a newsgroup, Outlook Express retrieves the most recent message headers (the text in the Subject line) from the news server. When you see a message you want to read, Outlook Express can download it for you. Figure 3-28 illustrates the dissemination of messages posted to a newsgroup.

Figure 3-28   POSTING TO A NEWSGROUP

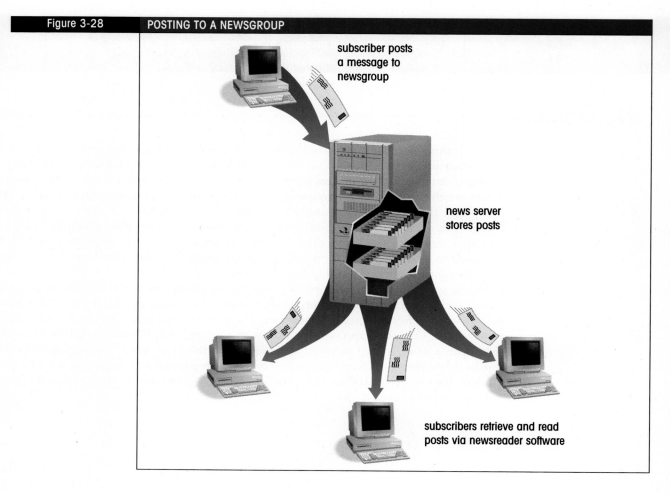

Newsgroup Names

Newsgroup names are defined based on a hierarchy of categories. Figure 3-29 shows a small part of this hierarchy.

Figure 3-29   EXAMPLES OF NEWSGROUP CATEGORIES IN THE NEWSGROUP HIERARCHY

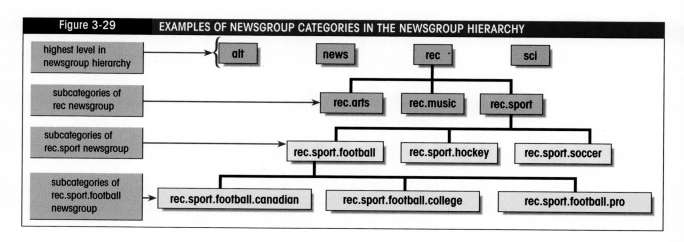

The highest level is the general category to which a topic belongs. Each category has a name (usually an abbreviation). For example, all recreational activities begin with the name "rec." Newsgroups that deal with the arts, music, sports, and so on are within the recreational category. Within the sports category you might find categories such as football, hockey, and soccer. Within the football category you might find categories such as Canadian football, college football, and professional football. The newsgroup for college football has a name consisting of all codes of the hierarchy, separated by periods: "rec.sport.football.college."

Outlook Express identifies newsgroups by these somewhat cryptic names. Figure 3-30 shows sample newsgroup categories and newsgroups that might exist within those categories.

Figure 3-30	EXAMPLES OF NEWSGROUP NAMES	
CATEGORY	**DESCRIPTION**	**EXAMPLE**
alt	Alternative newsgroups of many different types	alt.guitar.bass for discussions about bass guitars
harvard	Newsgroups about Harvard University	harvard.course.math121 for discussions about the Math 121 course at Harvard
humanities	Newsgroups about topics in the humanities department, such as art and literature	humanities.lit.authors.shakespeare for discussions about the works of William Shakespeare
k12	Newsgroups about education K-12	k12.lang.japanese for discussions about Japanese language programs in K-12 schools
rec	Newsgroups about recreational activities	rec.autos.sport.indy for discussions about car racing at the Indy 500
uk	Newsgroups about the United Kingdom	uk.politics.electoral for discussions about electoral politics in the United Kingdom

Threads

When you subscribe to a newsgroup, you have access to all messages posted by all subscribers within a time frame established by the news server. Organizing your e-mail might seem an easy task when compared to organizing newsgroup messages, given that many people can post on numerous conversations in a given newsgroup. Newsreader software such as Outlook Express lets you organize the list of message headers so subscribers can follow many conversations without losing their flow.

Outlook Express by default sorts message headers into threads. A **thread** is a batch of messages that follow a single "line of conversation." One person posts a message, several people reply to it, more reply to the replies, and so on until the topic is dropped. Multiple threads can develop simultaneously, just as in a busy room there can be many conversations. Figure 3-31 illustrates how threads develop in a newsgroup.

Figure 3-31	THREADS YOU MIGHT FIND IN REC.ARTS.CALLIGRAPHY

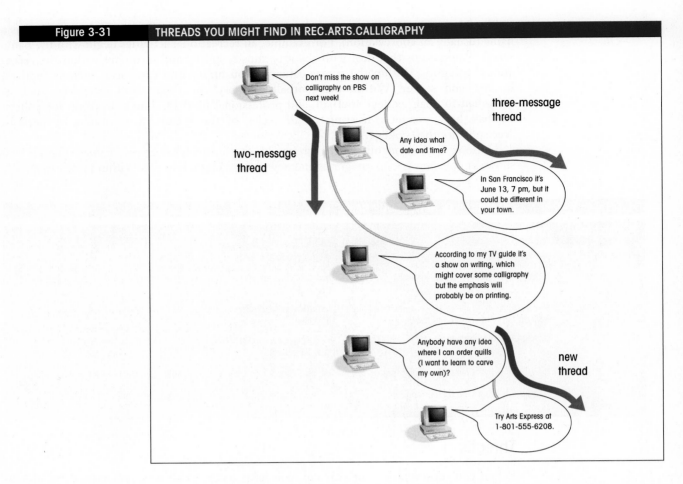

Most threads generate just a few posts, but some (especially on controversial topics) generate numerous posts over many days.

Setting Up a Newsgroup Account

To subscribe to a newsgroup you must first set up a newsgroup account with a news server. Outlook Express must download to your computer a copy of the list of all newsgroups supported by your news server, which could be time-consuming. After downloading the initial list, however, Outlook Express simply loads the list stored on your computer whenever you attempt to subscribe to a newsgroup.

You decide to spend your lunch hour exploring newsgroups. You have no particular goal in mind; you just want to get a feel for what's out there. It's possible that someone has already set up a newsgroup account on your computer; if so, you don't need to perform the next set of steps unless you want to set up an account for an additional news server. Because different news servers maintain different lists of newsgroups, some people have multiple news server accounts.

To set up a newsgroup account:

1. If necessary, launch Outlook Express.

2. Click **Tools**, then click **Accounts**.

3. Click the **News** tab.

4. Click the **Add** button, then click **News**. The Internet Connection Wizard starts. Follow the steps, supplying information where necessary. When you finish, click the **Finish** button.

   TROUBLE? If you aren't sure of your news server's name, check with your technical support person or contact your Internet Service Provider.

5. Click the **Close** button. When prompted to download the list of newsgroups on the server, click the **Yes** button. You must wait for the newsreader to download the names of all existing newsgroups on your news server; a message box informs you how many have been downloaded. This could take considerable time, depending on the speed of your Internet connection and the number of newsgroups your news server supports. Be prepared to wait 10 minutes or more. When all newsgroups have been downloaded, the Newsgroups window opens, displaying your news server's list of newsgroups.

   TROUBLE? If 15 minutes elapse, your Internet connection might be slow. Ask your technical support person whether you should continue to wait or whether there might be a problem with the connection. If you can determine that you are still receiving data (perhaps your computer indicates data transfer with a blinking icon in the Windows taskbar or you can see the number of newsgroups downloaded so far), continue to wait.

After you set up an account with a news server, you are ready to subscribe to any newsgroups the server supports. You decide to view the list of available newsgroups supported by your news server. The list you see depends on what newsgroups your server supports. If you added a news server account in the previous set of steps, that server's newsgroup list should appear, and you can skip the next steps.

To view the list of newsgroups your server supports:

1. Click the news server whose newsgroup list you want to view. News servers are listed at the bottom of the Folder list.

2. If you do not currently subscribe to any newsgroups, a message box asks if you would like to view a list of newsgroups now. Click the **Yes** button. If this message box doesn't appear, click the **Newsgroups** button. You might need to click More Buttons to locate this button. The Newsgroups window opens. See Figure 3-32.

| Figure 3-32 | **LIST OF NEWSGROUPS** |

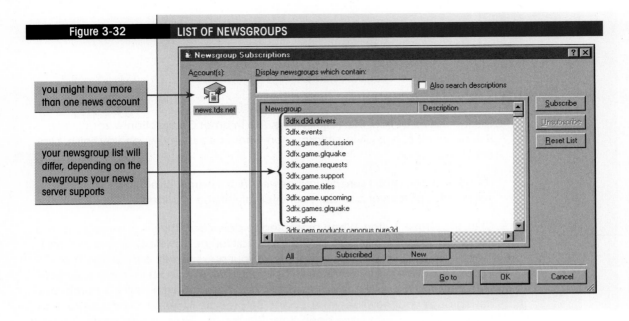

you might have more than one news account

your newsgroup list will differ, depending on the newgroups your news server supports

The list of newsgroups appears in alphabetical order. If you want the most current list of newsgroups (new ones are added all the time), you can click the Reset List button.

Subscribing to a Newsgroup

To subscribe to a newsgroup you can either search for a particular one, as you'll see later, or you can navigate the list of newsgroups until you find the one you want. You decide to look at the newsgroups in the alt category, and when you find an interesting one, you'll subscribe to it.

To subscribe to a newsgroup:

1. Scroll down to the newsgroups that begin with "alt".

2. Scroll down the list of newsgroups in the alt category. The alt category contains many subcategories, such as alt.animals, alt.autos, and alt.books.

3. Scroll through the alt categories, and click a newsgroup that interests you.

   TROUBLE? If you can't find one that interests you, click one whose name is recognizable. This tutorial doesn't recommend a specific newsgroup to prevent a large batch of new members posting to and overloading a single newsgroup.

4. Click the **Subscribe** button. A subscribe icon 🗞 appears next to the newsgroup to show you are subscribed to it. You can subscribe to another newsgroup by clicking the newsgroup and again clicking the Subscribe button, but you won't do that now.

5. Click the **OK** button. The alt group you chose now appears in the message window. See Figure 3-33. Your group should be different.

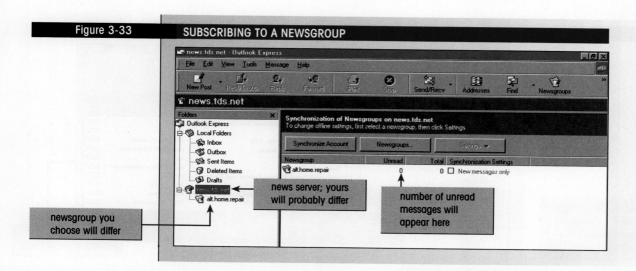

Figure 3-33 — SUBSCRIBING TO A NEWSGROUP

newsgroup you choose will differ

news server; yours will probably differ

number of unread messages will appear here

Now you are ready to open the newsgroup to which you just subscribed. Outlook Express downloads message headers (not the messages themselves, to save space) 300 at a time, although you can use the menu commands to download just new message headers, new messages, or all messages.

To download the first batch of message headers:

1. In the folder list, click the newsgroup to which you just subscribed. Your computer might take a few minutes to download the headers; the status bar reports the download progress. After the download is complete, the message headers appear in a list. Scroll through the list to view its contents. See Figure 3-34.

   TROUBLE? If the newsgroup you subscribed to has only a few messages, there might be no threads and you might have trouble understanding how threads work. Try subscribing to a different newsgroup.

   TROUBLE? If you are asked if you want to view new newsgroups, click the No button.

Figure 3-34   MESSAGE HEADERS

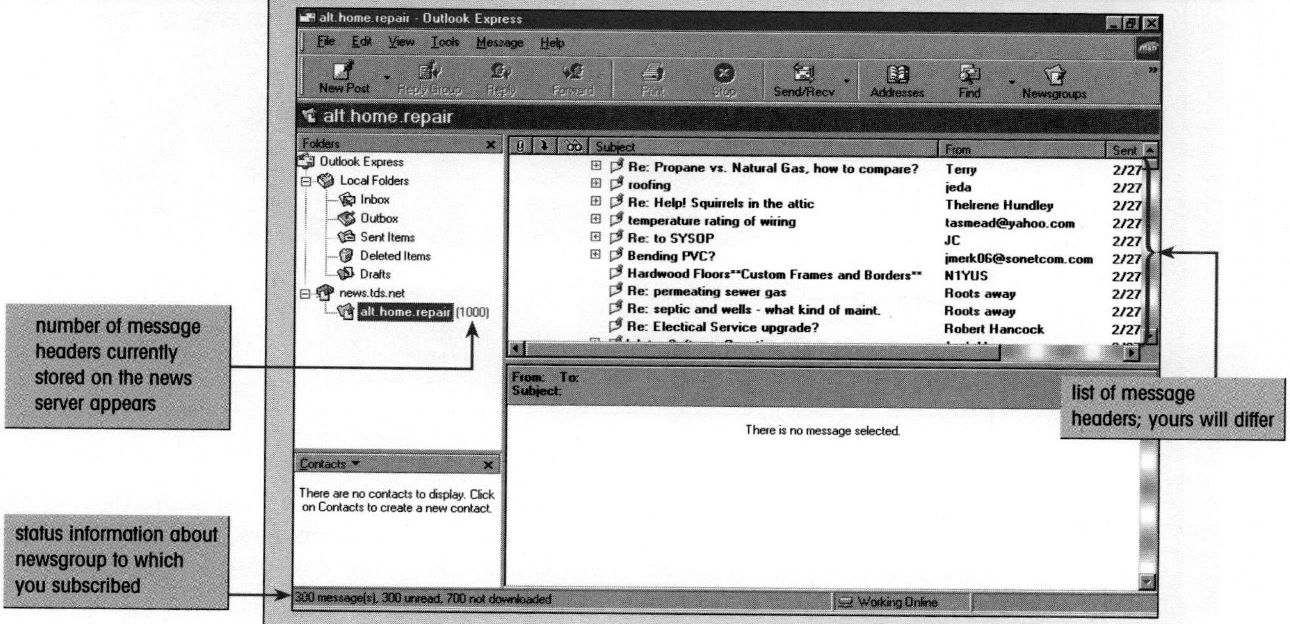

number of message headers currently stored on the news server appears

status information about newsgroup to which you subscribed

list of message headers; yours will differ

Now that you have subscribed, you can view the message headers you have retrieved and select the messages you want to read.

Working with Newsgroup Messages

You read a newsgroup message the same way you read an ordinary e-mail message: you either click it and the text appears in the preview pane, or you double-click it and the message opens in its own window. After the first message opens, you proceed through the list of messages using the Next button.

Sorting Newsgroup Posts

The order in which the message headers appear when you click Next depends on how they are sorted in the newsgroup list. By default, Outlook Express sorts message headers by the date sent and groups them by thread, but sorting in a different order can be helpful. For example, a newsgroup on a popular TV series might have regular posts from the series producer. If you want to read only those posts, you could sort by sender to locate all posts from the producer.

For now, you should make sure the sort order is by date sent and that messages are grouped by thread, so when you read your messages you can follow a thread of conversation. You can use the View menu to sort, or you can click the column heading buttons to sort by those columns.

To check the sort order:

1. Click **View**, then point to **Sort By**.

2. Click **Sent** to ensure the messages are sorted by date.

3. Click **View**, point to **Current View**, and, if it is not already checked, click **Group Messages by Conversation**.

Following a Thread

Outlook Express provides several visual clues to help track threads in a newsgroup's conversation. For example:

- A plus box ⊞ or minus box ⊟ preceding a message indicates the presence of a thread. ⊞ indicates the responses to the initial message are hidden, and ⊟ indicates that they are visible.
- Messages without ⊞ or ⊟ aren't part of a thread in the headers you downloaded; however, if you download more messages, they might be part of a thread. Messages that are part of a thread are usually preceded by Re:.
- Boldfaced messages have not yet been read; messages without boldface have.

Outlook Express also uses a set of icons that help you track messages. Figure 3-35 introduces some icons you'll see when you examine your newsgroup list; study them so you know how to interpret them.

Figure 3-35	MESSAGE ICONS

ICON	DESCRIPTION
	Message has not been opened.
	Message has been read.
	Thread has an unread message.
	Message is no longer available on the news server.

Now you're ready to read your newsgroup's messages. Because your message list will differ from the list shown in the figures, you'll have to adapt the steps to the newsgroup you selected.

To read the messages in a thread:

1. Scroll to locate a thread, preceded by ⊞.

2. Click ⊞ next to the first message in a thread to view the thread. Click any other ⊞ to view all messages in that thread.

3. Click the first message in the thread so its contents appear in the preview pane. Figure 3-36 shows a thread beginning with a message that asks about the disposal of fluorescent lightbulbs. Messages indented one level are replies to the first message in the thread. Messages indented two levels are replies to the messages indented one level, and so on.

Figure 3-36   VIEWING A THREAD

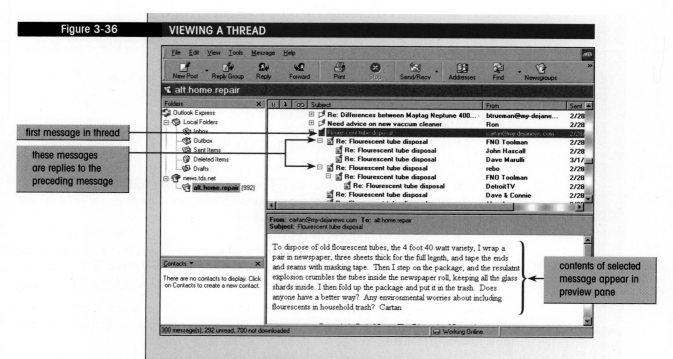

first message in thread

these messages are replies to the preceding message

contents of selected message appear in preview pane

4. Double-click the first message in the thread.

5. After you read the message, click the **Next** button ⬇. The next message in the thread appears. Click ⬇ to read the next few messages in the thread. Notice that the thread name at the top of the message area is the same as the subject of the original message. See Figure 3-37.

Figure 3-37   NEWSGROUP MESSAGE IN A THREAD

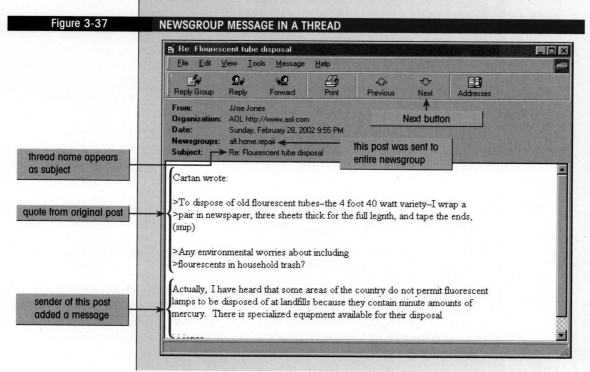

thread name appears as subject

quote from original post

sender of this post added a message

Next button

this post was sent to entire newsgroup

5. Continue viewing messages in the thread until you finish the thread. If there are too many messages, just view the first several messages. Now click the message window's **Close** button ☒ to return to the newsgroup's window. Notice that all message headers you read are no longer boldfaced, and observe how the icons have changed, according to the table in Figure 3-35.

As you read through the thread, you probably noticed that new posts often quote previous posts to which they are replying. When you respond to a post, quote as sparingly as possible to keep your message short. Some newsreaders do not let you post a message unless it contains more new material than quotations.

Downloading Additional Messages

If you like what you see in a newsgroup, you will probably want to download additional messages. Or you might read messages from a thread but find that you don't have the first message that initiated the conversation. Try downloading more of the messages in your newsgroup.

To download additional messages:

1. Make sure the newsgroup is open.

2. Click **Tools**, then click **Get Next 300 Headers**.

Outlook Express places the message headers in the list according to the current sort order. Thus, if you added headers belonging to a thread, Outlook Express places those headers in the correct position in the thread.

Posting a Message

After you read through some posts in a newsgroup, you might be ready to post your own message. You can post a follow-up message to a post you are currently reading, or you can post a message on a completely new topic. When you post a response, you can choose to:

■ Send a private e-mail message to the sender.
■ Post a response to the entire newsgroup.

In a newsgroup, you should usually reply to the group and not the sender, unless you have good reason for wanting the reply to be private. The idea of a newsgroup is that it is an open forum. Moreover, people don't want their personal e-mail account cluttered with e-mail from the newsgroup.

You should perform these next steps only if you have a valuable post to send to the newsgroup you chose. If you have nothing valuable to say, then read through these steps without performing them.

To post a reply to an existing message:

1. Select or open the message to which you want to reply.

2. Click the **Reply Group** button 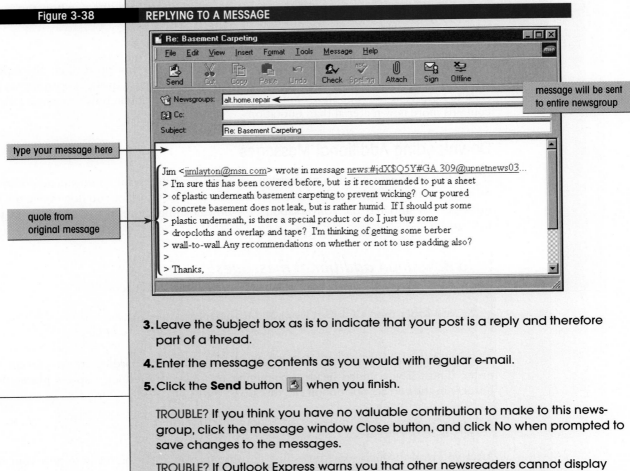. The message window opens with the group's address automatically inserted. See Figure 3-38.

Figure 3-38	REPLYING TO A MESSAGE

type your message here

quote from
original message

message will be sent
to entire newsgroup

3. Leave the Subject box as is to indicate that your post is a reply and therefore part of a thread.

4. Enter the message contents as you would with regular e-mail.

5. Click the **Send** button when you finish.

TROUBLE? If you think you have no valuable contribution to make to this newsgroup, click the message window Close button, and click No when prompted to save changes to the messages.

TROUBLE? If Outlook Express warns you that other newsreaders cannot display HTML messages and asks if it is OK to send it anyway, click OK.

6. Click the **OK** button if warned that it might take a while to post your message.

You have added your message to the list of newsgroup messages as a reply within a thread.

You can also raise a new issue in a newsgroup that might start a new thread, depending on whether other newsgroup members reply. Again, don't post a new message if you have nothing to say.

To post a new message:

1. Open the newsgroup, then click the **New Post** button. The newsgroup address is again filled in for you.

2. Enter a subject and the message contents.

3. Click the **Send** button.

> **TROUBLE?** If you have nothing important to post, cancel this message.
>
> **4.** Click the **OK** button if warned that it might take a while to post your message.
>
> **5.** Close all open messages.

If you asked a question or if your message is provocative enough to generate discussion, when you next download messages you might find responses to your message. Depending on how active the newsgroup is, you might receive a response within the hour, or you might have to wait a few days for a response.

Searching a Newsgroup

Outlook Express search features make finding the newsgroup and information you want easy. For example, within the Newsgroups window you can search your news server's list of newsgroups for a particular newsgroup. You hope to drive to California when you complete your internship, so you decide to look for newsgroups on surfing.

To search for a newsgroup on surfing:

1. Click the **Newsgroups** button 📷.

2. Type **surfing** in the Display newsgroups which contain box. After a moment a list of all newsgroups with "surfing" in their names appears. See Figure 3-39. You could click one of these newsgroups and then click the Subscribe button to subscribe to that group, but you won't do that now.

Figure 3-39	SEARCHING FOR A NEWSGROUP

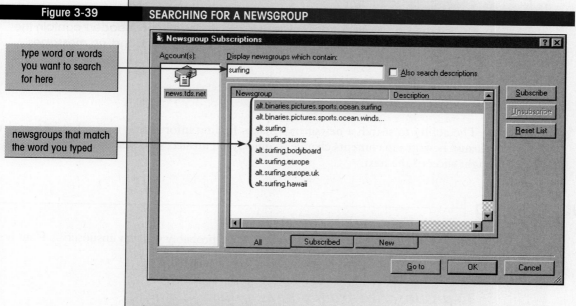

type word or words
you want to search
for here

newsgroups that match
the word you typed

3. Click the **Cancel** button.

Within a newsgroup, you can search for posts on particular topics. For example, perhaps you subscribed to a newsgroup of people who like backcountry camping because you want to camp in the Rocky Mountain National Park and want to find any recent discussions on that topic.

To search a newsgroup for messages on a topic:

1. If necessary, open the newsgroup.

2. Click the **Find** button 🔍. You might need to click More Buttons to locate this button.

3. Click the **Subject** box, then type a search word or words for the newsgroup you opened. See Figure 3-40.

| Figure 3-40 | LOCATING INFORMATION IN A NEWSGROUP |

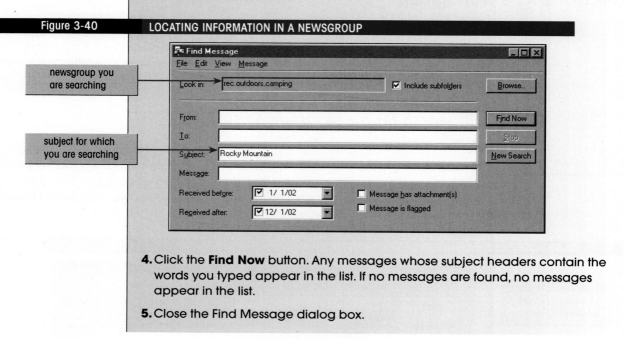

newsgroup you are searching

subject for which you are searching

4. Click the **Find Now** button. Any messages whose subject headers contain the words you typed appear in the list. If no messages are found, no messages appear in the list.

5. Close the Find Message dialog box.

The ability to search a newsgroup makes finding information easier, but be aware that because newsgroup contents change so quickly, an unsuccessful search you perform one day might succeed the next.

Unsubscribing

When you lose interest in a newsgroup, you will probably want to unsubscribe from it so it doesn't clutter your newsgroup list.

To unsubscribe from a newsgroup:

1. In either the Folder list or the display pane, right-click the newsgroup you joined in this tutorial.

2. Click **Unsubscribe**.

3. Click the **OK** button if asked if you are sure you want to unsubscribe from the newsgroup.

4. Click the **Close** button to exit Outlook Express.

Newsgroups can be an excellent source of information. Some newsgroups exist to support people going through hard times, such as coping with a serious illness. Others exist to exchange information and advice on challenges such as do-it-yourself home repair. Still others provide an open forum to discuss a hot topic, such as current election issues. The "conversation" in some newsgroups can become rather intense because people express themselves with less inhibition in an anonymous e-mail message than they tend to in face-to-face conversation. Insulting e-mail in newsgroups is so common that it even has a name: **flaming**. If you avoid taking and giving offense, however, your newsgroup experience will probably be positive.

Session 3.3 QUICK CHECK

1. True or false: Messages posted to a newsgroup are automatically forwarded to all subscribers.

2. A server that stores the messages posted to a newsgroup is called a(n) _____.

3. A friend who knows nothing about newsgroups sees "rec.arts.painting.oil" on your computer screen and asks you to explain what it means. Draw a diagram to accompany your explanation.

4. What is a thread?

5. What might you do to read only the posts written by a certain sender?

6. If no plus box ⊞ or minus box ⊟ appears next to a message header in the list of posts, what does that tell you?

7. What is flaming and why is it more prevalent in newsgroups than in public?

REVIEW ASSIGNMENTS

You completed your internship at Carey Outerwear, and you're back at school after an exciting weekend trip during which you actually climbed Mt. Rainier. You want to use some things you learned while in Seattle, especially about e-mail and newsgroups. You plan to e-mail a photo of Mt. Rainier to your instructor to show what you climbed, and then you want to add the addresses of your instructor and some of your friends to the Address Book. You also want to create folders to store your course-related e-mail. Finally, you want to explore more newsgroups to see if you can find one in which you would like to participate.

1. Make sure Outlook Express is properly configured to send and receive e-mail.

2. Create a new e-mail message to your instructor (your instructor will provide you with the e-mail address to use) and Cc it to yourself. Enter "From your student [name]" as

the subject (insert your name between the brackets). In the message area, write your instructor a message about what you hope to gain from taking this course.

3. Enter your instructor's name as a new contact in your Address Book.

4. Add the e-mail addresses of three friends to your Address Book. Create a group called "Friends," and add the names of your three friends.

Explore

5. Create a short message to the friends list you just created, and Cc the message to your instructor. Use the Ivy stationery template. Enter "Class assignment" as the subject, and explain briefly in your message that you are testing your e-mail system. (*Hint:* to use the Ivy stationery template, click the New Mail list arrow and then click Ivy.)

6. In the "Class assignment" message from the previous step, attach the Climb.bmp file in the Tutorial.03/Review folder on your Data Disk.

7. Send the Class assignment message. After you send it, open the Sent Items folder and then open the message you just sent.

8. Print the message you sent in Step 7.

9. Create a folder in the Inbox named "Courses." Within the Courses folder, create a folder for each course you are taking.

10. Create another folder in the Inbox named "Work" for storing e-mail related to work. On the back of the printout you created in Step 8, draw a picture of your folder hierarchy.

11. Delete the folders you created.

12. Subscribe to one of the newsgroups in the rec category.

13. Download the first batch of message headers in the newsgroup you just subscribed to.

14. Open any message and print it. On the back of the printout, write the full address of the newsgroup you subscribed to.

15. Search for all newsgroups on the topic basketball. On the back of your printout, write the addresses of a basketball newsgroup in the alt category and in the rec category, plus three additional addresses of any other basketball newsgroups in other categories.

CASE PROBLEMS

Case 1. E-mailing Freelancers at Custom Cartoons Custom Cartoons provides its clients with cartoon drawings for their promotions and advertisements. Often, when its own cartooning staff is busy with projects, Custom Cartoons contracts projects out to freelance cartoonists. Janey Killips has been assigned to manage a project for a jugglers guild that is hosting a conference in San Antonio next summer. Janey e-mails you and asks if you would be interested in the job. You will correspond with Janey via e-mail to get the job done.

If necessary, launch Outlook Express and then complete these steps:

1. Create a new message to janey@customcartoons.netez.com.

2. Enter "Jugglers Guild" in the Subject line, and type your own words in the message area.

3. In the message area, confirm your availability and willingness to do the job.

4. Send a copy of the message to your instructor. Use the Address Book entry you created in the Review Assignments.

5. Send a copy of the message to yourself as well.

Explore

6. Add formatting to the message. First, you make sure formatting is allowed. Click Format, then click Rich Text (HTML) so that the Formatting toolbar appears. In the message area, boldface at least one word and italicize at least one word. To boldface a word, you select it and then click the Bold button **B**. To italicize it, you select it and then click the Italic button *I*.

7. Now color one word red. Select the word, click the Font Color button, and then click the color red.

Explore

8. Attach the file Juggler.bmp, located in the Cases folder of the Tutorial.03 folder on your Data Disk, to the message. Explain in the message area that this file is a draft of a juggler cartoon.

9. Send the message.

10. Now check your mail. A copy of your message should appear. Open the message. Print the message and submit the printout to your instructor.

Case 2. Joining a Newsgroup at Camp Yahara George Hendriks, the maintenance person at Camp Yahara, a summer camp for children with special needs, hired you to help with summer maintenance jobs. Many outdoor facilities, such as the tennis courts, the lake dock, and the obstacle course, need work. Everyone who works at Camp Yahara has a computer with an Internet connection, and you ask George if he would mind if you spend a little time checking the Internet for advice on some of the repair projects. George replies that a second opinion never hurts, so you subscribe to the newsgroup alt.home.repair, which you know addresses many indoor and outdoor repair and maintenance problems.

If necessary, launch Outlook Express, then do the following:

1. Search for a group named alt.home.repair. If your search does not succeed, your news server doesn't support this newsgroup. Ask your instructor which newsgroup you should select.

2. Subscribe to the alt.home.repair newsgroup.

3. Open the newsgroup and download the first batch of message headers. If there are no messages, subscribe to a different newsgroup and repeat this step.

4. Scroll through the message headers until you locate a thread that looks like it might apply to any outdoor or indoor repair job underway at Camp Yahara.

5. Open the first message in the thread, and read it. Click the Next button to read through all messages in the thread.

6. Click the Forward Message button to forward the newsgroup message to your instructor; use the Address Book to enter your instructor's e-mail address in the To line.

7. Enter "Camp Yahara" in the Subject line.

8. In the message area, inform your instructor that you found this message in the alt.home.repair newsgroup.

9. Unsubscribe from the newsgroup.

Case 3. Corresponding with College Students You are interested in what's going on at other colleges and decide to subscribe to one of the many college newsgroups on the Internet. After you find a college newsgroup that interests you, you'll post a message to that newsgroup.

If necessary, launch Outlook Express, then do the following:

1. Search for all groups with the word "college."

2. Scroll through the list that appears until you find one that interests you. There are many such newsgroups, ranging from alt.art.college to alt.college.fraternities to soc.college.financial-aid, and so on.

3. Subscribe to the newsgroup that interests you.

4. Download the first batch of message headers.

Explore ▷ 5. Read through the messages until you find one to which you'd like to respond. Make sure you have something worthwhile to say; the newsgroup won't appreciate your writing a worthless post. Use the "flavor" of the messages you've read as your guide to tone and length.

Explore ▷ 6. Reply to one of the messages by posting a message to the entire newsgroup. Copy the message you post to your instructor. Send the message.

7. Wait at least a day. Open the newsgroup again and, if necessary, click Tools, then click Get Next 300 Headers. Locate your message and print it. Submit the printout to your instructor.

Explore ▷ 8. If you receive a response to your post, reply to that post and add another contribution to the newsgroup. Again, make sure you have something worthwhile to say.

Case 4. *Downloading a Decompression Utility* Many files that people attach to e-mail messages are **zipped** or compressed to save space. You want to locate a simple decompression utility so that when you receive a zipped, attached file in an e-mail message, you can unzip it. You'll first search for a file named pkz204g.exe, which is a version of pkzip, a popular decompression utility. After you find the file, you'll create a folder to store the file on a blank, formatted disk. Then you'll download the file into that folder on your blank disk. The pkz204g.exe file is a self-extracting file that decompresses or restores compressed files without a separate decompression utility. You'll restore the pkz204g.exe file, and then the decompression program will be available to run on any zip file you receive, either an attached file or a file you download from a Web site.

If necessary, launch Internet Explorer, then do the following:

1. Create a folder named pkzip on a blank, formatted disk. Do not use your Data Disk. To do this, minimize the Outlook Express window. Open My Computer, double-click 3½" Floppy (A:), click File, point to New, click Folder, type pkzip, press Enter, and then close My Computer.

2. Maximize the Internet Explorer window.

3. Click the Search button, then perform a search for the file pkz204g.exe.

Explore ▷ 4. Read through the links and click the one that looks most promising. A site whose name includes the word "utilities" or "archive" will probably have a copy of this file. After you locate a promising site, click the pkz204g.exe link. If you have trouble, ask your instructor for a workable site.

5. Save the file in the pkzip folder you created on the disk in drive A.

Explore ▷ 6. If you have a virus checker, run it on this file. If you don't, realize that you are taking a risk by running a program that you did not check. If you cannot find a virus-checking program on your computer or have trouble running it, ask your instructor for help.

7. Click the Start button on the Windows taskbar, then click Run.

Explore ▷ 8. Type a:\pkzip\pkz204g.exe in the Open box, then click the OK button. A DOS window opens because the program is a DOS utility, and the window shows the steps for decompressing the file. If you receive a message saying your disk is full, you'll need to copy the file you downloaded again onto a blank disk. After the program is decompressed, you are ready to run it. It decompresses into several files; one is pkunzip.exe, the decompression utility.

Explore

9. To run the pkunzip program, you click the Start button, click Run, type:
   a:\pkzip\pkunzip.exe
   and then type file path you want to unzip, followed by the location where you want to
   store the unzipped file. For example, if you have a file named flowers.zip on drive C and
   you want to unzip it and store it in a folder named c:\flowers, you would type:
   a:\pkzip\pkunzip.exe c:\flowers.zip c:\flowers
   The first "phrase" in this command names the decompression program you are running; the second names the file you are decompressing; and the third tells where you
   want to store the decompressed files.

LAB ASSIGNMENTS

This Lab Assignment is designed to accompany the interactive Course Lab called Internet
World Wide Web. To start the Lab, click the Start button on the taskbar, point to
Programs, point to Course Labs, point to New Perspectives Applications, then click
Internet World Wide Web. If you do not see Course Labs on your Programs menu, see
your instructor or technical support person.

E-mail that originates on a local area network with a mail gateway can travel the world.
That's why learning how to use it is so important. In this Lab you use an e-mail simulator,
so even if your school computers don't provide e-mail service, you will know the basics of
reading, sending, and replying to electronic mail.

E-mail

1. Click the Steps button to learn how to work with e-mail. As you proceed through the
   steps, answer all Quick Check questions that appear. After you complete the steps, you
   will see a Quick Check Summary Report. Follow the instructions on the screen to print
   this report.

2. Click the Explore button. Write a message to re@films.org. The subject of the message
   is "Picks and Pans." In the body of your message, describe a movie you have recently
   seen. Include the movie's name, briefly summarize its plot, and give it thumbs up or
   thumbs down. Print the message before you send it.

3. In Explore, look in your In Box for a message from jb@music.org. Read the message,
   then compose a reply indicating that you will attend. Carbon copy
   mciccone@music.org. Print your reply, including the text of JB's original message,
   before you send it.

4. In Explore, look in your In Box for a message from leo@sports.org. Reply to the message by adding your rating to the text of the original message as follows:

Equipment:	Your Rating:
Rollerblades	2
Skis	3
Bicycle	1
Scuba gear	4
Snowmobile	5

5. Print your reply before you send it.

QUICK CHECK ANSWERS

Session 3.1

1. user ID: pcsmith; host name: icom.net
2. Click Tools, click Accounts, click the Mail tab, click the account with your name, and then click the Properties button.
3. Sent Items folder
4. The recipient might interpret the uppercase letters as shouting.
5. backbone
6. Recipient's e-mail address is automatically inserted, subject is automatically inserted, and original message is quoted.

Session 3.2

1. False
2. A paper clip icon appears.
3. Click the folder's plus box ⊞.
4. They are returned as undeliverable.
5. False
6. Ctrl

Session 3.3

1. False
2. news server
3. The newsgroup is in the rec category, which stands for recreational. It is in the painting subcategory of the arts subcategory, and its subject is oil, probably oil painting.

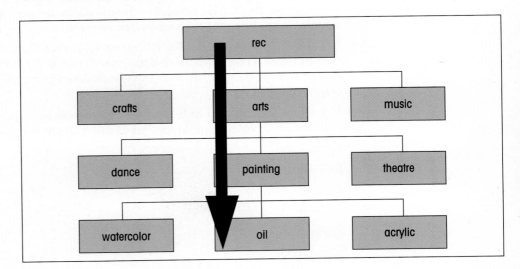

4. a batch of messages that follow a single "line of conversation"
5. sort by sender
6. It is not part of a thread in the message header list you downloaded.
7. insulting e-mail; because e-mail senders are anonymous

New Perspectives on

MICROSOFT INTERNET EXPLORER 5

TUTORIAL 4   IE 4.03

Developing Web Pages with FrontPage Express
Creating a Home Page at Avalon Books

TUTORIAL 5   IE 5.01

Creating a Hypertext Document
Creating a Web Presentation

Read This Before You Begin

To the Student

Data Disk

To complete the Introductory tutorials, Review Assignments, and Case Problems in this book, you need 1 Data Disk. Your instructor will either provide you with a Data Disk or ask you to make your own.

If you are making your own Data Disk, you will need **1** blank, formatted high-density disk. You will need to copy a set of folders from a file server or standalone computer or the Web onto your disk. Your instructor will tell you which computer, drive letter, and folders contain the files you need. You could also download the files by going to www.course.com, clicking Data Disk Files, and following the instructions on the screen.

The following table shows you which folders go on your disk, so that you will have enough disk space to complete all the tutorials, Review Assignments, and Case Problems.

Data Disk

Write this on the disk label
Student Disk 1: Level 2 Tutorials 4-5

Put these folders on the disk
Tutorial.04
Tutorial.05

When you begin each tutorial, be sure you are using the correct Data Disk. See the inside front or inside back cover of this book for more information on Data Disk Files, or ask your instructor or technical support person for assistance.

Using Your Own Computer

If you are going to work through this book using your own computer, you need:

- **Computer System** Microsoft Internet Explorer 5 and Windows 95/98 must be installed on your computer. This book assumes a complete installation of Internet Explorer 5.

- **Data Disk** You will not be able to complete the tutorials or exercises in this book using your own computer until you have a Data Disk.

- **Course Labs** See your instructor or technical support person to obtain the Course Lab software for use on your own computer.

Visit Our World Wide Web Site

Additional materials designed especially for you are available on the World Wide Web. Go to **http://www.course.com**.

To the Instructor

The Data files and Course Labs are available on the Instructor's Resource Kit for this title. Follow the instructions in the Help file on the CD-ROM to install the programs to your network or standalone computer. For information on creating Data Disks or the Course Labs, see the "To the Student" section above. Also, please note that students will need an Internet connection in order to complete the tutorials in this book.

You are granted a license to copy the Data Files and Course Labs to any computer or computer network used by students who have purchased this book.

In this tutorial you will:

- Create a Web page from scratch using FrontPage Express

- Format large sections of text using paragraph tags

- Create and format numbered and bulleted lists

- Format individual characters or words using character tags

- Insert and format lines and graphic images

- Create a Web page background

DEVELOPING
WEB PAGES WITH FRONTPAGE EXPRESS

Creating a Home Page at Avalon Books

CASE

Avalon Books

You work at Avalon Books, a large bookstore in the city of Lakeside. The store offers its customers more than books; it also includes reading rooms, play areas for the kids, and a small cafe. The bookstore sponsors special events such as author signings, poetry readings, and live music. The manager of Avalon Books, Mark Stewart, prepares paper flyers featuring the month's events, and the Avalon Books salespeople insert these flyers into the books customers purchase. However, Mark would like to publicize these events to a wider audience. He especially wants to reach those who have never visited the store or who haven't purchased a book recently and so are unaware of upcoming events. He has asked you to create a Web page to advertise Avalon Books on the World Wide Web. He plans to advertise his Web site in all his promotions.

The FrontPage Express component of Internet Explorer provides three methods to create a Web page. The Personal Home Page Wizard method walks you through a series of steps to create a home page. A second method requires using a **template**, a page created by someone else that you retrieve and use as a model for your own page. Although using a template relieves you from having to spend time on page design, you might find that your page ends up looking too similar to the page it was based on. You can use both the Personal Home Page Wizard and the templates to "jump start" your page by creating the page and then using FrontPage Express to modify it. A third method of creating a new page is starting from scratch with a blank page in FrontPage Express. You enter and format your own text and create your own design using the FrontPage Express tools.

After spending some time thinking about the project Mark has asked you to take on, you decide to use this third method to create the Avalon Books page.

SESSION 4.1

In this session, you will use FrontPage Express to create a Web page from scratch. You will learn how to work offline, to save your document, and to enter and then format text in your page.

Creating a New Page with FrontPage Express

The FrontPage Express component of Internet Explorer gives you the ability to create and edit intranet and Web documents. An **intranet document** is just like a Web page, except that it is available only to an internal network, not to all users on the Web. Thus, a company can make internal company documents available to employees so that they can access them just as they would a regular Web page, but people outside the intranet cannot. See Figure 4-1.

| Figure 4-1 | STORING A WEB PAGE ON THE INTERNET OR AN INTRANET |

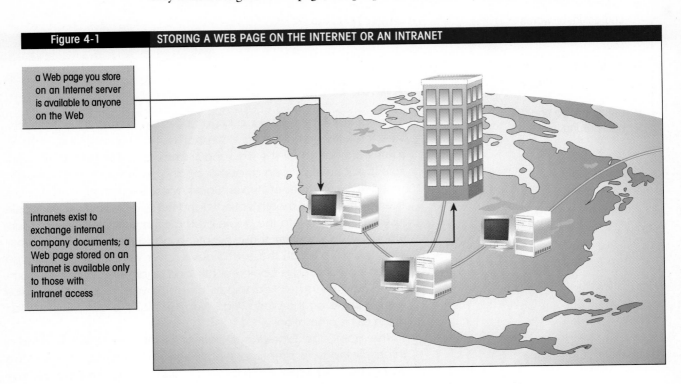

a Web page you store on an Internet server is available to anyone on the Web

intranets exist to exchange internal company documents; a Web page stored on an intranet is available only to those with intranet access

When you create a Web page, you need to decide if your audience will be only your local intranet, if you are on one, or the entire Internet community. Your content should always be dictated by your audience. Once you've created your page, Internet Explorer can help you publish it.

With FrontPage Express you can:

- Create Web documents from scratch, using composition aids.
- Edit and format your documents in a WYSIWYG (what you see is what you get) environment, so that you will see an immediate preview of how the final document will appear.
- Use familiar word processing features such as text formatting and table creation.
- Quickly and easily insert graphic objects and hypertext links into your document.
- Publish your document to a server.

Elements of a Web Page

Creating a Web page involves planning both the content and the appearance of the page. You can plan the content by asking questions like: What information do I want to convey? What links do I want to include?

Once you have settled on your content, you should plan your design. You can include colors, interesting fonts, a stylized background, graphics, and other design elements such as lines and tables. Keep in mind, however, that a browser takes much longer to retrieve a Web page that contains a lot of graphics. If your page takes too long to retrieve, your target audience might lose patience and skip your page.

Mark shows you a flyer he uses to advertise the bookstore's current events, shown in Figure 4-2. He suggests you use this flyer as a basis for the Web page contents.

Figure 4-2	MARK'S FLYER

Avalon Books

341 Gorham Avenue, Lakeside, IL (608) 555-4891

Avalon Books is Lakeside's premier bookstore. Come and curl up next to our cozy fire with a good book and a cup of one of our classic coffees. Meet with an author at one of our discussion sessions, or stop by for live music every Friday and Saturday night. Bring the kids any afternoon for storytime and snacks.

Come to Avalon Books for...

- The largest selection of books in the Midwest
- Comfortable reading rooms
- Coffee, wines, and delicious desserts as you read
- A computer lab for kids with the best educational software titles

This week's events

Monday, 10/7

Isaac Anderson discusses humor and science fiction and will sign copies of his new book, *The Time Traveler's Bar and Grill*

Wednesday, 10/9

The Avalon Reading Club will discuss Maureen Dawson's book, *Deconstructing Beethoven*

Friday, 10/11

Soft Jazz by Burns, Sutton, and Davis

The page that Mark sketched contains the following elements:

- A main heading and several subheadings at different levels
- A description of the contents and purpose of the page
- A bulleted list
- Horizontal line that improves the page's appearance
- A graphic image
- Text in different fonts and sizes
- Indented text

You decide to create this page from scratch, by first entering and formatting the text and then by creating a page design.

Going Offline

You can use many Internet Explorer features without actually being connected to the Internet—a plus if you are paying for your Internet connection. When you work without an Internet connection, you are working **offline**. When you start an Internet Explorer component, your computer might attempt to connect to the Internet. If you will be using only FrontPage Express without requiring any Internet resources, you could click the Cancel or Stop button on your Internet connection dialog box to halt the connection.

Starting FrontPage Express

How you start FrontPage Express depends on your circumstances. If you plan to use the Personal Home Page Wizard or to start from a blank page, you need to first start FrontPage Express from the Start menu. Alternatively, you can retrieve any page on the Web in the Internet Explorer browser and open it in FrontPage Express so that it functions as a template. Keep in mind that most Web pages contain copyrighted material that you cannot use without permission.

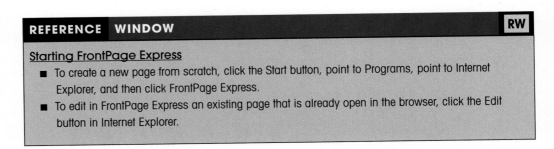

REFERENCE WINDOW   RW

<u>Starting FrontPage Express</u>
- To create a new page from scratch, click the Start button, point to Programs, point to Internet Explorer, and then click FrontPage Express.
- To edit in FrontPage Express an existing page that is already open in the browser, click the Edit button in Internet Explorer.

To create a new document in FrontPage Express:

1. Click the **Start** button ▓Start, point to **Programs**, then point to **Internet Explorer**.

2. Click **FrontPage Express**. If your computer attempts to connect to the Internet, you can cancel the connection. The FrontPage Express window opens to a blank page.

3. If necessary, click the **Maximize** button ▢ to maximize the FrontPage Express window. Figure 4-3 shows the maximized FrontPage Express window.

   TROUBLE? If you see the Forms toolbar in addition to the Standard and Format toolbar, don't worry. You'll learn how to hide it in a moment.

Figure 4-3	FRONTPAGE EXPRESS WINDOW

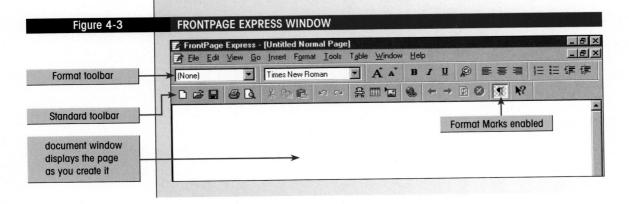

Format toolbar

Standard toolbar

document window displays the page as you create it

Format Marks enabled

FrontPage Express includes three toolbars: Format, Standard, and Forms. The Format toolbar includes tools that help you format your page; the Standard toolbar includes tools that help you compose your page; and the Forms toolbar includes tools that help you create a form on your page. Because the Avalon Books page won't use forms, you don't need to view the Forms toolbar.

To hide the Forms toolbar:

1. Click **View**.

2. Make sure both the **Standard Toolbar** and **Format Toolbar** options are preceded by a checkmark.

3. If the Forms Toolbar option is preceded by a checkmark, click **Forms Toolbar** to hide the Forms toolbar.

4. Click **View** once more and make sure the **Status Bar** and **Format Marks** options are both preceded by a checkmark.

Your screen should now match the screen in Figure 4-3.

Saving a Web Page

Before you actually begin entering text into your new document, you decide to save it. FrontPage Express lets you save the page directly to the Web or as a file on your disk. You aren't ready to publish the page on the Web, so you will save it as a file on your Data Disk. When you save your page, FrontPage Express gives you the opportunity to give a title to your page. Browsers viewing your page will display this title in the browser title bar.

You decide to enter Avalon Books as the page title and to save the page with the name "Avalon".

To save your Web page and assign it a title:

1. Place your Data Disk in the drive, click **File**, and then click **Save As**.

2. Type **Avalon Books** in the Page Title box. See Figure 4-4.

| Figure 4-4 | SAVING A WEB PAGE |

this title will appear to Web users

clicking OK would start publishing the page on the Web

location displays the path to your computer; yours will be different

click to save as a file on your Data Disk

Save As
Page Title:
Avalon Books
Page Location:
http://joan/avalon.htm
Tip
Please be sure your page has a title.
Click OK to save this page to the web.
OK
Cancel
Help
As File...

3. Click the **As File** button.

4. Click the **Save in** list arrow, then click the drive containing your Data Disk.

5. Open the **Tutorial.04** folder.

6. Replace the contents of the File name box with the word **Avalon**.

7. Click the **Save** button to save your new Web page document in the Tutorial.04 folder on your Data Disk.

Notice that the FrontPage Express title bar now displays the path A:\Tutorial.04\Avalon.htm. In the browser, however, the filename will not appear. Instead, the title you entered will appear.

Markup Tags

FrontPage Express works much like a word processor. There are, however, some important differences between a document created with a software program such as Microsoft Word and one created by FrontPage Express for use on the Web. When you create a document using FrontPage Express, you are actually creating a file that consists of HTML codes. **HTML**, which stands for Hypertext Markup Language, is the language in which a Web page is written. HTML uses special codes to describe how the page should appear on the screen. Figure 4-5 shows a Web page as it appears on your computer screen, and behind it, the underlying HTML code. It is this code that is actually transferred over the Web when someone accesses your page.

Figure 4-5	WEB PAGE AND THE HTML CODE IT EMPLOYS

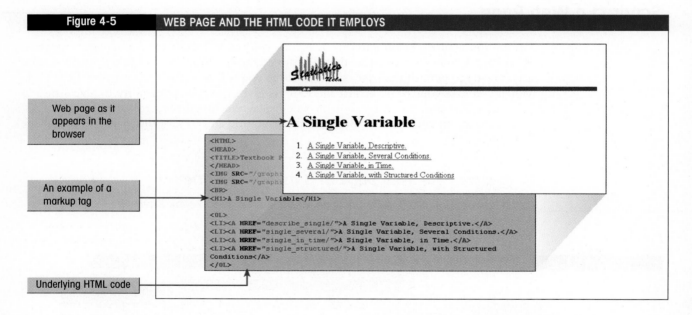

When the HTML code is transferred over the Web, the browser accessing the page interprets the code to determine the page's appearance and then displays the page according to its interpretation of the code. The appearance of each element in the page, such as a heading or a bulleted list, is indicated by a **markup tag**—a label within angle brackets that identifies the element to a browser. A tag with the label <H1>, for example, stands for "Heading 1" and indicates that the text that follows is a top-level heading in the document. Markup tags are necessarily very general so that many different kinds of browsers can read the document and determine how to display it. Not all browsers display text the same way. Some browsers, called **text-based browsers**, often can't display formatting such as bold or italics and might be able to display only one type of font. These browsers will display

Heading 1 text very differently from a browser like Internet Explorer that can display a variety of fonts and formatting. Figure 4-6 shows how two different browsers might interpret text formatted with a Heading 1 tag.

Figure 4-6	SAME HEADING AS IT APPEARS IN DIFFERENT BROWSERS

You can assign fonts and font sizes to text, just as you do in a word processor, but you should be aware that not all browsers will be able to display the font you choose. Suppose you format text with a Heading 1 tag with a 14-point bold Century Gothic font. If a browser on an operating system without Century Gothic installed retrieves your page, it will use the default font for the style you've assigned rather than Century Gothic. If you designed your page around interesting fonts, you could sell yourself short if the majority of browsers don't have your font.

As a Web page author, you don't have the same kind of control over your page's appearance as you would in creating a word-processed document. Although you can use different fonts and font sizes, the appearance of text is determined by the browser, not by you. Even with these limitations, you can still create interesting and visually attractive documents. And as the Web increases in popularity, new tags will be developed that give Web authors more flexibility and control in creating pages.

In creating your Avalon Books Web page, you'll be using tags with the following document elements:

- paragraphs
- individual characters
- graphic images

Some tags simply contain information about the document. Earlier, when you entered a title for the page, you were actually inserting a tag of this kind into your document. Although these tags do not show up on the page, they do appear in the HTML code. You can see this by viewing the source code, or the actual HTML tags, that define the document.

To view a page's source code:

1. Click **View**, then click **HTML**. The View or Edit HTML window opens. See Figure 4-7. Notice that the title you entered is actually part of a tag. When you enter your page's contents, it will appear between the Body tags.

Figure 4-7	HTML SOURCE CODE

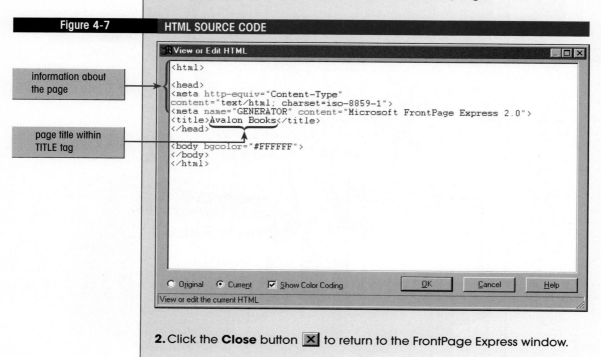

information about the page

page title within TITLE tag

2. Click the **Close** button ⊠ to return to the FrontPage Express window.

Entering and Formatting Text

You are now ready to start formatting the Avalon Books Web page to mirror the appearance of Mark's flyer. As you look over Mark's flyer from Figure 4-2, you identify the following elements:

- Main heading for the title
- Smaller heading listing store's address and phone number
- Heading for each of the two sections of the document
- Bulleted list of activities at the bookstore
- Bolded and italicized weekdays on which Avalon Books has scheduled events
- Indented descriptions of events
- Horizontal line separating headings
- Graphic that makes the page visually attractive

In trying to recreate this flyer on the Web, you will need to apply a tag to each of these elements: headings, bulleted lists, formatted text, indented text, and graphics. FrontPage Express makes it easy for you to choose the appropriate tags for each element. When you want to apply the style to an entire paragraph you choose a paragraph tag. When you want to apply a style to just a phrase, word, or character, you choose a character tag.

To start, you decide to apply the paragraph tags for the headings. HTML offers six different heading tags, labeled H1, H2, H3, and so on through H6. FrontPage Express has assigned a style name to each HTML tag and placed all available style names on a list that is available through the Format toolbar. The HTML tag H1, for example, appears as the Heading 1 style in this list. Figure 4-8 shows how a typical browser might display paragraphs with each of these heading tags applied.

| Figure 4-8 | HEADING STYLES AS THEY APPEAR IN BROWSER |

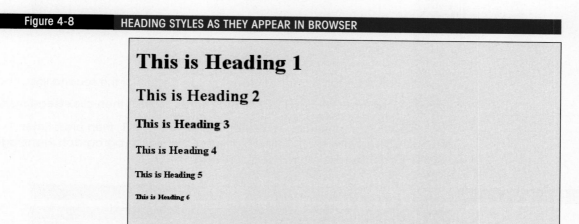

To apply a style to a paragraph, click anywhere in the paragraph and then choose the style you want from the Change Style list. You can apply a style before or after you type the paragraph, and you can apply a different style at any time.

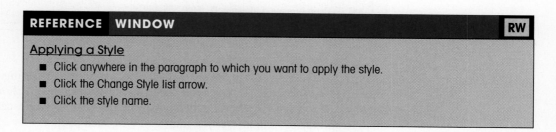

REFERENCE WINDOW   **RW**

Applying a Style
- Click anywhere in the paragraph to which you want to apply the style.
- Click the Change Style list arrow.
- Click the style name.

Applying Heading Styles

You decide to use the Heading 1 style (corresponding to the H1 HTML tag) for the page's main heading, "Avalon Books", and the Heading 4 style (corresponding to the H4 HTML tag) for the store's address and phone number.

To enter text and styles for the first two paragraphs:

1. Click the upper-left corner of the document window. The blinking insertion point indicates you are ready to type.

2. Click the **Change Style** list arrow on the Format toolbar. The list of available styles opens. Each style corresponds to an HTML tag. See Figure 4-9.

Figure 4-9   **CHANGE STYLE LIST**

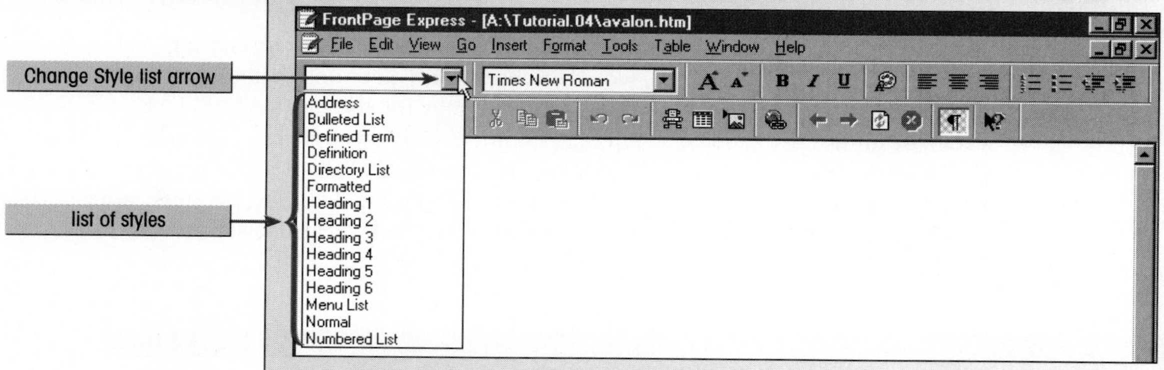

Change Style list arrow →

list of styles →

FrontPage Express - [A:\Tutorial.04\avalon.htm]

File Edit View Go Insert Format Tools Table Window Help

Times New Roman

Address
Bulleted List
Defined Term
Definition
Directory List
Formatted
Heading 1
Heading 2
Heading 3
Heading 4
Heading 5
Heading 6
Menu List
Normal
Numbered List

3. Click **Heading 1**.

4. Type **Avalon Books**, then press **Enter**. Now tag and enter the second line.

5. Click the **Change Style** list arrow on the Format toolbar, then click **Heading 4**.

6. Type **341 Gorham Avenue, Lakeside, IL (608) 555-4891**, then press **Enter**. Notice that because you applied a different style to this paragraph, FrontPage Express displays it differently. See Figure 4-10.

Figure 4-10   **ENTERING HEADINGS**

FrontPage Express - [A:\Tutorial.04\avalon.htm]

File Edit View Go Insert Format Tools Table Window Help

Normal   Times New Roman

paragraph formatted with Heading 1 style →

Avalon Books

341 Gorham Avenue, Lakeside, IL (608) 555-4891 ← paragraph formatted with Heading 4 style

Within each tag, you can make some additional choices regarding the appearance of text formatted with that tag. These choices are called **properties**. Although tag properties are not as extensive as what you may be accustomed to with word processors, you can still use them to add variety and interest to your text. One such property for a paragraph tag is alignment. Paragraphs can be left-, centered, or right-aligned.

You decide to center the two headings you just created to follow the format of the flyer.

To center the headings on the page:

1. Use the mouse to select the two headings.

TROUBLE? To select the two headings, drag the mouse with the left mouse button held down from the left side of the first heading to the right side of the second.

2. Click the **Center** button on the Format toolbar. Your headings are now centered.

You now add the next two headings to the page. Unlike the first two, they will be aligned with the left edge of the page.

To add additional headings:

1. Click the end of the second line and press **Enter**. The new line is also centered, so you need to set it to left alignment.

   TROUBLE? If you press Enter while the text is still highlighted, all your typing will disappear. Click the Undo button 🔄 and this time make sure you click the end of the second line before pressing Enter, as directed in Step 1.

2. Click the **Align Left** button 📄 on the Format toolbar.

3. Type **Come to Avalon Books for...**, then press **Enter**.

4. Type **This week's events**, then press **Enter**.

5. Select the two headings you just entered, then click **Heading 2** from the Change Style list. See Figure 4-11.

Figure 4-11   APPLYING HEADING 2 STYLE

these paragraphs
are centered

paragraphs formatted
with Heading 2 style

You've entered your headings, and now you want to enter the introductory paragraph on Mark's flyer.

Inserting Text with the Normal Style

Most Web pages include a descriptive paragraph that serves as an introduction to the page, usually in the Normal style. This text can describe the page, its goals, and its resources, or it can give brief instructions about how the page operates.

Unformatted sections of text such as descriptive or informational paragraphs are called **normal text**. You tag normal text with the Normal style. Inserting additional text into a Web page with FrontPage Express works much as it would with a word processor. Move the mouse pointer to the spot on the page where you want the new text to appear, click the left mouse button, press Enter if you want a new line, and then start typing the new text.

Mark's flyer includes a paragraph describing Avalon Books attractions. You are ready to enter this information into your Web page.

To add normal text to a page:

1. Click the end of the line containing Avalon's address and press **Enter**. When you press Enter, FrontPage Express automatically formats the next paragraph with the Normal style, as you can see from the Change Style list box.

2. Click the **Align Left** button 🗒 on the Format toolbar.

3. Type the following text into the document window:

   Avalon Books is Lakeside's premier bookstore. Come and curl up next to our cozy fire with a good book and a cup of one of our classic coffees. Meet with an author at one of our discussion sessions, or stop by for live music every Friday and Saturday night. Bring the kids any afternoon for storytime and snacks.

   Your page should now look similar to Figure 4-12, although your text might wrap differently.

Figure 4-12   ENTERING NORMAL TEXT

normal text

You are satisfied with your page so far. You decide to save your work and then take a break.

To save your changes to the Avalon Books Web page:

1. Click the **Save** button 🖫.

2. Click **File**, then click **Exit**.

Your Web page is well on its way. You've entered a page title, the page's headings, and normal text.

Session 4.1 QUICK CHECK

1. What is a WYSIWYG document?

2. Under what circumstances would you want to work offline?

3. The language in which a Web page is written is called _____.

4. What is the difference between a markup tag and a style?

5. Why might you choose not to use a special font in your page?

6. How does FrontPage Express differ from a word processor like Microsoft Word?

7. What style do you use for unformatted sections of text such as descriptive paragraphs?

SESSION 4.2

In this session you will learn how to enhance the appearance of your documents with numbered and bulleted lists, how to indent text, and how to format text using character formats.

Creating Lists

As you look over Mark's flyer, you notice the next thing you want to add is a list of attractions. You can use FrontPage Express to create two kinds of lists: a numbered list or a bulleted list. Use a numbered list, also called an **ordered list**, when you want to display, for example, chronological information such as a list of the steps needed to complete a task. Use a bulleted list, known as an **unordered list** because the order doesn't matter, to distinguish between items in the list with bullet symbols.

You decide to try both the numbered and bulleted list formats so you can decide how you want the list of Avalon Books attractions to appear on Mark's flyer. First, you must reopen the page you were working on in Session 4.1.

To reopen the Avalon Books page in FrontPage Express:

1. Restart FrontPage Express. You do not have to initiate an Internet connection nor load your home page.

2. Click the **Open** button.

3. If necessary, click the **From File** option button.

4. Click the **Browse** button, click the **Look in** list arrow, then locate and select the drive containing your Data Disk.

5. Open the **Tutorial.04** folder, click **Avalon.htm**, then click the **Open** button.

Creating a Numbered List

You decide to enter the list of Avalon attractions first as a numbered list using the Numbered List style. This style has its own toolbar button that you use instead of the Change Style list.

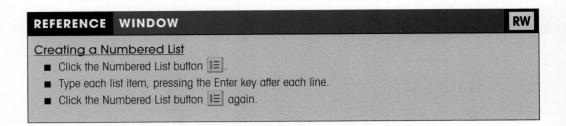

REFERENCE WINDOW   **RW**

Creating a Numbered List
- Click the Numbered List button.
- Type each list item, pressing the Enter key after each line.
- Click the Numbered List button again.

To create a numbered list:

1. Click the end of the **Come to Avalon Books for...** heading, then press **Enter**.

2. Click the **Numbered List** button on the Format toolbar. The number 1 appears.

3. Type **The largest selection of books in the Midwest**, then press **Enter**.

4. Continue entering the following items in the list, each on its own line:

   Comfortable reading rooms

   Coffee, wines, and delicious desserts as you read

   A computer lab for kids with the best educational software titles

   The Avalon Books page should now appear as shown in Figure 4-13.

   TROUBLE? If you pressed Enter after the last item in the list, press the Backspace key to remove the extra blank line.

Figure 4-13	ENTERING A NUMBERED LIST

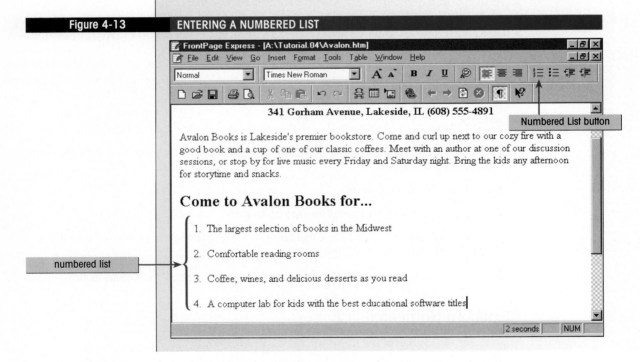

Viewing Your Page in the Browser

You should periodically save your page and open it in your browser to ensure that it looks the way you want it to. Usually it will look the same in the browser as it does in FrontPage Express, but not always. Some Web page creators like to test their pages in several browsers, such as different versions of Internet Explorer and Netscape Navigator, before they publish them so they are sure the page looks good regardless of the browser or version. You can open a page in Internet Explorer even when it is already open in FrontPage Express. If you make changes to your page in FrontPage Express, you can save the page and then use the Refresh button to view the changes in Internet Explorer.

To view the Avalon Books page in the Internet Explorer browser window:

1. Click the **Save** button 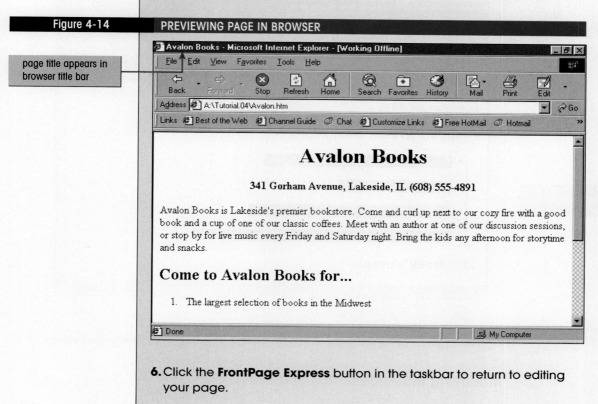 to save your changes to the page.

2. Launch Internet Explorer. You don't have to connect to the Internet to open a page from your disk, so cancel the connection if it is initiated. You might need to click the Work Offline button.

3. Click **File**, then click **Open** In the Internet Explorer window.

4. Click the **Browse** button and locate and select the Avalon.htm file in the Tutorial.04 folder of your Data Disk.

5. Click the **Open** button, then click the **OK** button. The page appears in Internet Explorer as shown in Figure 4-14. Notice that the Internet Explorer title bar displays the page's title, Avalon Books. This is how your page will look to other Internet Explorer users, although different browsers might display it differently.

   TROUBLE? If your Internet Explorer window is configured differently than the one shown in Figure 4-14, don't worry.

| Figure 4-14 | PREVIEWING PAGE IN BROWSER |

page title appears in
browser title bar

Avalon Books - Microsoft Internet Explorer - [Working Offline]

File Edit View Favorites Tools Help

Back   Forward   Stop   Refresh   Home   Search   Favorites   History   Mail   Print   Edit

Address A:\Tutorial.04\Avalon.htm   Go

Links Best of the Web   Channel Guide   Chat   Customize Links   Free HotMail   Hotmail

Avalon Books

341 Gorham Avenue, Lakeside, IL (608) 555-4891

Avalon Books is Lakeside's premier bookstore. Come and curl up next to our cozy fire with a good book and a cup of one of our classic coffees. Meet with an author at one of our discussion sessions, or stop by for live music every Friday and Saturday night. Bring the kids any afternoon for storytime and snacks.

Come to Avalon Books for...

1. The largest selection of books in the Midwest

Done   My Computer

6. Click the **FrontPage Express** button in the taskbar to return to editing your page.

Creating a Bulleted List

A bulleted list uses bullets instead of numbers. Like the numbered list, you apply it using one of the toolbar buttons on the Format toolbar. You decide to format your list as a bulleted list to see how it appears.

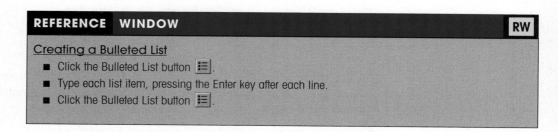

REFERENCE WINDOW   RW

Creating a Bulleted List
- Click the Bulleted List button ⊞.
- Type each list item, pressing the Enter key after each line.
- Click the Bulleted List button ⊞.

To format a list as a bulleted list:

1. Select the list of attractions by dragging the mouse over all the items in the list.
2. Click the **Bulleted List** button ⊞ on the Format toolbar. The list changes to a bulleted list of items as shown in Figure 4-15.

Figure 4-15   CREATING A BULLETED LIST

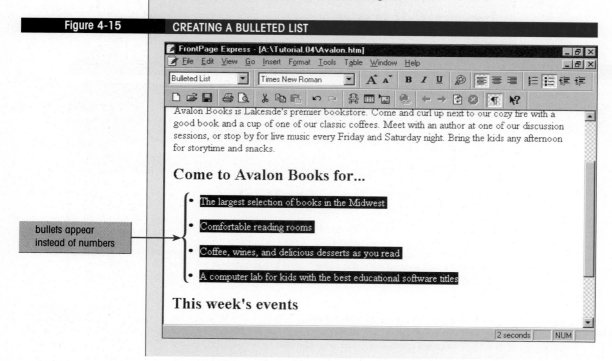

bullets appear instead of numbers

You decide to leave the list as a bulleted list, because it is not in any particular order.

Modifying the Appearance of a List

FrontPage Express allows you to choose a different symbol for bulleted lists or a different numbering format for numbered lists, although you should be aware that not all browsers will properly display the formats you choose, but will instead revert to the standard bulleted or numbered style. The bullet symbol is one of the properties of the bulleted list style. Some properties, such as the alignment property, can be accessed with toolbar buttons, but not all properties have corresponding toolbar buttons; you can access those properties by clicking the selected text with the right mouse button and choosing the appropriate properties option from the popup menu that opens.

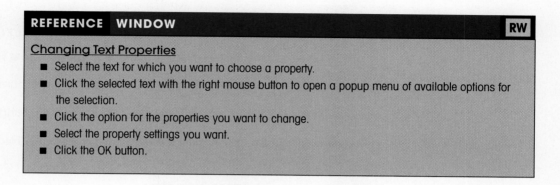

REFERENCE WINDOW   RW

Changing Text Properties
- Select the text for which you want to choose a property.
- Click the selected text with the right mouse button to open a popup menu of available options for the selection.
- Click the option for the properties you want to change.
- Select the property settings you want.
- Click the OK button.

You decide to replace the bullet symbol in your list of attractions with a symbol that more closely approximates the square bullet symbol used in Mark's flyer.

To change the bullet symbol:

1. If necessary, select the bulleted list, then right-click the selection.

2. Click **List Properties** from the popup menu.

3. Click the solid square bullet style from the available styles. See Figure 4-16.

Figure 4-16   CHANGING BULLET STYLE

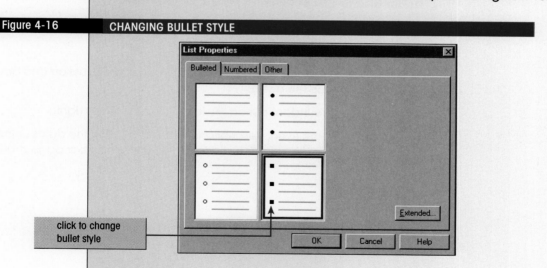

click to change bullet style

4. Click the **OK** button. The items in the list are now preceded by the new bullet style.

You like the way the bulleted list looks. You're now ready to start entering upcoming events.

Indenting Text

If you want to offset text from the left edge of the page, you can do so by indenting the text using the Indent buttons ▤ and ▤ on the toolbar.

Based on Mark's flyer you decide to indent the descriptions of the upcoming events. First you enter the text describing the upcoming events.

To enter the week's events and indent the descriptions:

1. Click the end of the heading "This week's events", then press **Enter**.

   TROUBLE? If you can't see this heading, scroll down the document window.

2. Verify that the Normal style is applied by checking the Change Style list box.

   TROUBLE? If the style does not appear as Normal, select the Normal style from the Change Style list box.

3. Type **Monday, 10/7**, then press **Enter**.

4. Type the following, then press **Enter**:

   Isaac Anderson discusses humor and science fiction and will sign copies of his new book, The Time Traveler's Bar and Grill

5. Continue typing the following information into the document window, pressing **Enter** after each line.

   Wednesday, 10/9

   The Avalon Reading Club will discuss Maureen Dawson's book, Deconstructing Beethoven

   Friday, 10/11

   Soft Jazz by Burns, Sutton, and Davis

6. Select the line or lines describing the Isaac Anderson discussion and book signing (do not include the date).

7. Click the **Increase Indent** button ▤ to shift the line to the right.

8. Indent the rest of the event descriptions in the list, leaving the dates unindented. Click the page when you're finished to deselect the text. Your page should look like Figure 4-17.

Figure 4-17   **INDENTING TEXT**

indented text

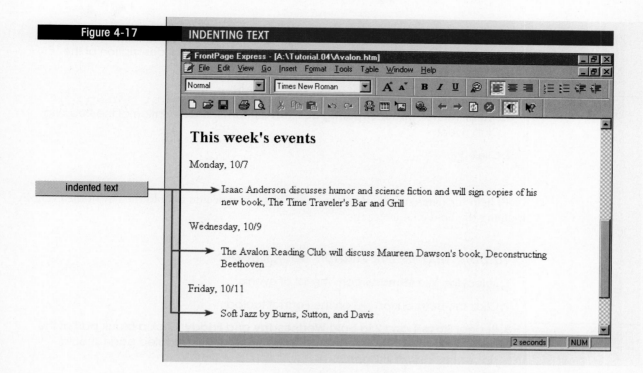

You realize that some of the events include book titles, which need to be italicized. To do this, you need to work with character tags.

Applying **Character Tags**

Although you can't change the definition of a style like "Heading 1", you can alter the appearance of individual characters. The HTML formats that you can apply to characters are called **character tags**. FrontPage Express allows you to use character tags to italicize your text, bold it, change its font type and size, or display it in a different color.

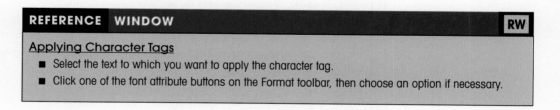

REFERENCE WINDOW   **RW**

Applying Character Tags
- Select the text to which you want to apply the character tag.
- Click one of the font attribute buttons on the Format toolbar, then choose an option if necessary.

Changing Font Attributes

A **font attribute** is a characteristic of a font that you can change, including its font type, size, color, and whether it is in bold or italics. Font attributes are represented in FrontPage Express by toolbar buttons on the Format toolbar. The descriptions of the upcoming events include book names that should be italicized.

To italicize text in the Avalon Books page:

1. Select the text **The Time Traveler's Bar and Grill** from the description of the Isaac Anderson discussion.
2. Click the **Italic** button *I* on the Format toolbar.
3. Select the text **Deconstructing Beethoven** from the description of the Reading Club event.
4. Click *I*.

To help the dates stand out better on the page, you decide to bold the day of the event by applying the bold character tag.

To bold text in the Avalon Books page:

1. Select the text **Monday** from the list of events.
2. Click the **Bold** button **B** on the Format toolbar.
3. Repeat Steps 1 and 2 to bold **Wednesday** and **Friday**. Click a blank part of the page to deselect the text when you are finished. The updated page should appear as shown in Figure 4-18.

| Figure 4-18 | APPLYING CHARACTER TAGS |

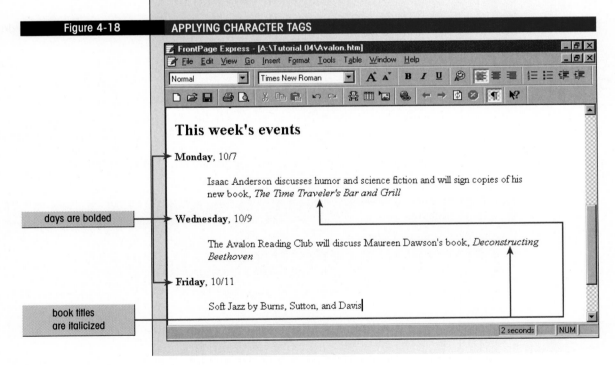

days are bolded

book titles are italicized

Changing Font Type Size

The type of font and its size are additional font attributes you can change. You have already seen how to change the font size of an entire paragraph by applying one of the heading styles, and individual browsers might change font types based on those headings. To change the font size or type of individual characters, not necessarily entire lines or paragraphs, you use the Font list and the text size buttons on the Format toolbar.

Looking at your page, you decide to increase the size of the Avalon Books heading. At present it is formatted with the Heading 1 tag. You would like the text to be larger, but there isn't another heading tag that will display the text in a larger font, so you will change its text size attribute. You decide not to change the font type, because you don't want your page design to rely on a font that other browsers might not support.

To increase the size of the Avalon Books heading:

1. Scroll to the top of your Web page, then select the text **Avalon Books** from the first line of your page.

2. Click the **Increase Text Size** button [A] on the Format toolbar. The font size is increased accordingly. Figure 4-19 shows the updated page heading.

Figure 4-19   INCREASING FONT SIZE

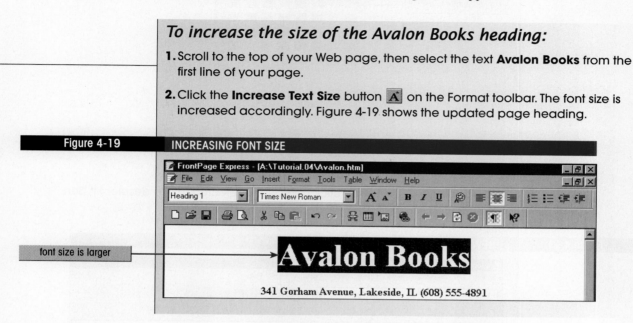

font size is larger

The heading looks better, but you'd like to emphasize it further by using color.

Changing Font Color

Another way of adding emphasis and interest to the text on your page is to use different colors by applying the Text Color character tag to selected text. FrontPage Express allows you to choose colors from a palette of colors. The default color of text in your Web document is black.

You decide to change the color of the first two lines of the page to red to give them greater emphasis.

To change the text color:

1. Select the first two headings on the page.

2. Click the **Text Color** button [icon] on the Format toolbar.

3. Click the red color shown in Figure 4-20.

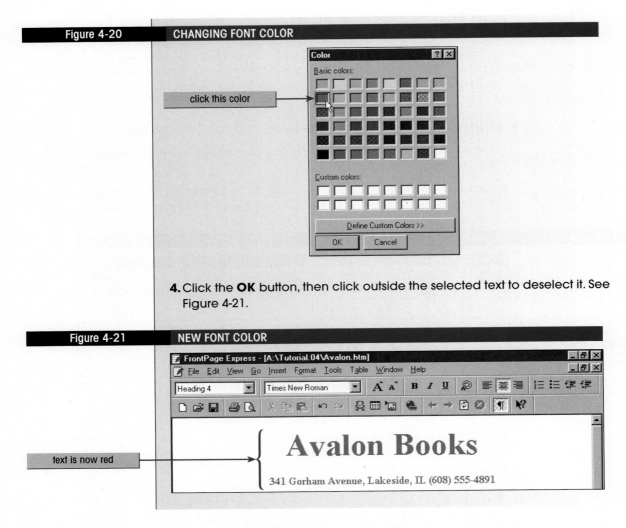

Figure 4-20 — CHANGING FONT COLOR

click this color

Figure 4-21 — NEW FONT COLOR

text is now red

4. Click the **OK** button, then click outside the selected text to deselect it. See Figure 4-21.

The first two headings now appear in red.

Applying Multiple Character Tags

So far you've been changing one character property at a time using the buttons on the Format toolbar. You can apply more than one character tag at a time using the Font dialog box. You open this dialog box the way you open any properties dialog box: by right-clicking the selected text and choosing the appropriate properties option from the popup menu that appears. You then make the selections you want in the property sheets and apply them all at once by clicking the OK button.

Mark stops by and looks at the work you've done. He's pleased with the use of color on the page and would like you to change the color for the two other headings. He thinks they should be italicized as well. You can change the font style, size, and color properties all at the same time.

To apply multiple character tags using the Character Properties sheet:

1. Select the line **Come to Avalon Books for...** .

2. Right-click the selection, then click **Font Properties** from the popup menu.

3. In the Font dialog box, click **Italic**.

4. Click the **Color** list arrow, then click **Blue**, as shown in Figure 4-22.

| Figure 4-22 | SETTING CHARACTER PROPERTIES |

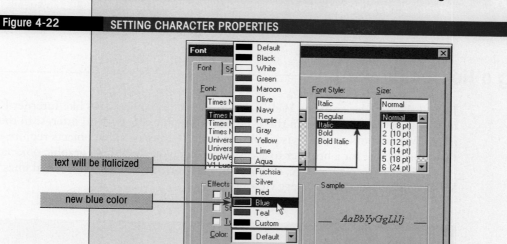

text will be italicized

new blue color

5. Click the **OK** button.

6. Select the heading **This week's events**, then repeat Steps 2 through 5.

You're finished modifying the text on the Avalon Books page. You decide to take a break. Save your changes to the file and close FrontPage Express. In the next session you'll add graphic elements to the page.

To save your changes and then exit FrontPage Express and Internet Explorer:

1. Click the **Save** button 💾.

2. Click **File**, then click **Exit**. Your Web page is saved to your Data Disk. Close Internet Explorer if necessary.

You've finished entering the text of the Avalon Books Web page, and you've formatted it so that the important parts are most noticeable.

Session 4.2 QUICK | CHECK

1. How do you change the symbol FrontPage Express uses in bulleted lists?

2. Name three font attributes you can change in FrontPage Express.

3. Why might you decide not to specify a different font, such as Century Gothic, for a heading?

4. How would you change the font size, font color, and appearance for a section of text without opening several dialog boxes?

5. How would you change the color of text on your page to green?

SESSION 4.3

In this session you will learn how to insert graphic elements on your page, including graphical lines, images, and a background. You will also learn how to modify the properties of these graphical elements.

Inserting a Horizontal Line

Part of the popularity of the Web is due to the ability of browsers like Internet Explorer to display graphic objects within the Web page. Graphic objects lend interest to the page and allow Web authors to share visual information. Because graphic objects require more time than normal text for a browser to access, however, you should use graphic objects sparingly.

To give shape to your page, consider adding horizontal lines. Horizontal lines divide the Web page into sections for easy viewing.

REFERENCE WINDOW   **RW**

Inserting a Horizontal Line
- Click the end of the paragraph below which you want to insert the line.
- Click Insert, then click Horizontal Line.
- To change the line's appearance, right-click the horizontal line and click Horizontal Line Properties from the popup menu. Make any changes you want, then click the OK button.

Mark's flyer includes horizontal lines, and he would like his Web page to feature them as well. You decide to add a horizontal line separating the name and address of the bookstore from the rest of the page.

To insert a horizontal line:

1. Restart FrontPage Express and open the Avalon Books page into the FrontPage Express window.

2. Click the end of the heading containing address information for Avalon Books.

3. Click **Insert**, then click **Horizontal Line**. A horizontal line appears on the page.

You can use the Horizontal Line Properties dialog box to change your line's width, height, alignment, and appearance. Figure 4-23 describes the properties you can change.

Figure 4-23	LINE PROPERTIES
PROPERTY	**DESCRIPTION**
Width	The width of the line is expressed either as a percentage of the window or in the number of pixels, where a pixel is a single dot or point on your monitor's screen. Therefore setting the line width to 100% means the line will stretch the full width of the document window. If you want the line to always stretch across the document window, you should use the percent of window option. If you are trying to define the line width so that it is the same for all browsers, you should use the pixels option.
Height	The height of the line is always expressed in pixels, with a default height of two pixels.
Alignment	Lines can be left-, centered, or right-aligned on the page.
Color	You can specify a color from the color palette.
Shadow	A line can appear with or without shading, which gives the line an illusion of depth.

Figure 4-24 shows several examples of lines whose appearance varies depending on the properties they use.

Figure 4-24	EXAMPLES OF LINE STYLES

Default line

Centered, 50% of screen wide, 6 pixels high, shadow

Centered, 50% of screen width, 6 pixels high, no shadow

Left aligned, full screen width, 15 pixels high, shadow

Left aligned, full screen width, 15 pixels high, no shadow

You decide to modify the appearance of the line you just created so it looks more like the one in Mark's flyer.

You might find that your line settings already match these; if that is the case, read the steps without performing them.

To change the properties of a horizontal line:

1. Right-click the horizontal line, then click **Horizontal Line Properties**.

2. Type **325** in the Width box, then click the **Pixels** option button.

   TROUBLE? The Width and Height boxes use spin arrows to ease number entry. You can click the up spin arrow or down spin arrow to change the value. Alternately, you can simply click the box and type the new entry.

3. Change the Height box to **3** to set the line's height to three pixels.

4. Verify that the **Center** alignment option button is selected.

5. Make sure the **Solid line (no shading)** check box is deselected. The completed Horizontal Line Properties dialog box should appear as shown in Figure 4-25.

Figure 4-25	CHANGING LINE PROPERTIES

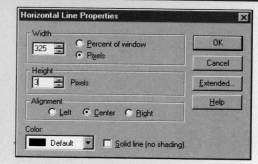

6. Click the **OK** button, then click outside the horizontal line. Figure 4-26 displays the revised horizontal line.

Figure 4-26   LINE WITH NEW PROPERTIES

revised horizontal line

You are pleased with the appearance of the page so far, and are now ready to add a graphic image to the page so that it matches Mark's flyer.

Adding Graphic Images to a Web Page

Most Web browsers can display two types of graphics: inline images and external images. An **inline image** appears directly on the Web page your browser has accessed. To ensure that your inline image is displayable by most browsers, you should use either the GIF or JPEG graphics file formats. If you have a graphic in a different format, you should convert it to a GIF or a JPEG file to ensure that most browsers can display it.

An **external image** is not displayed on the Web page itself. Instead, a link—either a textual or graphical link—appears on the page that represents the image. Figure 4-27 shows the difference between inline and external images.

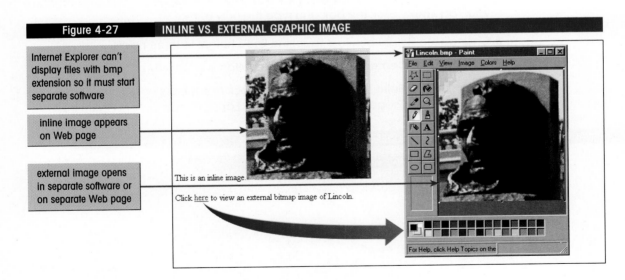

Figure 4-27   INLINE VS. EXTERNAL GRAPHIC IMAGE

Internet Explorer can't display files with bmp extension so it must start separate software

inline image appears on Web page

external image opens in separate software or on separate Web page

If you have used an external image on your page, a browser accessing that page either displays it on a separate page in the browser or loads software to display the image. Thus, external images have the disadvantage of requiring extra software or linking to an extra Web page, and someone reading your page must activate a link to view the image. But external images are not limited to the GIF or JPEG formats.

GIF File Formats

GIF files come in two formats: interlaced or noninterlaced. When you create your GIF file in your graphics program, you'll need to decide which format you want to use. The difference between the two formats lies in how your browser displays the graphic as it loads the page. With a **noninterlaced** GIF, the image appears one line at a time, starting from the top of the image and working down to the bottom. Figure 4-28 shows this effect. If the graphic is a large one, it might take several minutes for the entire image to appear. People who access your page might find this annoying if the part of the graphic they are interested in is located at the bottom.

Figure 4-28	NONINTERLACED IMAGE AS BROWSER RETRIEVES IT

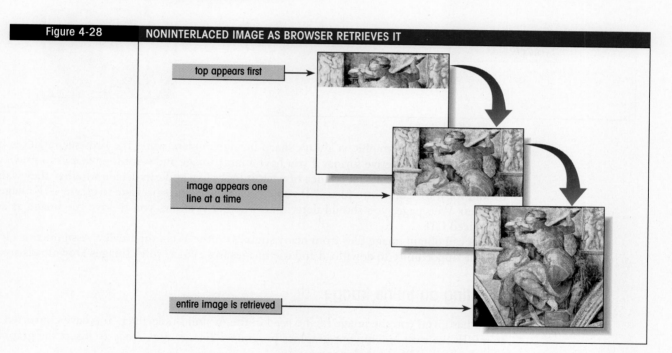

With an **interlaced** GIF, the image appears "stepwise." For example, every fifth line might appear first, followed by every sixth line, and so forth through the remaining rows. As shown in Figure 4-29, the effect of interlacing is that the graphic starts out as a blurry representation of the final image, only gradually coming into focus.

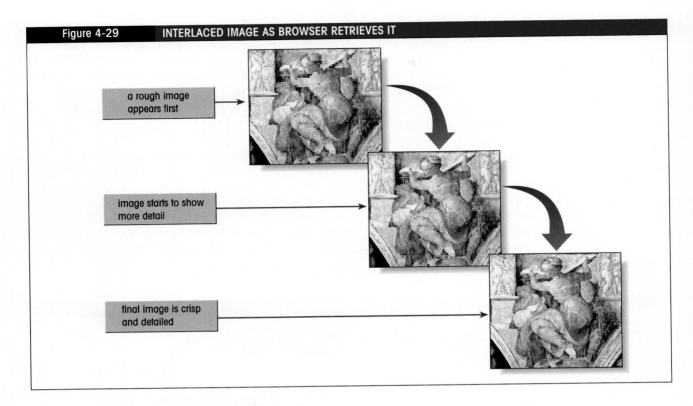

Figure 4-29   INTERLACED IMAGE AS BROWSER RETRIEVES IT

a rough image
appears first

image starts to show
more detail

final image is crisp
and detailed

A noninterlaced graphic is always sharp but incomplete while the browser retrieves it. Interlacing is an effective format if you have a large image and want to give users a preview of the final image. They get an idea of what it looks like and can decide whether they want to wait for it to "come into focus." If you are using a graphics package to create GIF images for your Web page, you should determine whether it allows you to save the image as an interlaced GIF.

You can obtain image files from many sources on the Web; the Review Assignments give you the opportunity to download and use images from Microsoft's Images Downloads area.

Inserting an Inline Image

Mark has given you the image file he used in the Avalon Books flyer. You have converted it to a GIF file with one of your graphics programs. You are now ready to insert the graphic into the Avalon Books Web page.

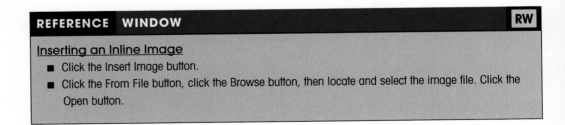

REFERENCE WINDOW   **RW**

Inserting an Inline Image
- Click the Insert Image button.
- Click the From File button, click the Browse button, then locate and select the image file. Click the Open button.

You want to place Mark's graphic to the left of the introductory paragraph.

To insert an inline image:

1. Click the beginning of the opening paragraph describing the bookstore to place the insertion point.

2. Click the **Insert Image** button 🖾 on the Standard toolbar. The Image dialog box opens. Make sure the **From File** option button is selected.

3. Click the **Browse** button, then locate and select the **Book.gif** file located in the Tutorial.04 folder on your Data Disk.

4. Click the **Open** button. The book graphic is inserted onto the page as shown in Figure 4-30.

| Figure 4-30 | INSERTED GRAPHIC |

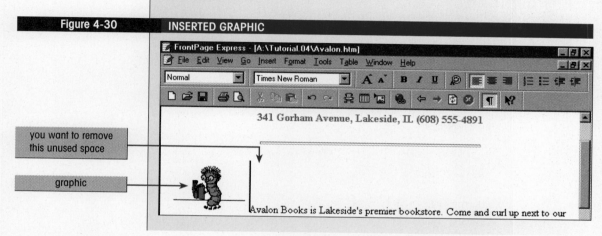

you want to remove this unused space

graphic

You notice there is a large amount of white space above the paragraph, and you decide to solve that problem.

Setting Image Properties

FrontPage Express gives you some control over how the image appears on your page. You can change the size of the image, add a border, change the distance between the graphic and surrounding text, and modify how the graphic is aligned relative to surrounding text.

Figure 4-31 shows examples of some of the options FrontPage Express provides for aligning the graphic with the surrounding text. Text can appear at the bottom, middle, or top of the graphic, or you can place the image at either the right or left page margin, and have the adjacent text wrap around the image. For larger graphics, you will probably want to choose either of the latter two options, allowing the text to wrap. If the image is small and you want to have it appear as part of the surrounding text, you will probably employ the bottom, middle, or top options.

Figure 4-31	EXAMPLES OF ALIGNED TEXT

ALIGNMENT	APPEARANCE
Top alignment	Avalon Books is Lakeside's premier bookstore. Come and curl up next to our cozy fire with a good book and a cup of one of our classic coffees. Meet with an author at one of our discussion sessions, or stop by for live music every Friday and Saturday night. Bring the kids any afternoon for storytime and snacks.
Middle alignment	Avalon Books is Lakeside's premier bookstore. Come and curl up next to our cozy fire with a good book and a cup of one of our classic coffees. Meet with an author at one of our discussion sessions, or stop by for live music every Friday and Saturday night. Bring the kids any afternoon for storytime and snacks.
Bottom alignment	Avalon Books is Lakeside's premier bookstore. Come and curl up next to our cozy fire with a good book and a cup of one of our classic coffees. Meet with an author at one of our discussion sessions, or stop by for live music every Friday and Saturday night. Bring the kids any afternoon for storytime and snacks
Right alignment	Avalon Books is Lakeside's premier bookstore. Come and curl up next to our cozy fire with a good book and a cup of one of our classic coffees. Meet with an author at one of our discussion sessions, or stop by for live music every Friday and Saturday night. Bring the kids any afternoon for storytime and snacks.
Left alignment	Avalon Books is Lakeside's premier bookstore. Come and curl up next to our cozy fire with a good book and a cup of one of our classic coffees. Meet with an author at one of our discussion sessions, or stop by for live music every Friday and Saturday night. Bring the kids any afternoon for storytime and snacks.

For large graphics you can use FrontPage Express to specify alternative images for the graphic. An **alternative image** is an image that gives users something to look at as they wait for the browser to finish retrieving the larger image from the Web server. You might, for example, want to include a lower-resolution version of the graphic that loads more quickly. You can also specify text that appears as the browser retrieves the graphic image. This is useful for users who are accessing your page with a text browser incapable of displaying the image. In those cases, they can still read your text description.

Another option to consider for your graphic is the space between the graphic and the surrounding text. As shown in Figure 4-32 you can set up your page to have the text closely hugging the graphic or you can add extra space between the image and the text.

Figure 4-32	SPACING BETWEEN IMAGE AND TEXT

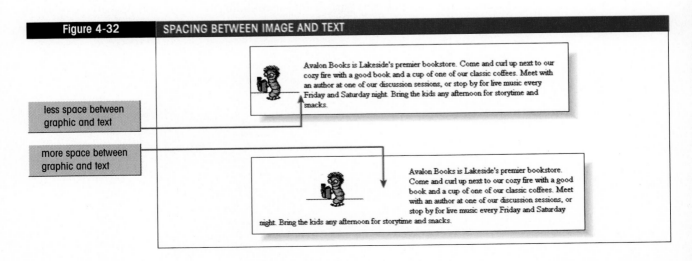

less space between graphic and text

Avalon Books is Lakeside's premier bookstore. Come and curl up next to our cozy fire with a good book and a cup of one of our classic coffees. Meet with an author at one of our discussion sessions, or stop by for live music every Friday and Saturday night. Bring the kids any afternoon for storytime and snacks.

more space between graphic and text

Avalon Books is Lakeside's premier bookstore. Come and curl up next to our cozy fire with a good book and a cup of one of our classic coffees. Meet with an author at one of our discussion sessions, or stop by for live music every Friday and Saturday night. Bring the kids any afternoon for storytime and snacks.

Considering these various options for your graphic, you decide to place the graphic to the left of the paragraph. This will remove much of the blank space between the horizontal line and the start of the paragraph. You also decide to add space between the graphic and the text in the paragraph. Finally, you decide to include a text description of the graphic.

To modify the properties of an inline image:

1. Right-click the inline image, then click **Image Properties**. The Image Properties dialog box opens to the General tab; notice the image is identified as an inter-laced GIF.

2. In the Alternative Representations area, click the **Text** box and type **Come to Avalon Books!**

3. Click the **Appearance** tab. In the Layout area, click the **Alignment** list arrow, then click **left**.

4. Set the Horizontal Spacing spin box to **5** to increase the space around the image to five pixels. The completed dialog box should look like Figure 4-33.

Figure 4-33	MODIFYING INLINE IMAGE PROPERTIES

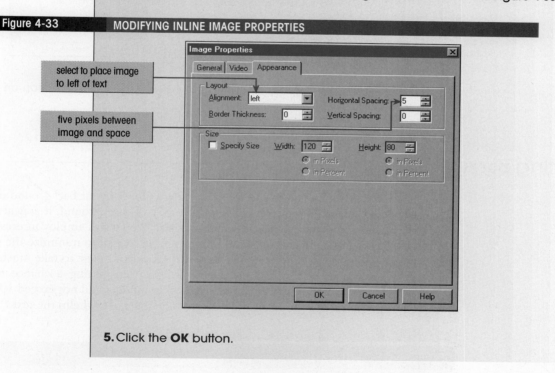

select to place image to left of text

five pixels between image and space

5. Click the **OK** button.

You decide to save your changes and view the page with the Internet Explorer browser to make sure everything looks good.

To view your changes in the browser:

1. Click a blank area of the page to deselect the image, then click the **Save** button on the Standard toolbar.

2. Launch Internet Explorer.

3. Open the **Avalon.htm** page in the Internet Explorer browser. Figure 4-34 displays the revised Avalon Books page in the browser.

Figure 4-34   INLINE IMAGE IN BROWSER

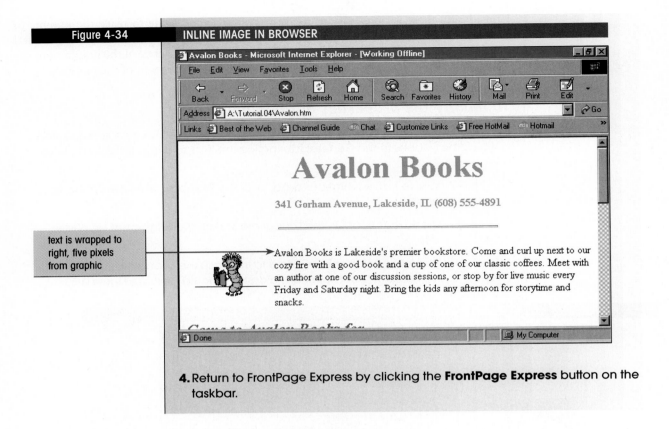

text is wrapped to right, five pixels from graphic

4. Return to FrontPage Express by clicking the **FrontPage Express** button on the taskbar.

Setting **Background Properties**

FrontPage Express allows you to specify a particular color for your background or a particular background image. When you use a graphic as your background, it appears over and over in a pattern across the document window. Many Web pages employ interesting background images to great effect. You should, however, be careful to minimize the size of the graphic image you use. A large graphic image will cause your page to take much longer to load, causing some users to cancel the page before even getting a chance to view it. Generally, the size of a graphic used for a page background should not exceed 30 kilobytes. You should also be careful not to let the background image overwhelm the text.

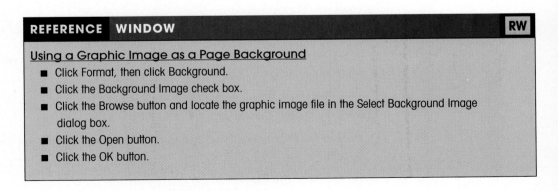

REFERENCE WINDOW   RW

Using a Graphic Image as a Page Background
- Click Format, then click Background.
- Click the Background Image check box.
- Click the Browse button and locate the graphic image file in the Select Background Image dialog box.
- Click the Open button.
- Click the OK button.

You've created an image for the Avalon Books background using the store logo. You've been careful to make the image small and unobtrusive.

To change the background of your Web page:

1. Click **Format**, then click **Background**.

2. Click the **Background Image** check box.

3. Click the **Browse** button.

4. On the Other Location tab, make sure the **From File** option button is selected. Click **Browse**, and then locate and select the file **AB.gif** in the Tutorial.04 folder on your Data Disk.

5. Click the **Open** button, then click the **OK** button.

The image background appears throughout the background. Save the page to your Data Disk and view the final version in the Internet Explorer browser.

To view the final version of your work:

1. Click the **Save** button 🖫.

2. Click the Avalon Books–Microsoft Internet Explorer browser button on the taskbar.

3. In Internet Explorer, click the **Refresh** button 🔁 to reload the page. Figure 4-35 displays the final version of the page.

Figure 4-35   **FINAL AVALON BOOKS PAGE IN BROWSER WINDOW**

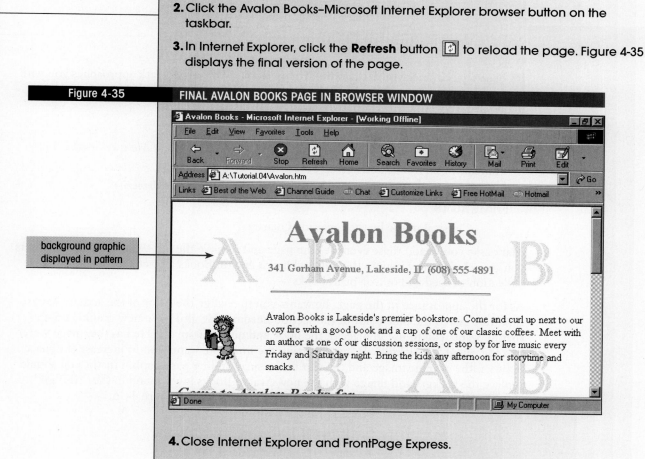

background graphic displayed in pattern

4. Close Internet Explorer and FrontPage Express.

Mark is pleased with the final version of the page and will contact his Internet Service Provider about posting it on the store's Internet account. Because you've done such a good job creating this page, he asks that you be responsible for keeping the page up-to-date. Because creating the page was so easy with FrontPage Express, you quickly agree.

Session 4.3 QUICK CHECK

1. Explain the difference between expressing line width in percent of window vs. pixels.

2. What is the difference between an inline graphic and an external graphic?

3. Name two file formats you can use for inline graphics.

4. If you want to use a Windows Bitmap image (file extension bmp) as an inline image on your Web page, what should you do to it first?

5. What is the difference between an interlaced graphic and a noninterlaced graphic?

6. How would you set up a horizontal line so that it is centered on a page and covers 25% of the width of the document window?

7. What should you watch out for when using a graphic image for your page background?

8. If you display a picture on your Web page, why might you want to enter a text description of that picture?

REVIEW ASSIGNMENTS

It's been a week since you created the Avalon Books Web page. Mark approaches you with a list of things he wants to have added and changed on the page. In the upcoming week, the bookstore will host the following events:

Monday, 10/14

A lecture given by Professor Patricia Fuller on *The Art of Maurice Sendak*

Thursday, 10/17

Peter Daynes will sign copies of his new book, *Glencoe Memories*

Friday, 10/18

Classical music by the Lakeside Quartet

Mark asks you to add these events to the page and remove the old event list. He also wants you to include a new item in the bulleted list of Avalon Books attractions: "An impressive collection of used and out-of-print books".

As for the appearance of the page, he wants you to change the color of the activity days so that they match the blue color of the section heading. He also has a new graphic image that he wants you to use in place of the book and quill pen image. He has the image stored in a file called "Book2.gif". When inserting the image he wants you to increase the space between the graphic image and the text in the surrounding paragraph. Finally, you should replace the background image with the new Avalon Books logo, found in the "AB2.gif" file. The final version of this page should appear as shown in Figure 4-36.

Figure 4-36

Avalon Books

341 Gorham Avenue, Lakeside, IL (608) 555-4891

Avalon Books is Lakeside's premier bookstore. Come and curl up next to our cozy fire with a good book and a cup of one of our classic coffees. Meet with an author at one of our discussion sessions, or stop by for live music every Friday and Saturday night. Bring the kids any afternoon for storytime and snacks.

Come to Avalon Books for...

- The largest selection of books in the Midwest
- Comfortable reading rooms
- Coffe, wines and delicious desserts as you read
- A computer lab for kids with the best educational software titles
- An impressive collection of used and out-of-print books

This week's events

Monday, 10/14

A lecture given by Professor Patricia Fuller on *The Art of Maurice Sendak*

Thursday, 10/17

Peter Daynes will sign copies of his new book, *Glencoe Memories*

Friday 10/18

Classical music by the Lakeside Quartet

To complete this review assignment:

1. Open the "Avalon.htm" file that you created in this tutorial in FrontPage Express.

2. Save the page as "Avalon2" to the Review folder on your Data Disk. As you save the page, change the title to "Avalon Books 2".

3. Add the item "An impressive collection of used and out-of-print books" to the end of the bulleted list.

4. Delete the outdated events list and replace it with the new events list. Use the same indentation.

5. Change the color of the day to match the color of the section heading.

Explore 6. Replace the "Book.gif" graphic with the "Book2.gif" graphic found in the Review folder of the Tutorial.04 folder on your Data Disk. To replace a graphic, right-click the old graphic, click Image Properties, click the Browse button, and then locate and select the new graphic.

7. Change the horizontal spacing around the graphic to 9 pixels but leave the graphic to the left of the paragraph so the text wraps to the right.

8. Replace the "AB.gif" background graphic with the "AB2.gif" graphic in the Review folder of the Tutorial.04 folder on your Data Disk.

9. Save the Web page.

10. View the revised page in the Internet Explorer browser.

11. Print a copy of the page for your instructor.

CASE PROBLEMS

Case 1. Creating a Web Page for the River Bar Seafood Restaurant   You work as a manager at the River Bar Seafood Restaurant in Woolworth, Missouri. The owner, Gwen Foucoult, has asked you to create a Web page listing the weekly specials at the restaurant. She shows you a printout of what she wants on the page, shown in Figure 4-37.

Figure 4-37

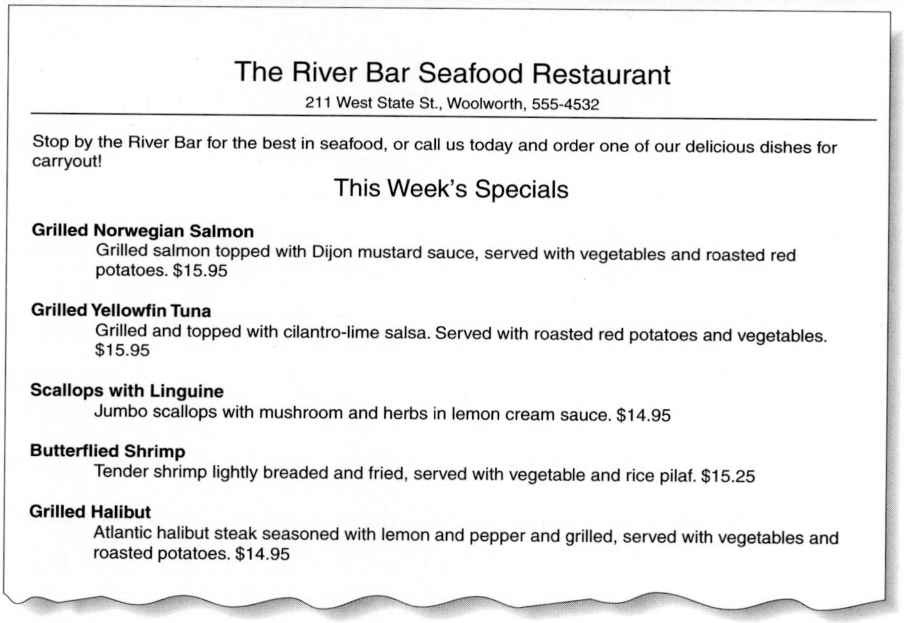

The River Bar Seafood Restaurant
211 West State St., Woolworth, 555-4532

Stop by the River Bar for the best in seafood, or call us today and order one of our delicious dishes for carryout!

This Week's Specials

Grilled Norwegian Salmon
Grilled salmon topped with Dijon mustard sauce, served with vegetables and roasted red potatoes. $15.95

Grilled Yellowfin Tuna
Grilled and topped with cilantro-lime salsa. Served with roasted red potatoes and vegetables. $15.95

Scallops with Linguine
Jumbo scallops with mushroom and herbs in lemon cream sauce. $14.95

Butterflied Shrimp
Tender shrimp lightly breaded and fried, served with vegetable and rice pilaf. $15.25

Grilled Halibut
Atlantic halibut steak seasoned with lemon and pepper and grilled, served with vegetables and roasted potatoes. $14.95

Using Figure 4-37 as a guide, create the River Bar page.

To complete this case problem:

1. Open FrontPage Express to a blank page.

2. Save the page as "Seafood.htm" to the Cases folder in the Tutorial.04 folder on your Data Disk. Give the page the title, "River Bar Specials".

3. Enter the text shown in Figure 4-37.

Explore

4. Format and center the main heading using the Heading 2 style. Then apply an interesting, applicable font to it.

5. Format and center the restaurant address using the Heading 5 style.

6. Insert a horizontal line after the restaurant address. Use the default line style.

7. Enter a brief description of the restaurant in the Normal style.

8. Format and center the heading, "This Week's Specials" with the Heading 3 style.

9. Format and left-align the name of each dish with the Heading 4 style.

10. Indent the description of each dish.

11. Use the graphic file "Fish.gif," located in the Cases folder of the Tutorial.04 folder on your Data Disk, as a background for your page.

12. Save your changes to the page.

13. Print the page for your instructor. On the back of the printed page, write the name of the font you used to format the main heading in Step 4.

Case 2. Displaying a Lecture Outline   You are the teaching assistant for history professor, Clifford Foote. Starting this semester, he is putting his lecture outlines on the Web for students to view. He wants you to create the lecture outline for his September 22 lecture on Abraham Lincoln's life prior to the Civil War.

To create such a page you will have to use numbered lists. With FrontPage Express you specify the symbol used for the list items. You can use Roman Numerals (I, II, III, IV...), capital letters (A,B,C...), numbers (1,2,3...), and so forth. For Professor Foote's lecture outline, you will format major points with the Roman Numerals format. You will also indent minor points, listing them with capital letters.

The professor also has a photo from the Lincoln mausoleum that he wants you to place on the page. The photo has been saved to the file "Lincoln.gif".

The page should include a heading for the history course, the professor's name, and the date of the lecture. The professor also wants you to place the text on a solid blue background. The complete Web page should look like Figure 4-38.

Figure 4-38

U.S. History 1722 - 1872

Professor: Clifford Foote

Lecture outline from September 22

Life of Lincoln

I. Early Life
   A. Born 1809 in Hodgenville, KY
   B. Moved to Spencer County, IN in 1811
   C. Settled in Macon County, IL in 1831
   D. Worked as a rail splitter and grocery store clerk
   E. Captain in Black Hawk war in 1832
II. Politician and Lawyer
   A. Defeated in run for state legislature in 1832
   B. Elected to state legislature in 1834 as a Whig
   C. Admitted to the bar in 1837 and joined law partnership
   D. Served in U.S. Congress from 1846-1848
III. Rise to national prominence
   A. Campaigned for newly-formed Republican party in 1856
   B. Lincoln-Douglas debates in 1858
   C. House Divided Speech in 1858
   D. Republican presidential nominee in 1860
   E. Elected president in 1860

To complete this case problem:

1. Open a blank document in FrontPage Express.

Explore
2. Set the page background color to Aqua. To do this, use the Background tab on the Page Properties dialog box, click the Background list arrow, and select Aqua.

3. Save the page as "Lincoln.htm" to the Cases folder in the Tutorial.04 folder on your Data Disk and specify "September 22 lecture" as the title.

4. Type the main heading "U.S. History 1722–1872," formatted with the Heading 1 style and centered on the page.

5. Change the color of the main heading to red (second row, first column in the list of basic colors).

6. Type the secondary heading "Professor: Clifford Foote," formatted with the Normal style and centered.

7. Bold the title of professor.

8. Type "Lecture outline from September 22," formatted with the Normal style, italicized, and left-aligned.

9. Type "Life of Lincoln," formatted with the Heading 3 style and left-aligned.

Explore
10. Enter the three main outline heads as a numbered list, and use the Roman Numeral style for the list items. You can change ordered list styles on the Numbered tab of the List Properties dialog box.

Explore
11. Within each main point, enter the subpoints and indent them.

12. Format the indented subpoints as a numbered list using the capital letter style.

13. At the beginning of the line reading "Life of Lincoln" insert the "Lincoln.gif" image, available in the Cases folder of the Tutorial.04 folder on your Data Disk.

14. Format the image so that the image will be placed to the right of the text.

 15. Add a 2-pixel horizontal border to the image. Use the Border Thickness spin box.

16. Save your completed page.

17. View the page in the Internet Explorer browser and print the page.

18. Hand in the printout to your instructor.

Case 3. *Using Preformatted Text on the Weber State Weather Page*   You are in charge of a weather page at Weber State University. You use a program that creates temperature charts like the one shown in Figure 4-39.

Figure 4-39

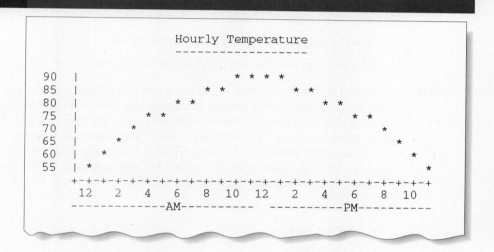

This chart uses a monospace font, which allots the same amount of space to each character. Because it is a monospace font, the characters in the chart are perfectly aligned. The normal font used by most Web browsers, however, is not monospace. Using the normal font would result in a chart that is out of alignment. You can solve this problem by using another of the styles provided with FrontPage Express called "Formatted." The Formatted tag displays text in a monospace font. The temperature chart has been placed in the file "Temp.txt" in the Cases folder of the Tutorial.04 folder on your Data Disk. By copying the temperature chart from the Temp.txt file and pasting it into FrontPage Express, try to create a Web page detailing the previous day's temperature variations.

To complete this case problem:

1. Open FrontPage Express to a blank page.

2. Save the page as "Temp" in the Cases folder in the Tutorial.04 folder on your Data Disk and enter "Weber State Weather Page" as the page title.

3. Return to the document window and type the text "Yesterday's Temperature Chart" at the top of the page.

4. Format the heading with the Heading 1 style and center it on the page.

5. Beneath the heading, type yesterday's date.

6. Center the date and format it with the Heading 5 style.

7. Insert a horizontal line beneath the date.

Explore   8. Start Notepad (click the Start button, point to Programs, point to Accessories, and then click Notepad). Open the file "Temp.txt" in the Cases folder of the Tutorial.04 folder on your Data Disk.

Explore   9. Copy the temperature chart (click Edit, click Select All, click Edit again, and then click Copy).

10. Close Notepad and return to the Temp page.

Explore   11. Insert a new paragraph underneath the horizontal line and format it with the Formatted tag on the Change Style list.

12. Click the Align Left button to align any formatted text with the left edge of the window.

Explore   13. Paste the temperature chart into the new line (click Edit, then click Paste).

14. Save the changes you made to the Temp page.

15. View the page in the Internet Explorer browser.

16. Print the page and hand in the printout to your instructor.

Case 4. Creating a Realty Listing   You work as a real estate agent for TK Realty. Just recently your company has started putting listings on the World Wide Web. You're responsible for creating your own listing. One of the houses you want to create a Web page for is a lake-front house located at 22 Northshore Drive. The owners have given you this description, which they want placed on the page: "This is a must see. Large waterfront home overlooking Lake Mills. It comes complete with 3 bedrooms, a huge master bedroom, hot tub, family room, large office, and three-car garage. Wood boat ramp. Great condition."

The main points about the house are:

- 2,300 sq. feet
- 15 years old
- Updated electrical and heat
- Asking price: $230,000

You also have a photo of the house, saved as "House.jpg" in the Cases folder on the Tutorial.04 folder on your Data Disk. Using this information, create a page describing the house to interested house-hunters. You may choose any design for the page, but it must include the following elements:

1. A main heading

2. The photo of the house

3. A bulleted list describing the features of the house

4. A paragraph containing the owner's description

5. Information on how to contact you, in italics

You can make your page more interesting by inserting lines or other graphics that you download off the Web. Start Internet Explorer, and connect to the http://www.msdn.microsoft.com/downloads page. This page is maintained by Microsoft, and features free graphics, sounds, and other objects useful to Web page designers. Click the clip art link and then browse through the graphics and download a horizontal line and an image or two to include on your page, perhaps as a background. Figure 4-40 shows the Images page. If you are unable to locate this page, ask your instructor for a more current URL.

Figure 4-40

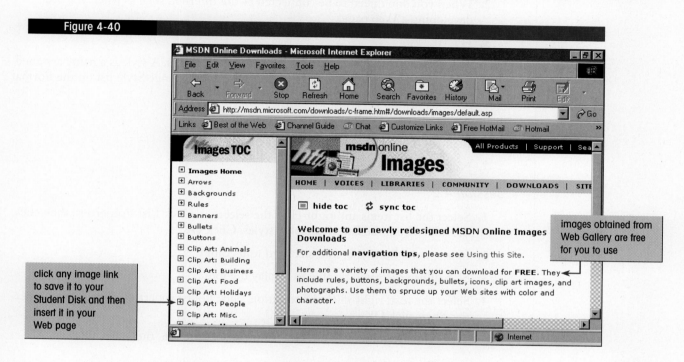

click any image link to save it to your Student Disk and then insert it in your Web page

images obtained from Web Gallery are free for you to use

Save the page you create in the Cases folder on the Tutorial.04 folder on your Data Disk with the name "Realty". When you submit the page to your instructor, indicate which graphics or objects you used from the Microsoft site.

QUICK CHECK ANSWERS

Session 4.1

1. "What you see is what you get" allows you to see how the final document will appear as you develop your page.

2. When you don't need to be connected to the Internet, such as when you are developing a Web page.

3. HTML

4. A markup tag is an HTML label within angle brackets. A style is a name assigned by FrontPage Express to a tag that appears in the Change Style list on the Format toolbar.

5. Not all browsers will be able to view it.

6. It allows only options supported by HTML.

7. Normal

Session 4.2

1. Select the list items and right-click the selection. Click List Properties, then click the bullet from the list of available styles. Click OK.

2. Italics, bold, font type, font size, and font color

3. Not all browsers will be able to display the font.

4. Select the text, right-click the selection, click Font Properties, change the properties, then click OK.

5. Select the text, click the Text Color button, click green, then click OK.

Session 4.3

1. Percent of window indicates what percentage of the window the line will extend across; pixels indicates the number of pixels the line will occupy.

2. Browser displays inline graphic on the page while a separate application must start to display an external graphic.

3. GIF and JPEG

4. Convert it to GIF or JPEG format.

5. A noninterlaced graphic appears one line at a time, starting from the top of the image and working down. In an interlaced graphic, the image appears stepwise with the image coming gradually into focus.

6. Right-click the line, click Horizontal Line Properties, enter 25 in the Width box, and choose Percent of window as the width option. Click OK.

7. That the graphic is not so large that it makes the page take longer to display and that it is not too distracting from the main text on the page.

8. So users know the picture's content without having to view the image itself.

OBJECTIVES

In this tutorial you will:

- Create bookmarks within a Web page

- Create hypertext links to bookmarks on the same Web page

- Learn the principles of structuring a Web site

- Create links to other Web pages on the same computer

- Create links to bookmarks on other Web pages

- Create links to other Web pages on the Internet

- Create links to e-mail addresses

- Explore publishing a page on the Web

CREATING A HYPERTEXT DOCUMENT

Creating a Web Site

CASE

The Findlay Farmhouse Bed and Breakfast

Prince Edward Island in Canada is a popular summer vacation spot. The island is known for its natural beauty and peaceful setting. Visitors to the island can choose their lodging from several attractive inns and picturesque bed and breakfasts. One of the most popular bed and breakfasts on the island is the Findlay Farmhouse outside of Summerside. The proprietors, Ian and Fiona Findlay, have owned the inn for many years. Several years ago they bought a computer to help manage their business, and recently they set up an Internet connection. The Findlays want to advertise their bed and breakfast on the Internet in hopes that it will generate new business. Fiona has started creating a page for the Findlay Farmhouse, and she hopes you can help finish it.

Fiona explains that she has organized information about the Findlay Farmhouse and its surroundings into five topics, each with a Heading 2 style heading, with the following titles:

- Your home on Prince Edward Island
- What are they saying about us?
- Area attractions
- How do I get there?
- For more information

Fiona tells you that she has also created two supplementary Web pages, Bio and Events, which contain information on the Findlay family and area events. She would like users to be able to access the Bio and Events pages from the Findlay Farmhouse page. She would also like users to be able to jump to other pages on Prince Edward Island from the Findlay Farmhouse page, as well as to be able to send her e-mail messages. You tell her she can accomplish all this with hypertext links. Then you suggest that she could make her page, which is rather long, more user-friendly by adding links that help users move more easily around the page. Fiona agrees that would be a good idea, so the two of you get to work.

SESSION 5.1

In this session you'll learn how to create bookmarks within a Web page and to create hypertext links to those bookmarks.

Setting Bookmarks

As you've seen by browsing the Web, Web pages contain hypertext, or links that you can select, usually by clicking a mouse, to jump instantly to another location. In addition to making access to other documents easy, hypertext links provide some important organizational benefits.

For example, when your Web page is too long to fit on a single screen, you can help users quickly locate the information they need by providing hypertext links to important points within the page. A typical screen can display only a small section of a long page, and this could be a problem for users in a hurry. Because many Web users glance at a page and then move on, you should make your page's topics as accessible as possible. You can do this by placing links at the beginning that point to the main topics on the page. When readers click the link, they jump to that section of the document.

To create links that jump to a specific point on a Web page, you must first insert a bookmark at the destination location. A **bookmark**, also called an **anchor** or **target**, is a reference point that identifies a specific location on the page. Once you insert a bookmark, you can then refer to that particular location. You create the link and indicate the bookmark to which the link points. Figure 5-1 illustrates how the bookmark you create will work as a reference point for a link.

Figure 5-1	LINK POINTING TO BOOKMARK WITHIN THE SAME WEB DOCUMENT

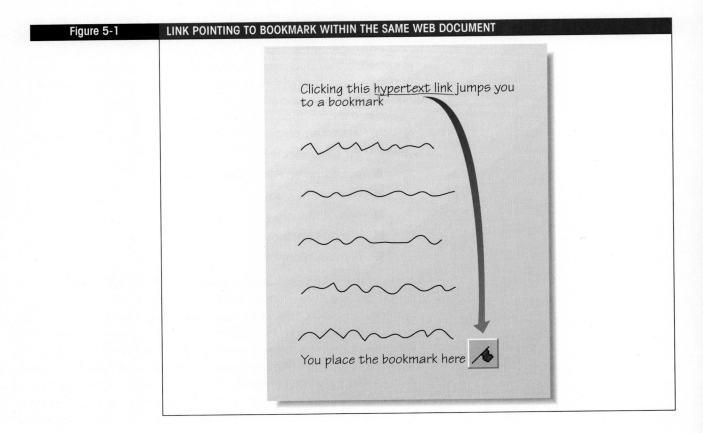

Bookmarks do not appear in the browser, but you can view them in FrontPage Express. For the Findlay Web page, you decide to create five bookmarks—one bookmark at each of the five section headings of the document. You can then create links at the beginning of the page that point to each of the five bookmarks. A user can click one of the links to jump to the bookmark it targets without having to scroll through the page to reach it. Figure 5-2 shows the location of the five bookmarks you will create on the Findlay Web page.

Figure 5-2	BOOKMARKS IN THE FINDLAY WEB PAGE

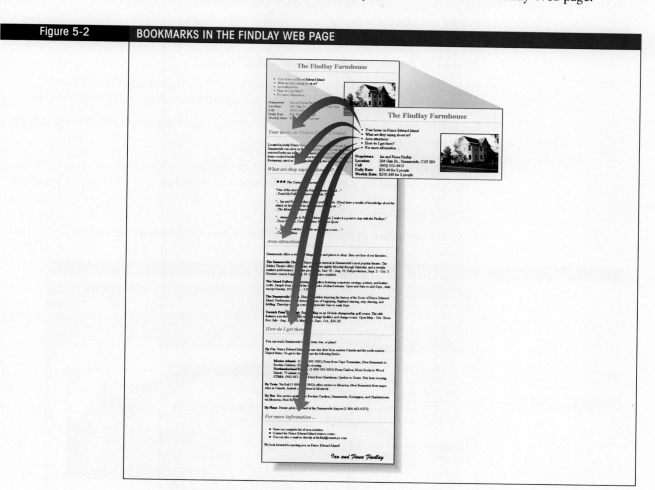

Fiona stored her page as Findlay.htm. You'll open the file and save it with a new name, Findlay2.htm, so you don't alter the contents of the original—just in case.

To open the Findlay.htm file in FrontPage Express and save it with a new name:

1. Launch FrontPage Express and insert your Student Disk in the drive.

2. Click the **Open** button 🖿.

3. Click the **Browse** button, locate and select the **Findlay** file from the Tutorial.05 folder on your Data Disk, and then click the **Open** button.

4. Click **File**, then click **Save As**.

5. Click the **As File** button.

6. Type **Findlay2** in the File name box, then click the **Save** button.

7. Scroll down the entire page to view the location of the five section headings.

First you will create the five bookmarks. FrontPage Express makes it very easy for you to create a bookmark. The first bookmark you create will be for the heading "Your home on Prince Edward Island".

To set a bookmark in your Web page:

1. Scroll the page to the first section heading, "Your home on Prince Edward Island". Make sure you are viewing the section heading, not the bulleted list.

2. Click at the start of the section heading to place the blinking insertion point at the beginning of the line.

TROUBLE? If you click too far to the left of the section heading, you highlight the heading. Make sure the blinking insertion point is just to the left of the heading.

3. Click **Edit**, then click **Bookmark**.

4. Type **Your home** in the Bookmark Name box as shown in Figure 5-3.

Figure 5-3	SETTING A BOOKMARK

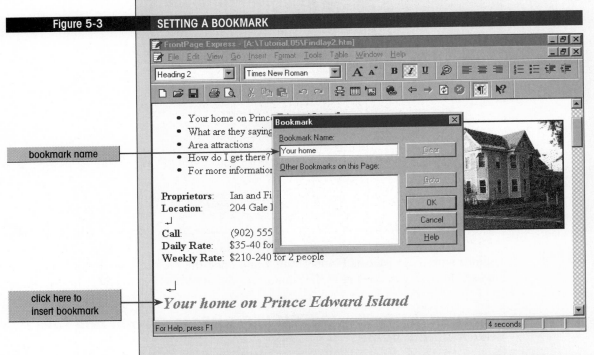

bookmark name

click here to
insert bookmark

5. Click the **OK** button. FrontPage inserts a bookmark icon before the section heading. See Figure 5-4.

TROUBLE? If you don't see the paragraph and other document markings shown in Figure 5-4, click the Show/Hide ¶ button so that it is selected. When the Show/Hide ¶ button is selected, FrontPage Express displays document markings that identify hard paragraphs and other page elements.

| Figure 5-4 | BOOKMARK IN FRONTPAGE EXPRESS |

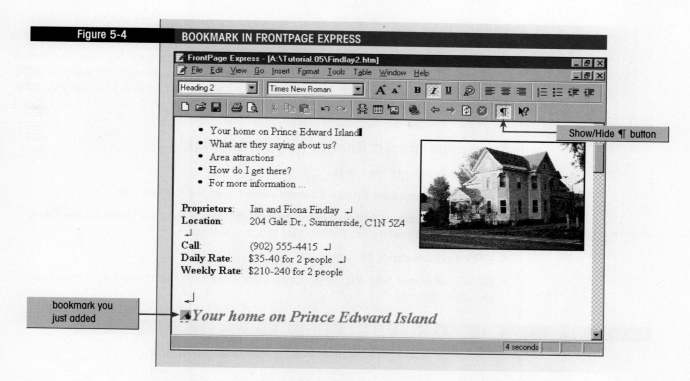

The bookmark icon ![icon] indicates the presence of a bookmark on a Web page. This icon appears only in FrontPage Express—not in the browser. If you ever forget the name you gave the bookmark, you can right-click it and click Bookmark Properties to view the bookmark name.

You're ready to add the rest of the bookmarks, one for each section heading. You can type in any characters or blank spaces into the bookmark name. Be sure you pay attention to case. A bookmark named "home" is different from one named "HOME".

To add the other section heading bookmarks:

1. Scroll down to the heading, "What are they saying about us?" then click the left side of the heading.

2. Click **Edit**, click **Bookmark**, type **Reviews**, and then click the **OK** button.

3. Scroll down to the heading, "Area attractions", then click the left side of the heading.

4. Add a bookmark named **Attractions**.

5. Scroll down to the heading, "How do I get there?" then add a bookmark named **Travel**.

6. Scroll down to the heading, "For more information", then add a bookmark named **More Info**.

Now all five bookmarks are in place. You are ready to create hypertext links to the bookmarks.

Creating Hypertext Links to Bookmarks

You can change existing text to a hypertext link by simply selecting the text, then clicking the Create or Edit Hyperlink button ![icon] and indicating the bookmark to which you want the link to point.

Creating Links

The Findlay Farmhouse page begins with a bulleted list that corresponds to the five section headings. By changing the items in this list to hypertext links, you enable users to jump directly to a bookmark. You begin by creating the link to the first section heading, which has a bookmark named Your home.

To change the list item to a hypertext link:

1. Scroll to the top of the page.

2. Select **Your home on Prince Edward Island** from the bulleted list.

3. Click the **Create or Edit Hyperlink button** 🖱. Make sure the Open Pages tab is selected and the Findlay Farmhouse page is selected.

4. Click the **Bookmark** list arrow.

5. Click **Your home** from the list of named bookmarks in the current document, as shown in Figure 5-5.

Figure 5-5	SELECTING A BOOKMARK FOR A HYPERTEXT LINK

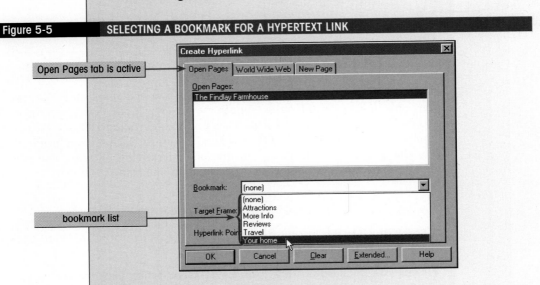

Open Pages tab is active

bookmark list

6. Click the **OK** button, then click the page to deselect the link. The text, "Your home on Prince Edward Island", is now underlined and in a different color.

7. Move the mouse pointer over the linked text. Notice the link's target appears in the status bar. See Figure 5-6.

Figure 5-6   HYPERTEXT LINK YOU JUST ADDED

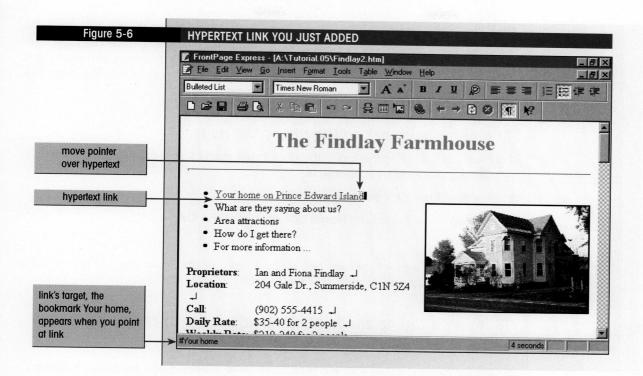

move pointer
over hypertext

hypertext link

link's target, the
bookmark Your home,
appears when you point
at link

Note that the name of the bookmark is prefaced by a pound sign (#). All bookmark names are prefaced by this symbol to differentiate them from other names such as filenames or document locations.

Using the same technique you just learned, turn the other items in the bulleted list to hypertext links.

To convert the rest of the list to hypertext links:

1. Select **What are they saying about us?**, then link the text to the **Reviews** bookmark.

2. Select **Area attractions**, then link the text to the **Attractions** bookmark.

3. Select **How do I get there?**, then link the text to the **Travel** bookmark.

4. Select **For more information...**, then link the text to the **More Info** bookmark. Figure 5-7 shows the completed list of hypertext links.

Figure 5-7   INSERTED LINKS

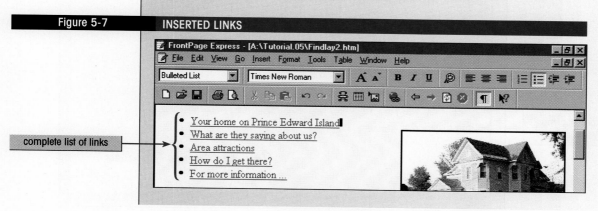

complete list of links

Users can now use the bulleted list to jump to any heading on the Findlay page. You notice that there is no easy way of returning to the top of the Findlay Farmhouse page, aside from scrolling. You realize that it might be helpful to include a hypertext link pointing to the top of the page. This is a common feature of long pages. To create this hypertext link, you first must create a bookmark at the top of the page.

To add a bookmark to the top of the page:

1. If necessary, scroll to the top of the document, then click to the left of the main heading, **The Findlay Farmhouse**.

2. Click **Edit**, then click **Bookmark**.

3. Type **Top** in the Bookmark Name box, then click the **OK** button.

Now you create a new hypertext link at the bottom of the document that points to the bookmark you just created at the top of the page.

To insert a link to the bookmark at the top of the document:

1. Scroll down to the bottom of the page.

2. Click at the end of the line: **We look forward to meeting you on Prince Edward Island!** then press **Enter**.

3. Type **Return to the top of the page**, then select the line you just typed.

4. Click the **Create or Edit Hyperlink button** 🔗.

5. On the Open Pages tab, click **Top** from the list of bookmarks.

6. Click the **OK** button. Figure 5-8 displays the linked text that appears on the Web page.

| Figure 5-8 | LINK TO THE TOP OF THE PAGE |

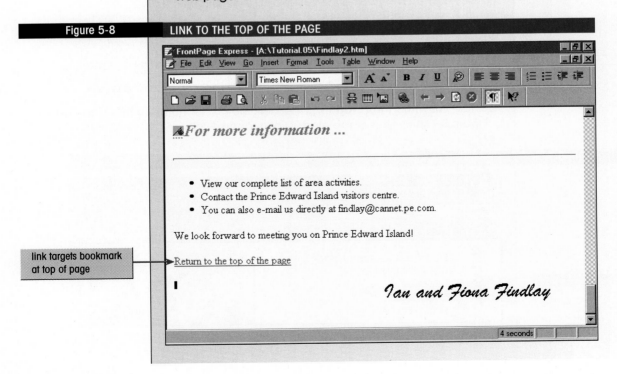

link targets bookmark
at top of page

You are finished adding links that help users navigate the Findlay page.

Testing Links

Once you have entered links into a hypertext document, you should test them in the Internet Explorer browser to make sure they target the correct bookmarks.

To test the links in the Internet Explorer browser:

1. Click the **Save** button 🖫 and then start the Internet Explorer browser and open the Findlay2 page in the Tutorial.05 folder on your Student Disk in the browser. You don't need to connect to the Internet to open this page from your Student Disk. You can now verify that your hypertext links are working correctly.

2. Move the mouse pointer over the list item, **Your home on Prince Edward Island**. The mouse pointer changes to 🖑 and the status bar shows the target. See Figure 5-9.

Figure 5-9	TESTING A LINK

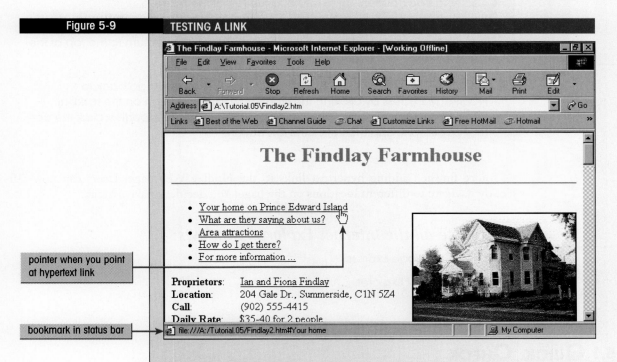

pointer when you point
at hypertext link

bookmark in status bar

3. Click the **Your home on Prince Edward Island** link. The browser jumps to the Your home bookmark and displays the Your home on Prince Edward Island heading. See Figure 5-10.

Figure 5-10	JUMPING TO A LINK'S DESTINATION

location of Your home bookmark; bookmark icon doesn't appear in browser

> Findlay2 - Microsoft Internet Explorer - [Working Offline]
>
> File   Edit   View   Favorites   Tools   Help
>
> Back   Forward   Stop   Refresh   Home   Search   Favorites   History   Mail   Print   Edit
>
> Address file:///A:/Tutorial.05/Findlay2.htm#Your home   Go
>
> Links   Best of the Web   Channel Guide   Chat   Customize Links   Free HotMail   Hotmail   »
>
> *Your home on Prince Edward Island*
>
> Located in lovely Prince County, this picturesque Victorian home on a 2.3 acre farm near Summerside can serve as the perfect home as you tour the island. Stay in one of our beautifully

4. Click the **Back** button to return to the top of the page.

5. Repeat Steps 2–4 with the other links on the page to verify that they are all working properly. After you test the For more information link, return to the top of the page by clicking the Return to the top of the page link.

TROUBLE? If you discover a link that is not working properly, go back to FrontPage Express by clicking the FrontPage Express button on the taskbar. Right-click the link in FrontPage Express, click Hyperlink Properties, click the correct bookmark, and then click the OK button.

You're finished adding hypertext links to the Findlay Web page. Users can now efficiently navigate to different locations on the page. You decide to take a break.

To close all the Internet Explorer windows:

1. Close FrontPage Express.

2. Close Internet Explorer.

Session 5.1 QUICK CHECK

1. What is a bookmark? When is it necessary?

2. How do you create a bookmark with FrontPage Express?

3. Are bookmark names case sensitive or case insensitive?

4. How is the presence of a bookmark indicated in a URL?

5. Where do you test links?

SESSION 5.2

In this session you will create a Web site that consists of several documents connected together with hypertext links. You'll learn how to control the development of such multi-document structures through the technique of storyboarding.

Principles of Storyboarding

When you are developing a Web page, one of the first things you must ask yourself is whether you intend to develop and include additional pages on related topics. A structure that contains the primary Web page, additional related pages, and the hypertext links that allow users to move among the pages, is known as a **Web site**. Web sites are usually created by the same person or group, and the pages within a Web sites usually have the same look and feel.

When you plan your Web site, you should determine exactly how you want to relate the pages using hypertext links. Charting the relationship between all the pages in your Web site is a technique known as **storyboarding**. Storyboarding your Web pages before you create links helps you determine which structure will work best for the type of information you're presenting and helps you avoid some common problems. You want to make sure readers can navigate easily from page to page without getting lost.

Fiona reminds you that she has developed two other pages for the Findlay Farmhouse Web site: Bio, a directory of people on the island, and Events, a list of activities and organizations in the area. Fiona would like readers who access her page to be able to reach either of these pages from the main Findlay Farmhouse page, as shown in Figure 5-11.

Figure 5-11	FINDLAY FARMHOUSE WEB SITE

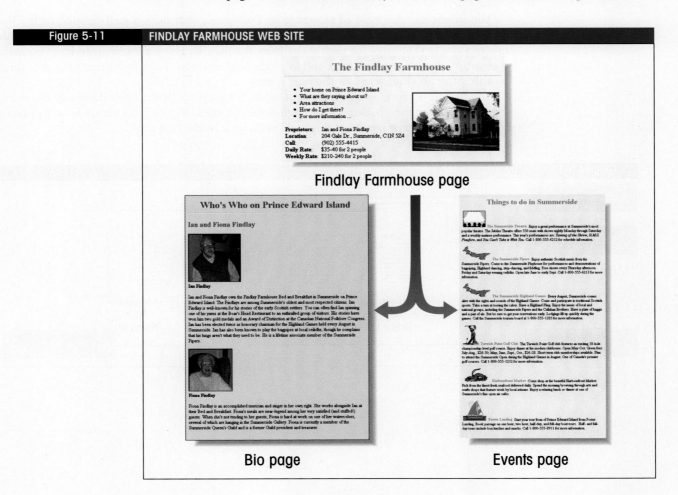

Findlay Farmhouse page

Bio page   Events page

You tell Fiona she should think about the basic principles of structuring Web presentations to decide how to link the three pages together.

Linear Structures

Web sites can be structured in a number of ways. Examining basic structures can help you decide how to design your Web site. Figure 5-12 shows a storyboard for one common structure, the **linear structure**, in which each page is linked to the next and previous pages in an ordered chain of pages.

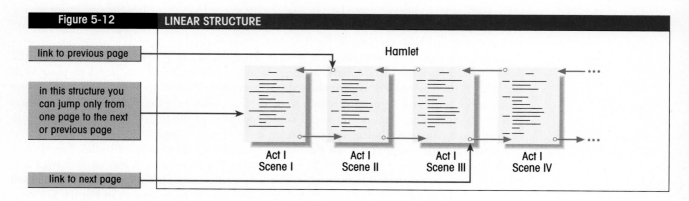

Figure 5-12   **LINEAR STRUCTURE**

You might use this type of structure in Web pages that have a well-defined order. For example, if you are trying to create a Web presentation of Shakespeare's *Hamlet*, you could create a single Web page for each scene from the play. By using a linear structure, you make it easy for users to progress back and forth through the play. Each hypertext link takes them to either the previous scene or the next scene.

You might, however, want to make it easier for users to return immediately to the opening scene rather than backtrack through several scenes. Figure 5-13 shows how you could include a link in each page that jumps directly back to the first page.

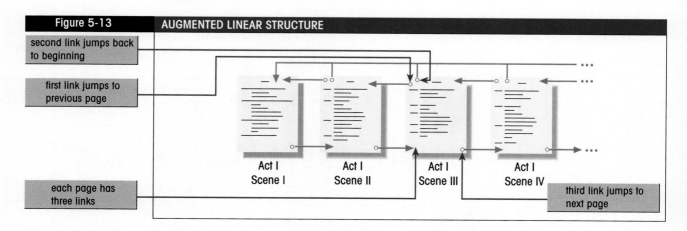

Figure 5-13   **AUGMENTED LINEAR STRUCTURE**

Hierarchical Structures

Another popular structure is the hierarchical structure of Web pages shown in Figure 5-14. A **hierarchical structure** starts with a general topic that includes links to more specific topics. Each specific topic includes links to yet more specialized topics, and so on. In a hierarchical structure, users can move easily from the general to the specific and back again.

Figure 5-14   HIERARCHICAL STRUCTURE

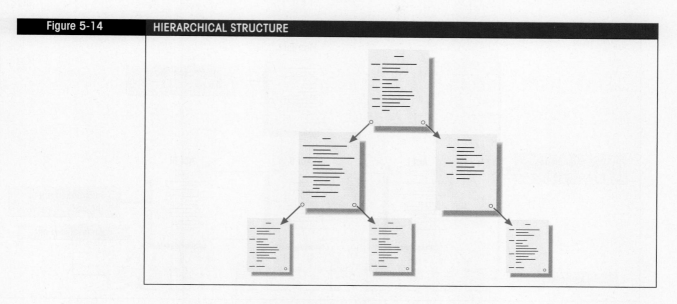

As with the linear structure, including a link to the top of the structure on each page gives users an easy way back to the hierarchy tree. Figure 5-15 shows a storyboard for this kind of Web site.

Figure 5-15   AUGMENTED HIERARCHICAL STRUCTURE

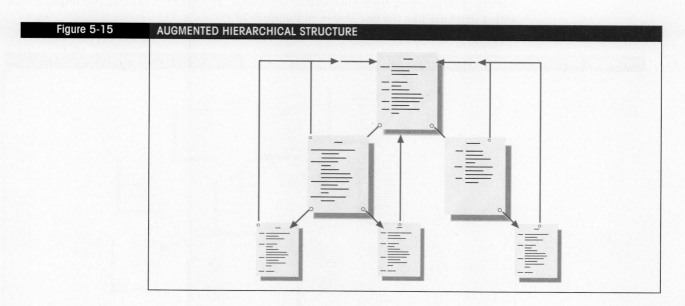

Mixed Structures

You can also combine structures. Figure 5-16 shows a hierarchical structure in which each page level is related in a linear structure. You might use this system for the *Hamlet* Web site to let the user move from scene to scene linearly or from a specific scene to the general act to the overall play.

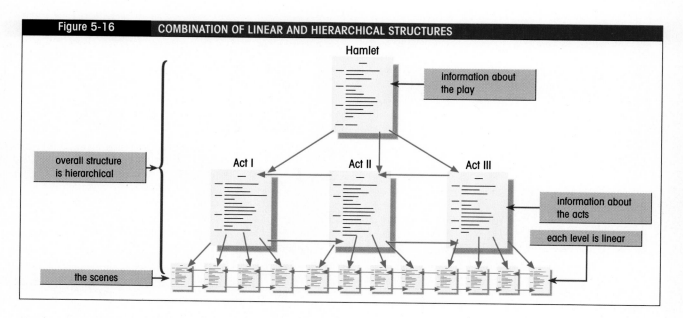

Figure 5-16   COMBINATION OF LINEAR AND HIERARCHICAL STRUCTURES

As these examples show, a little foresight can go a long way in making your Web pages easier to use. The best time to organize a structure is when you first start creating multiple pages and those pages are small and easy to manage. If you're not careful, you might end up with a structure like the one shown in Figure 5-17.

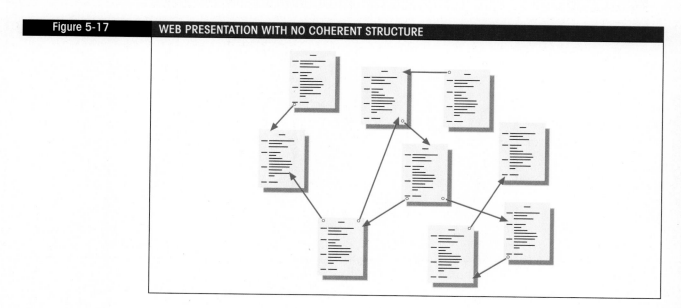

Figure 5-17   WEB PRESENTATION WITH NO COHERENT STRUCTURE

Many of the pages in this Web site are isolated from one another, and there is no clear path from one document to another. A user won't know what content to expect when jumping from one link to another. Nor are users ever sure if they have viewed all possible pages.

Creating Links to Other Documents

You and Fiona discuss the type of structure that will work best for the Findlay Farmhouse Web presentation. Fiona wants users to access the Findlay Farmhouse page first, and then both the Bio page and the Events page from the Findlay Farmhouse page. To make navigation easy, she wants hypertext links on both the Bio and Events pages that jump back to the Findlay Farmhouse page. Fiona doesn't see a need to include a hypertext link between the Bio page and the Events page. Based on her recommendations, you draw the storyboard shown in Figure 5-18. Fiona looks it over and agrees that this is what she had in mind.

Figure 5-18   STRUCTURE OF THE FINDLAY FARMHOUSE WEB PRESENTATION

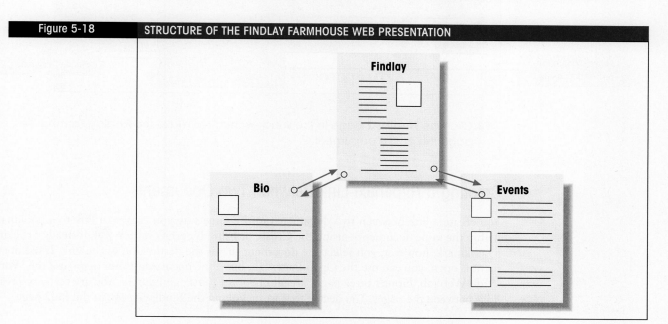

Opening Multiple Documents

Fiona's Web site has three pages, and you'd like to be able to work with all of them at once. Like most word processors, with FrontPage Express you can have several documents open at once; you use the Window menu to switch from document to document. You need to open Findlay2 (the page you were working on in Session 5.1), Bio, and Events, and then you need to save Bio as Bio2 and Events as Events2, so you don't alter the original files.

To open and rename the Findlay files:

1. Start FrontPage Express.

2. Click the **Open** button 📂.

3. Locate and open **Findlay2.htm** in the Tutorial.05 folder on your Data Disk.

4. Locate and open **Bio.htm** from the Tutorial.05 folder on your Data Disk.

5. Click **File**, click **Save As**, then click the **As File** button.

6. Type **Bio2** in the File name box, then click the **Save** button.

7. Locate and open **Events.htm** from the Tutorial.05 folder on your Data Disk.

8. Save the Events file as **Events2**.

9. Click **Window** on the menu bar. Figure 5-19 shows the Events2 page as the active document, with the other open pages listed on the bottom of the Window menu.

TROUBLE? If an untitled Normal page is also open, click that window on the Window menu and then close that window before you proceed.

Figure 5-19	OPENING MULTIPLE WEB DOCUMENTS

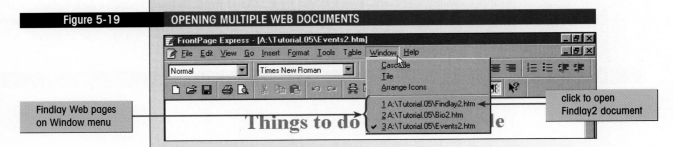

Findlay Web pages on Window menu

click to open Findlay2 document

10. Click the **Findlay2** page in the Window menu to make the Findlay Farmhouse page the active document.

Creating a Hypertext Link Between Two Documents

You create a link between two documents in the same way you created a link to a bookmark within the same document—using the Create or Edit Hyperlink button 🔗. Instead of clicking a bookmark, however, you select the document that is the destination of the link. If the document is open, you can use the Open Pages tab, but if the document is not open, use the World Wide Web tab. Fiona's three pages are all open in FrontPage Express. You are ready to create links between the pages. You decide to start by linking the Findlay2 page to the Bio2 page.

To create a hypertext link to the Bio2 page:

1. Locate the Proprietors information just below the bulleted list at the top of the page.

2. Select the text **Ian and Fiona Findlay**.

3. Click the **Create or Edit Hyperlink** button 🔗.

4. On the Open Pages tab, click **Ian and Fiona Findlay**, the title of the Bio2 page. See Figure 5-20.

Figure 5-20	CREATING A LINK TO ANOTHER DOCUMENT

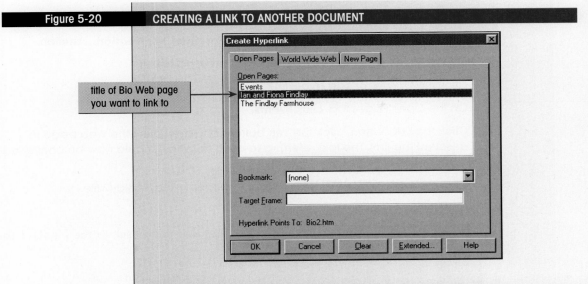

title of Bio Web page
you want to link to

5. Click the **OK** button. FrontPage Express warns you that this is a local file. Click the **Yes** button to acknowledge the warning.

6. Click the Web page to deselect the link.

7. Point to the link and notice the status bar. The Findlay Farmhouse page now displays the text as a hypertext link as shown in Figure 5-21.

Figure 5-21	TARGET FOR THIS LINK IS A DIFFERENT WEB DOCUMENT

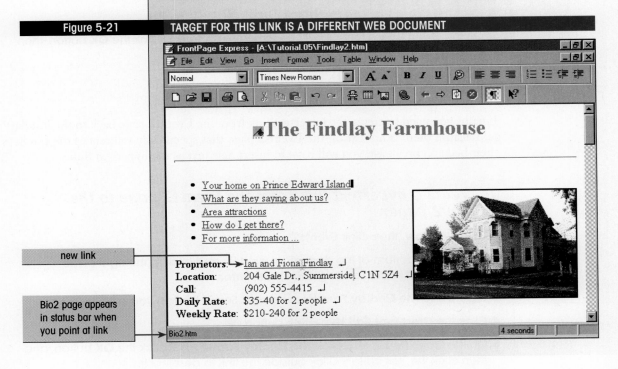

new link

Bio2 page appears
in status bar when
you point at link

Clicking the link shown in Figure 5-21 will jump you to the Bio2 page in your browser. You'll test this link later. Now you are ready to create a hypertext link to the Events2 page.

To create a hypertext link to the Events2 page:

1. Scroll down the document window to the **For more information...** section.

2. Select the text **View our complete list of area activities**.

3. Click the **Create or Edit Hyperlink** button 🐾.

4. On the Open Pages tab, click **Events**.

5. Click the **OK** button, click the **Yes** button, and then click the Web page to deselect the link. The text referring to area activities should now be converted to hypertext.

6. Click the **Save** button 💾 to save your changes to the Findlay2 file.

Now insert links in the Bio2 and Events2 pages that point back to the Findlay2 page. Start with the Bio2 page first.

To create a hypertext link from the Bio2 page to the Findlay2 page:

1. Click **Window**, then click the **Bio2** page.

2. Select the text **Findlay Farmhouse Bed and Breakfast** located in the paragraph below the picture of Ian Findlay.

3. Click the **Create or Edit Hyperlink** button 🐾.

4. On the Open Pages tab, click **The Findlay Farmhouse**. Click the **OK** button, then click the **Yes** button.

5. Click the **Save** button 💾.

Finally, you need to create the hypertext link from the Events2 page back to the Findlay2 page. Because there is no text on the Events2 page that specifically references the Findlays or their bed and breakfast, you will have to insert new text as the hypertext link.

To create a hypertext link from the Events2 page to the Findlay2 page:

1. Click **Window**, then click **Events2**.

2. Scroll to the bottom of the document window and click to the right of the description of Foster Landing, then press **Enter**.

3. Type **Go to the Findlay Farmhouse page**. Select the text you just typed.

4. Click the **Create or Edit Hyperlink** button 🐾.

5. On the Open Pages tab, click **The Findlay Farmhouse**, click the **OK** button, and then click the **Yes** button. Click outside the link to deselect it.

6. Click the **Save** button 💾.

The hypertext links between the pages in the Findlay Farmhouse Web presentation are now in place.

Testing Hypertext Links to Other Documents

Now that the hypertext links are in place, you should return to the Findlay Farmhouse page in the browser and then test the links among the three pages to verify that they are working properly.

To test your links:

1. Start the Internet Explorer browser and open the Findlay2 page in the browser.

2. Click the hypertext link **Ian and Fiona Findlay**. The Bio2 page opens in the browser.

3. Scroll down the document window and click the hypertext link, **Findlay Farmhouse Bed and Breakfast**. You return to the Findlay Farmhouse page.

4. Click the **For more information...** hypertext link to jump down the Findlay Farmhouse page to that heading.

5. Click the hypertext link, **View our complete list of area activities**. The Events2 page is displayed in the browser.

6. Scroll to the bottom of the document window and click the hypertext link, **Go to the Findlay Farmhouse page**. You return to the Findlay Farmhouse page.

The links are working properly.

Creating Links to Bookmarks Within Other Documents

You can create links not just to other documents, but also to specific points within documents. The destination point must have a bookmark, and the hypertext link you insert must point to that bookmark. You already know how to link to bookmarks within the same document, but now you'll see how to link to bookmarks in a different document.

You and Fiona discuss creating links from the individual items on the Findlay Farmhouse page that correspond to events on the Events page. You both agree that it would be a good idea. To save you time, the Events page already contains bookmarks for the theatre, bagpiping, golf, and so on. Using those bookmarks, you decide to add links from activities mentioned on the Findlay2 page to the corresponding activity on the Events2 page.

To insert a link to an event on the Events2 page:

1. Return to FrontPage Express and use the Window menu to return to the **Findlay2** page.

2. Scroll to the **Area attractions** section.

3. Select the text **The Summerside Theatre**, then click the **Create or Edit Hyperlink** button 🕮 .

4. On the Open Pages tab, click **Events**.

5. Click the **Bookmark** list arrow. A list of bookmarks on the Events2 page appears. See Figure 5-22.

Figure 5-22	LIST OF BOOKMARKS IN EVENTS2 PAGE

name of page to which
you are linking

list of bookmarks in
Events2 page

6. Click the **Theatre** bookmark. The bookmark name is appended to the filename, separated by a pound sign (#). See Figure 5-23.

Figure 5-23	FILENAME AND BOOKMARK

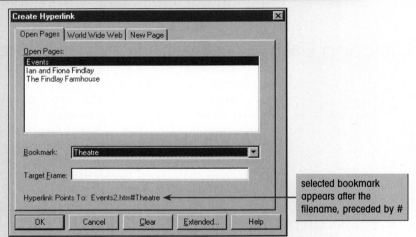

selected bookmark
appears after the
filename, preceded by #

7. Click the **OK** button, then click the **Yes** button.

8. In a similar manner, link **The Summerside Pipers** to the **Pipers** bookmark and
Turwick Point Golf Club to the **Golf** bookmark.

9. Save the changes to the Findlay Farmhouse page, then click **The Findlay
Farmhouse** Internet Explorer button on the taskbar. The Findlay2 page should
still be open. Click the **Refresh** button 🗗.

10. Scroll to and then test each of the three links you added in the Area Attractions
section and verify that you jump to the appropriate bookmarks in the Events2
page. Click the **Back** button ⬅ each time you test a link to return to the Findlay
Farmhouse page.

TROUBLE? If a link does not jump to the correct place, open the Findlay2 page in FrontPage Express, right-click the link, click Hyperlink Properties, then verify that the correct document and bookmark is specified. If it isn't, delete it, then repeat the previous set of steps as necessary to correct the link.

You have now inserted links to the Findlays' Web page that make it easy for users to navigate through the presentation. You decide to take a break.

To close all the Internet Explorer windows:

1. Close the browser.

2. Close FrontPage Express.

Session 5.2 QUICK CHECK

1. What is storyboarding? Why is it important in creating a Web site?

2. What is a linear structure? Draw a diagram of a linear structure and give an example of how to use it.

3. What is a hierarchical structure? Draw a diagram of a hierarchical structure and give an example of how to use it.

4. How do you create a hypertext link to another open document with FrontPage Express?

5. How do you create a hypertext link to a bookmark in another open document with FrontPage Express?

SESSION 5.3

In this session you will learn how to create hypertext links to Web pages on the Internet and to an e-mail address. Finally, you'll learn about publishing your Web site.

Linking to Web Pages

Until now you've worked with files all located on the same computer. However, you make use of the real power of the Web when you start linking your document with Web pages on other computers located anywhere from across the hall to across the world. The technique for creating a hypertext link to a Web page on a different computer is very similar to the technique you use to link to documents on your computer, except that instead of specifying the document's filename, you have to specify the page's URL.

As you have seen, a URL is the address of a page on the World Wide Web. If the URL you are targeting includes additional bookmarks within the page, you can add that bookmark to the URL so the link points to a specific location in the document. For example, the URL you might enter for a section of a page on majors at MidWest University might be: http://www.mwu.edu/course/info.html#majors

Figure 5-24 dissects the structure of this URL.

Figure 5-24	PARTS OF URL	
PARTS OF URL	**INTERPRETATION**	
http	The communications protocol. Between the protocol and the Internet host name, type a separator, usually a colon followed by a double slash (://).	
www.mwu.edu	The Internet host name for the computer storing the Web document.	
course	The folder containing the Web document.	
info.html	The filename of the Web document.	
#majors	The bookmark in the document, preceded by a pound sign (#).	

Some Web page URLs, such as http://www.microsoft.com/, do not include the filename section. In cases where the filename is missing, the name of the file is assumed to be index.html, but you don't need to specify that in the URL you enter on your page.

Inserting a Hypertext Link to a Web Page

Fiona would like the Findlay Farmhouse page to include a link that points to a Prince Edward Island information page. The URL for this page is http://www.gov.pe.ca. The text for this link is already in place at the bottom of the page.

To insert a link to a page on another computer:

1. Open **Findlay2** from the Tutorial.05 folder in FrontPage Express.

2. Scroll down to the **For more information...** section at the bottom of the page.

3. Select the text **Contact the Prince Edward Island visitors centre**.

4. Click the **Create or Edit Hyperlink** button 📖.

5. If necessary, click the **World Wide Web** tab.

6. Make sure the Hyperlink Type list box displays http. Type **http://www.gov.pe.ca** in the URL box as shown in Figure 5-25.

Figure 5-25   SPECIFYING A URL AS THE LINK TARGET

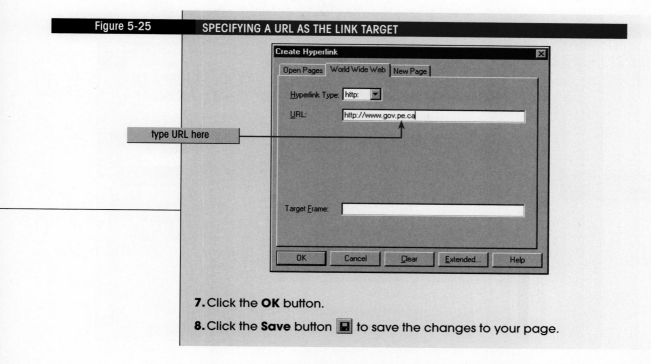

type URL here

7. Click the **OK** button.

8. Click the **Save** button 🖫 to save the changes to your page.

As usual, you should test your link. To test a link on another computer, you will need to connect to the Internet.

To test this hypertext link:

1. Start Internet Explorer and connect to the Internet.

2. Open Findlay2 in the Internet Explorer browser.

3. Scroll to the bottom of the Findlay Farmhouse page, then click the **Contact the Prince Edward Island visitors centre** hypertext link. The information page appears as shown in Figure 5-26.

TROUBLE? If the page does not appear, it could be because you are not connected to the Internet or that the Web server that is storing this page is not working. If the page looks different from the one shown in the figure, it could be because the page has changed since the time this tutorial was written. Ask your instructor if you should create a different link.

Figure 5-26   PRINCE EDWARD ISLAND PAGE

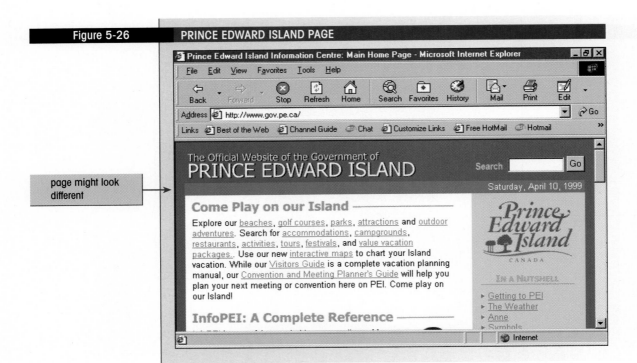

page might look
different

Users of the Findlay page will now be able to access Prince Edward Island information directly.

Creating a Link Using Drag and Drop

FrontPage Express offers an even easier way to add links to your Web page. The **drag and drop** technique involves dragging a hypertext link from the Internet Explorer browser window and dropping it into the FrontPage Express window. This useful technique helps you avoid typing errors, because you don't have to type long and complicated URLs. The Findlays would like a link to a page featuring attractions on the island. The tourism page that you just accessed includes a page with such information. You can drag the link to that page directly into your document.

To create a link through dragging and dropping:

1. Resize the Prince Edward Island Internet Explorer window and The Findlay Farmhouse FrontPage Express window so that you can see both on your desktop.

   TROUBLE? To rearrange the two windows, you can right-click a blank area of the taskbar and then click Tile Windows Vertically.

2. Click within the FrontPage Express window to make it the active window.

3. Add a new list item in the FrontPage Express window by clicking the end of the item, "Contact the Prince Edward Island visitors centre" at the bottom of the page, then pressing **Enter**. See Figure 5-27.

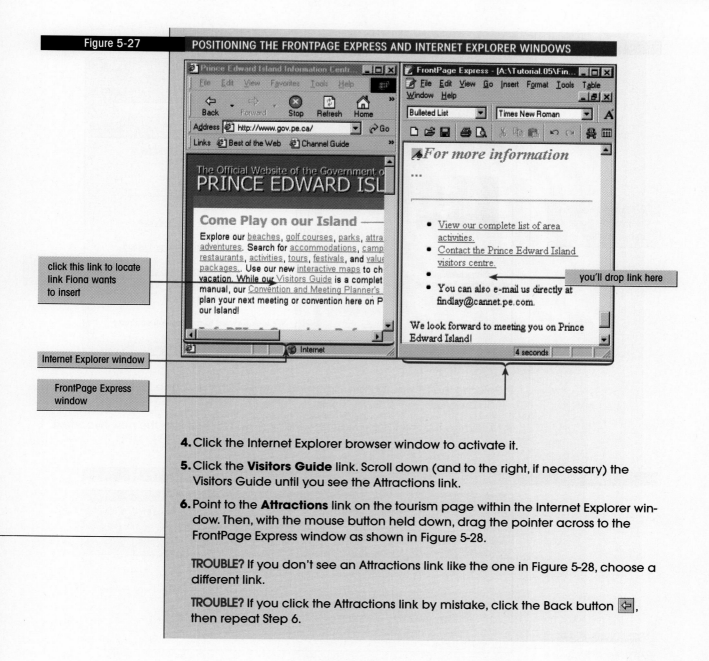

Figure 5-27   POSITIONING THE FRONTPAGE EXPRESS AND INTERNET EXPLORER WINDOWS

click this link to locate link Fiona wants to insert

you'll drop link here

Internet Explorer window

FrontPage Express window

4. Click the Internet Explorer browser window to activate it.

5. Click the **Visitors Guide** link. Scroll down (and to the right, if necessary) the Visitors Guide until you see the Attractions link.

6. Point to the **Attractions** link on the tourism page within the Internet Explorer window. Then, with the mouse button held down, drag the pointer across to the FrontPage Express window as shown in Figure 5-28.

TROUBLE? If you don't see an Attractions link like the one in Figure 5-28, choose a different link.

TROUBLE? If you click the Attractions link by mistake, click the Back button ⬅, then repeat Step 6.

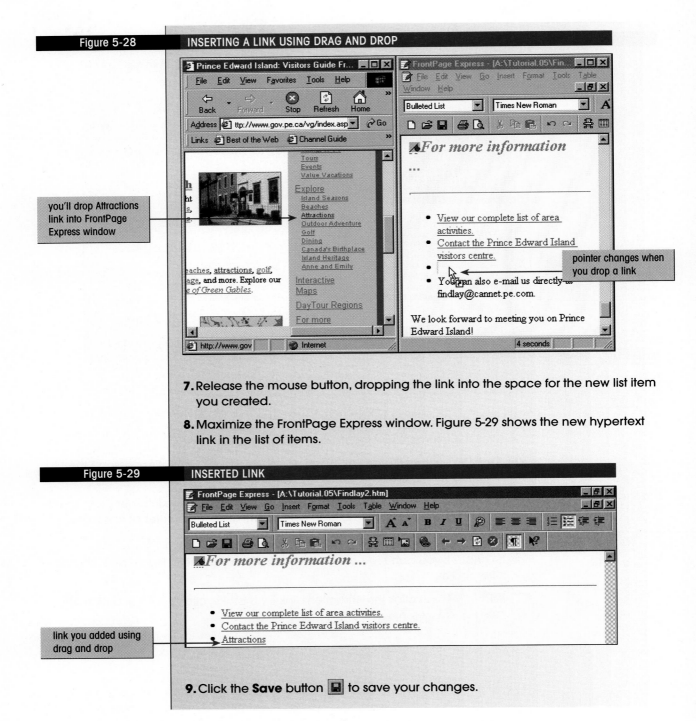

Figure 5-28   INSERTING A LINK USING DRAG AND DROP

you'll drop Attractions link into FrontPage Express window

pointer changes when you drop a link

7. Release the mouse button, dropping the link into the space for the new list item you created.

8. Maximize the FrontPage Express window. Figure 5-29 shows the new hypertext link in the list of items.

Figure 5-29   INSERTED LINK

link you added using drag and drop

9. Click the **Save** button 🖫 to save your changes.

As usual, you should confirm that the link you just created works.

To check your new hypertext link:

1. Return to the browser and maximize the browser window.

2. Click the **Back** button ⇦ until you return to The Findlay Farmhouse page.

3. Click the **Refresh** button 🔄.

4. Scroll to the bottom of the page, then click the **Attractions** link. The Attractions page appears as shown in Figure 5-30.

TROUBLE? If the page that appears looks different, don't worry. The links and pages at this site might have changed since this book was published.

Figure 5-30   **TARGET OF LINK YOU DRAGGED AND DROPPED**

5. Now return to the FrontPage Express window.

You've successfully inserted hyperlinks to two different Prince Edward Island pages.

Linking to an E-mail Address

You can link to other Internet resources besides Web pages, such as FTP servers or e-mail addresses. Many Web authors include their e-mail address on their Web pages so that they can receive direct feedback from people who use the page. The URL for an e-mail address is:

   mailto:e-mail_address

where *e-mail_address* is the Internet e-mail address of the user. For example, if a user's e-mail address is davis@mwu.edu, the URL for this address is mailto:davis@mwu.edu. When someone reading the page clicks this e-mail address link, the browser starts an e-mail program from which the user can create and send an e-mail message. Not all browsers can work with the e-mail hypertext link.

In order to make it easy for people to contact them, the Findlays have included their e-mail address on their Web page. You suggest that they make this a hypertext link.

To create a link to an e-mail address:

1. In the FrontPage Express window, if necessary, scroll to the bottom of the page. Select the text **findlay@cannet.pe.com** from the For more information... section.

2. Click the **Create or Edit Hyperlink** button 🔗.

3. On the World Wide Web page, click the **Hyperlink Type** list arrow, then click **mailto**.

4. Type **mailto:findlay@cannet.pe.com** in the URL box, as shown in Figure 5-31.

Figure 5-31	CREATING AN E-MAIL LINK

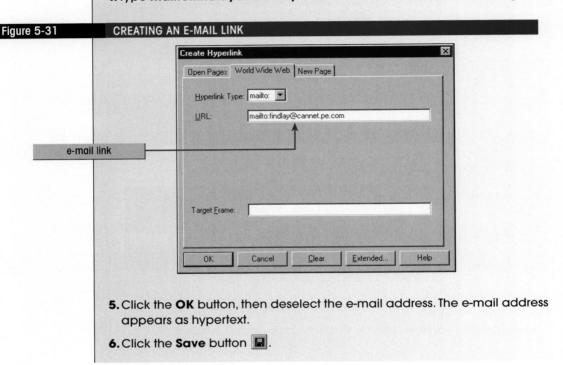

5. Click the **OK** button, then deselect the e-mail address. The e-mail address appears as hypertext.

6. Click the **Save** button 💾.

Now you should test this link to verify that it works properly. When you click an e-mail link, Internet Explorer automatically opens the New Message window: the same one you used with Outlook Express.

To test your e-mail address link:

1. Open the Internet Explorer browser and click the **Back** button ⬅ until The Findlay Farmhouse page appears.

2. Click the **Refresh** button 🔄.

3. Scroll to the bottom of the page, if necessary, and click **findlay@cannet.pe.com**. The New Message window opens and the address you clicked automatically appears in the To box as shown in Figure 5-32. At this point you could enter a message and send it off. For now, you should simply exit without sending anything (the e-mail address is fictional).

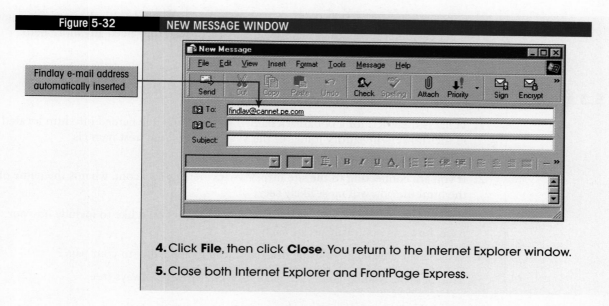

Figure 5-32   NEW MESSAGE WINDOW

Findlay e-mail address
automatically inserted

4. Click **File**, then click **Close**. You return to the Internet Explorer window.

5. Close both Internet Explorer and FrontPage Express.

The Findlay Farmhouse home page is now complete.

Publishing a Web Page

Ian and Fiona are very pleased with the final appearance of the Findlay Farmhouse home page. They are now ready to publish it on their Web site so that the general public can access it. To publish a page on the Web, you must first have space on a Web server. Your Internet Service Provider (ISP)—the entity through which you have Internet access—usually has a Web server available for your use. Because each ISP has a different procedure for storing Web pages, you should contact your ISP to learn its policies and procedures. Generally, you should be prepared to do the following:

- Make sure the filenames of your documents exhibit the correct case. For example, if your page refers to "Ian.gif" make sure the filename is Ian.gif, not ian.gif.

- Find out from your ISP the name of the folder into which you'll be placing your HTML documents.

- Work with your ISP to select a name for your site on the Web (such as http://www.findlays.com). Choose a name that will be easy for customers and interested parties to remember and return to.

- If you select a special name for your Web site, register it at http://www.internic.net. Registration is necessary to ensure that any name you give to your site is unique and not already in use by another party.

- Add your site to the indexes of search pages on the Web. This is not required, but it will make it easier for people to find your site. Each search facility has different policies regarding adding information about Web sites to their index. Be aware that some will charge a fee to include your Web site in their list.

The Findlays have already worked with their ISP to acquire and register the name www.findlays.com. They are ready to publish their page on the Web.

Ian and Fiona thank you for all your help. They decide to work with the page for a few days and get customer feedback. Then they'll let you know if they need any more help.

Session 5.3 QUICK CHECK

1. What is the URL for a bookmark named #petunia in a file named info.htm located in the /flowers/inventory folder of the Web server whose host name is www.ftd.com?

2. If you are connecting to the site http://www.cinemagreats.com, what is the name of the html file you will most likely see?

3. If you are connected to a page containing a link that you'd like to include on your page, how can you easily create such a link?

4. What is the advantage of using drag and drop to add a link to your page?

5. True or false: Adding your Web page to Web indexes is always free.

TUTORIAL ASSIGNMENT

Ian and Fiona have had a chance to work with the page you created. They would like you to make the following changes:

■ Add a link to the Events2 page that takes the user from the bottom of the page to the top.

■ On the Events2 page, include a note that Ian Findlay is honorary chairman of the Highland Games. Include a link to the Bio2 page.

■ Include a link on the Events2 page that points to the official Prince Edward Island list of events and attractions located at http://www.gov.pe.ca/vg/attractions.asp.

To complete this tutorial assignment:

1. Open the Events2.htm file in FrontPage Express.

2. Insert a bookmark named "Top" at the beginning of the main heading.

3. Scroll to the bottom of the page and add a new line, "Return to the top of the page".

4. Link the text to the bookmark named "Top" that you just created.

5. Scroll up to the description of the Summerside Highland Games. Add the following text to the end of the paragraph:
"You can also contact Ian Findlay, this year's honorary chairman, care of the Findlay Farmhouse Bed and Breakfast."

6. Open the Bio2 page, return to Events2, and select the text "Ian Findlay" from the sentence you just entered. Link the sentence to the Bio2 page in the Tutorial.05 folder.

7. Scroll down to the bottom of the page and add a new line:
"For more events and attractions, go to the Prince Edward Island list of current attractions".

Explore   8. Select the text "Prince Edward Island list of current attractions", locate the Attractions page on the Prince Edward Island Visitor Guide, and link it to the URL of that page.

9. Save your changes to the "Events2.htm" file.

10. Open the Events2 page in the browser and confirm that the links are working properly.

11. Print the page.

12. Hand in the printout to your instructor.

CASE PROBLEMS

Case 1. The Author Series at Avalon Books   Avalon Books is adding a new set of pages to their home page that will include biographical information for authors making appearances at the bookstore. They've asked you to set up the hypertext links between the bookstore's home page and the biographical pages.

To complete this case problem:

1. Start FrontPage Express and open the file "Avalon3.htm", located in the Cases folder in the Tutorial.05 folder on your Data Disk.

2. Save the file as "Avalon4" in the Cases folder.

3. Scroll down to the list of the coming week's events.

4. Select the text "Sandy Davis" and create a hypertext link to the file "Sd.htm", located in the Cases folder in the Tutorial.05 folder on your Data Disk. *Hint:* When you link to a file that is not open in FrontPage Express, use the World Wide Web tab and choose File as the Hyperlink Type. Then enter the file path and filename.

5. Select the text "John Sheridan" and create a hypertext link to the file "Js.htm" in the Cases folder in the Tutorial.05 folder on your Data Disk.

6. Save your changes to the Avalon4 file.

7. Open the file in the Internet Explorer browser and confirm that the links are working correctly.

8. Print the Avalon4 page.

9. Hand in the printout to your instructor.

Case 2. Creating a List of Movie Reviewers   You want to create a Web page for the Film School that lists pages containing reviews and synopses of major movies. You've received a list of existing pages and their URLs from your instructor. See Figure 5-33.

Figure 5-33

Page Name	URL
America Cinema	http://www.geocities.com/Hollywood/2171/
Washington Post Reviews	http://www.washingtonpost.com/wp-srv/searches/movies.htm
All-Movie Guide	http://www.allmovie.com/amg/movie_Root.html
Roger Ebert on Movies	http://www.suntimes.com/ebert/ebert.html
The A-List Movie Reviews	http://www.geocities.com/Hollywood/Hills/1197/a-list.html
The Best Video Guide	http://www.99lives.com/
BoxOffice Online	http://www.boxoff.com/

Create a Web page of this list. Format the list as a bulleted list. Make each page name a hypertext link to the appropriate Web page. Add the title "Movie Review Pages" at the top of the Web page, and then publish the page when you are finished.

To complete this case problem:

1. Open a blank document in FrontPage Express.

2. Save the page as "Movie.htm" in the Cases folder in the Tutorial.05 folder on your Data Disk, with a title of Movie Review Pages.

3. Type the main heading "Movie Review Pages", formatted with the Heading 1 style and centered on the page.

4. Create a bulleted list of the page names shown in Figure 5-38.

5. Select each item in the list and link the entire text in the item to the URL specified in Figure 5-38.

6. Save your changes to the file.

7. View the file in the Internet Explorer browser and confirm that each link is working correctly.

8. Create a printout of your Web page.

9. Hand in the printout to your instructor.

Case 3. Personnel Pages at First City Bank   The systems manager at First City Bank is creating Web pages listing company employees and their positions. Figure 5-34 shows one such page, which details the bank's loan officers.

Figure 5-34

First City Bank

Loan Officers

Loan Officer, Linda Keller

Loan Officer, Laura Flint

Assistant Loan Officer, Mary Taylor

Each photo on the page is linked to another page that gives more detail about the employee. The three employee pages are located on your Data Disk in the Cases folder in the Tutorial.05 folder with the filenames Keller.htm, Flint.htm, and Taylor.htm. Create the page shown in Figure 5-34, including the hypertext links to these three files.

To complete this case problem:

1. Open a blank document in FrontPage Express.

2. Save the page as "Bank.htm" in the Cases folder in the Tutorial.05 folder on your Data Disk, with First City Bank Loan Officers as the page title.

3. Type the main heading "First City Bank", formatted with the Heading 1 style and centered on the page.

4. Insert a horizontal line after the main heading that covers the width of the page.

5. Type the title "Loan Officers", formatted with the Heading 2 style and left-aligned on the page.

6. Insert the graphic image file "Keller.gif" on the first line below the Loan Officers heading.

7. Type "Loan Officer, Linda Keller" to the right of her photo.

8. Insert the graphic image file "Flint.gif" on the next line.

9. Type "Loan Officer, Laura Flint" to the right of her photo.

10. Insert the graphic image file "Taylor.gif" on the next line.

11. Type "Assistant Loan Officer, Mary Taylor" to the right of her photo.

Explore   12. Select each of the three photos, and using the Create or Edit Hyperlink button, link the photos to the files Keller.htm, Flint.htm, and Taylor.htm. *Hint:* When you link to a file that is not open in FrontPage Express, use the World Wide Web tab and choose File as the Hyperlink Type. Then enter the file path and filename.

13. Save your changes to the file.

14. Open the "Bank.htm" file in the Internet Explorer browser and verify that the links are working properly.

15. Print a copy of your page.

16. Hand in your printout to your instructor.

Case 4. *Create Your Own Web Presentation*   Create a Web presentation about yourself. There should be three pages in the presentation. The first page should deal with your interests. Include an ordered list of your top-ten favorite Web pages. The second page should deal with your coursework. Include a bulleted list detailing your previous courses. The third page should be a résumé page that you could submit to an employer. Include short summaries of your work experience and educational background. Create hypertext links between the three pages including links to specific points within each page using bookmarks. The appearance of the page is up to you. Use whatever colors, page backgrounds, or inline images you think are appropriate.

QUICK CHECK ANSWERS

Session 5.1

1. A bookmark is a reference point on a page that identifies a specific location; it is necessary when you want to link to that location.

2. Click where you want the bookmark or highlight the text you want to use as the bookmark, click Edit, and then click Bookmark.

3. Case sensitive.

4. With a pound sign #.

5. In the Internet Explorer browser.

Session 5.2

1. Storyboarding is the technique of creating a graphical representation of the pages and links in a Web presentation. Storyboarding is important in creating a coherent and user-friendly structure.

2. A linear structure is one in which Web pages are linked from one to another in a direct chain. Users can go to the previous page or to the next page in the chain, but not to a page in a different section of the chain.

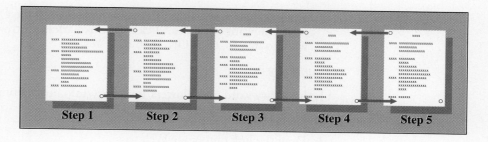

You could use a linear structure in a Web page presentation that included a series of steps that the user must follow, such as in a recipe or instructions to complete a task.

3. A hierarchical structure is one in which Web pages are linked from general to specific topics. Users can move up and down the hierarchy tree.

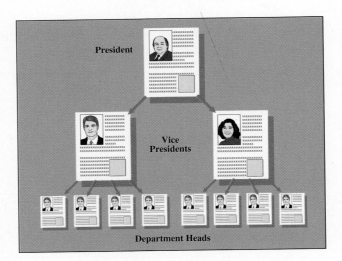

A company might use such a structure to describe the management organization.

4. Click the Create or Edit Hyperlink button, click the Open Pages tab, click the page you want to link to, click OK, then click Yes.

5. Click the Create or Edit Hyperlink button, click the Open Pages tab, click the page you want to link to, click the Bookmark list arrow, click the bookmark you want to link to, click OK, then click Yes.

Session 5.3

1. http://www.ftd.com/flowers/inventory/info.htm#petunia

2. index.html

3. Drag the link onto your Web page.

4. You are less likely to make a typographical error.

5. False.

In this appendix you will:

- Download the Internet Explorer software

- Install Internet Explorer

- Add Internet Explorer components

- Review available Internet Explorer tools

DOWNLOADING AND INSTALLING INTERNET EXPLORER

Using Windows Update to Download the Internet Explorer Software

Microsoft makes the Internet Explorer software available in several different ways. The Windows operating system includes the Internet Explorer software, so if you are using Windows, you probably already have a version of Internet Explorer on your computer. However, Microsoft upgrades its software regularly to take advantage of new technology, and you might want to acquire a more recent version than that available with the Windows software. You can purchase a more recent version of Internet Explorer and install it from a CD-ROM, or you can download it directly from the Windows Update page on Microsoft's Web site.

Downloading the Internet Explorer Software

The Windows Update page is an online extension of the Windows software. Available from the Windows Start menu, Windows Update makes available the current version of the Internet Explorer software. It also makes available other Microsoft software, including critical and recommended updates to the Windows operating system that ensure your computer is running the most current software and is protected against product irregularities called **bugs**. Microsoft constantly updates its Web site, and the steps you need to take to locate this page might change. If you use the steps in this appendix as a general guide and read the Microsoft pages for information, you should be able to locate the software successfully.

When you connect to the Windows Update page, it asks for permission to examine your computer and determine what software you already have and what you still need. You then choose what you want to download, and it installs a small Setup program that facilitates the download process.

To locate the Download page and provide the necessary information:

1. If necessary, connect to the Internet.

2. Click the **Start** button ![Start] and then click **Windows Update**. Your browser starts and connects to the Windows Update page. Maximize the browser window. See Figure A-1.

   TROUBLE? If a message box appears informing you that critical updates are available for your computer, click the Notify Me Later button. Critical updates are files that Microsoft strongly recommends you install on your computer. You can get them at any time by returning to Windows Update. For now, though, you want to install the Internet Explorer software.

| Figure A-1 | WINDOWS UPDATE PAGE |

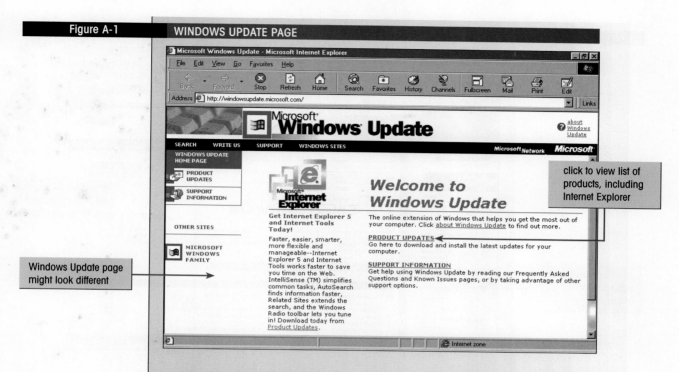

Windows Update page
might look different

click to view list of
products, including
Internet Explorer

3. Click the **Product Updates** link, which appears somewhere on the Windows Update page.

TROUBLE? If you can't locate this link, search for a similar link until you locate the Internet Explorer product. Read through the remainder of the appendix so you know roughly how software updates work. Microsoft might have changed its update procedure since this appendix was written.

TROUBLE? If a Security Warning message box appears and asks if you want to install the Microsoft Active Setup program, click Yes.

4. When Windows Update asks if you want it to determine what components are installed on your computer, click **Yes**. Windows Update examines the files on your computer and lists updates that are not installed. See Figure A-2.

Figure A-2	WINDOWS UPDATE SOFTWARE LIST

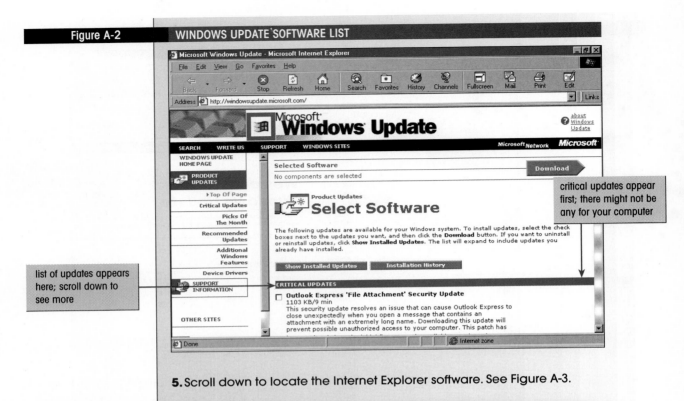

list of updates appears here; scroll down to see more

critical updates appear first; there might not be any for your computer

5. Scroll down to locate the Internet Explorer software. See Figure A-3.

Figure A-3	SELECTING INTERNET EXPLORER

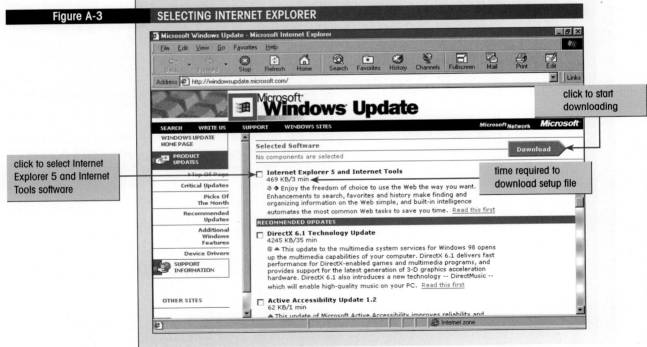

click to select Internet Explorer 5 and Internet Tools software

click to start downloading

time required to download setup file

6. Click the **Internet Explorer 5 and Internet Tools** check box to select it.

7. Click the **Download** button. Windows Update gives you the opportunity to view instructions on the download or to start the download right away.

   TROUBLE? If the Download Checklist appears immediately after Step 6, skip Step 7.

8. Click the **Start Download** button. Windows Update begins to download the Setup program to your computer. Figure A-4 shows the progress bar you will see as the Setup program downloads.

   TROUBLE? If additional instructions or information appear, read through the information and make additional choices as necessary.

| Figure A-4 | DOWNLOADING INTERNET EXPLORER 5 AND INTERNET TOOLS SOFTWARE |

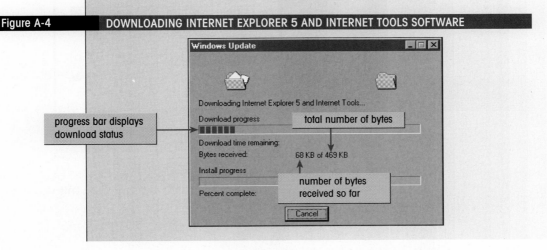

After the Setup program is loaded on your computer, Windows Update runs it and begins setting up the software on your computer. You first must accept the license agreement. Then you choose the type of installation you want. You can choose either the Typical or the Minimal/Custom installation. If you choose Typical, you include the Internet Explorer browser, Outlook Express, Windows Media Player, and other multimedia enhancements. If you choose Custom, you can choose one of three default installations (Minimal, Typical, or Full), or you can scroll through the list of tools and select only those you want.

The actual download can take some time, depending on how much software you are downloading. Be prepared to wait one or more hours, depending on the speed of your Internet connection.

To download the software:

1. Windows Update displays the license agreement; click the **I accept the agreement** option button as shown in Figure A-5.

Figure A-5	LICENSE AGREEMENT

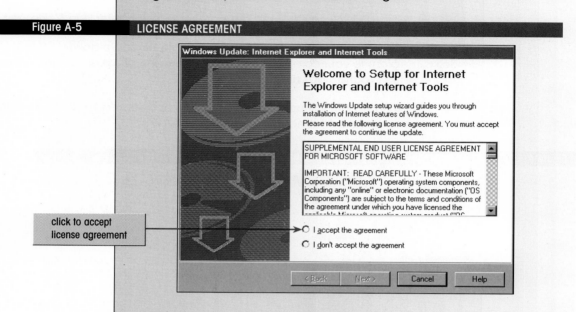

click to accept
license agreement

2. Click the **Next** button. Windows Update asks what components you want to download. See Figure A-6.

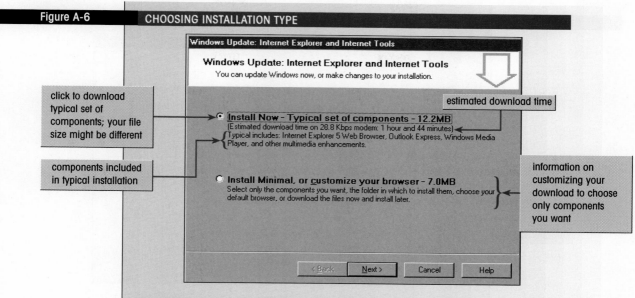

Figure A-6 CHOOSING INSTALLATION TYPE

click to download typical set of components; your file size might be different

components included in typical installation

estimated download time

information on customizing your download to choose only components you want

3. Make sure the **Install Now—Typical set of components** option button is selected, and then click the **Next** button. Windows Update begins downloading the components. See Figure A-7.

TROUBLE? If for some reason the download is halted, perhaps because you cancelled the download or your Internet connection was disrupted, Windows Update warns you and asks if you want to place an icon on your desktop that lets you resume the interrupted download. Click Yes and then when you reestablish an Internet connection, double-click the download icon on your desktop. If you do not place the icon on your desktop, the next time you attempt to download the Internet Explorer software, Windows Update searches for files you might have already downloaded, and continues downloading from where you left off.

Figure A-7   DOWNLOADING INTERNET EXPLORER COMPONENTS

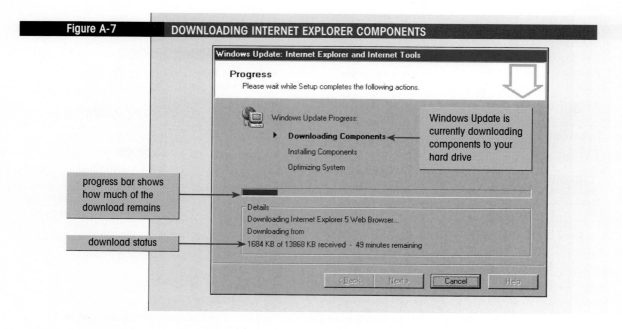

progress bar shows how much of the download remains

download status

Installing Internet Explorer

After the software is downloaded, the Setup program automatically begins to install it. See Figure A-8.

Figure A-8   INSTALLING INTERNET EXPLORER SOFTWARE

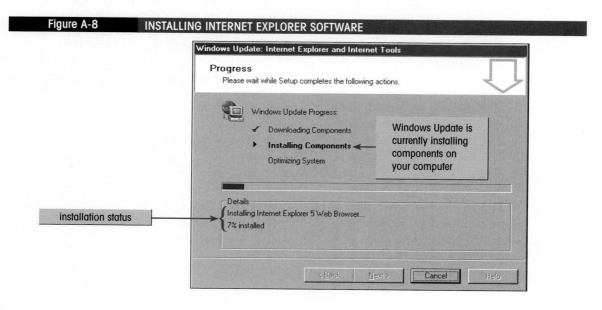

installation status

You need to act only when requested.

To complete the Setup program:

1. Windows Update informs you that you need to restart your computer. Save any work open in other programs, and close all applications, as directed.

2. Click **Finish**.

3. If an Install Complete dialog box appears informing you that Internet Explorer 5 and Internet Tools were installed successfully, click **OK**.

4. Windows Update prompts you to restart your computer. Click **OK**. Windows Update restarts your computer automatically.

   TROUBLE? If your computer doesn't restart, you might have to restart it manually. Exit Windows, then turn the computer off and on again.

5. When Windows restarts, log on to your network account if required. Setup runs automatically and updates your system settings. This can take several minutes.

6. When Setup is finished, you return to the Windows desktop.

7. Launch Internet Explorer. The first time you start Internet Explorer, the Internet Explorer Welcome screen usually appears, as shown in Figure A-9. Because Microsoft frequently changes its pages, yours might look different.

Figure A-9   **INTERNET EXPLORER WELCOME PAGE**

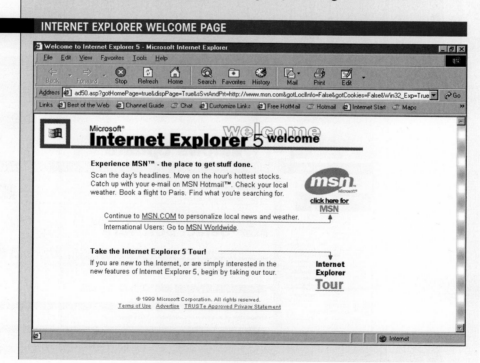

Adding Components

Depending on how you installed Internet Explorer (Typical, Minimal, or Custom), you might not have all components of the product. You can easily add components by re-connecting to the Windows Update page. Windows Update analyzes your system and displays a list of all components you have not yet installed. You can also view the entire list of components and their status on your computer. You can then choose to download and install any revised or new components.

To add components:

1. Click **Start** and then click **Windows Update**.

2. Click the **Product Updates** link.

3. Click **Yes** when asked if Windows Update can analyze your computer. After the analysis is complete, the WIndows Update page displays a list of components and informs you which are already installed on your computer, which components have available upgrades, and which components are not installed. Blank check boxes precede updates you don't have.

4. Click the **Show Installed Updates** button to view the updates you have already installed. See Figure A-10.

Figure A-10	VIEWING UPDATES LIST

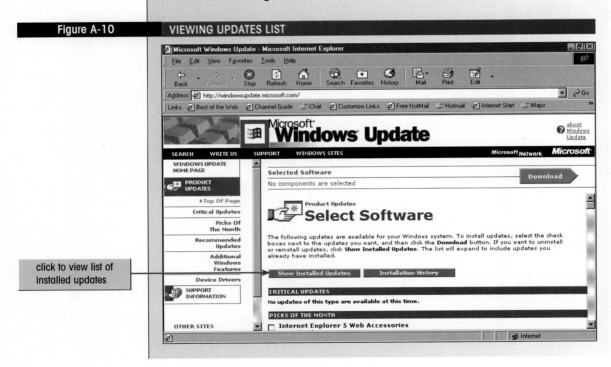

click to view list of installed updates

5. Scroll down the updates list to view the status of each component on your computer. See Figure A-11.

Figure A-11

STATUS OF UPDATES ON YOUR COMPUTER

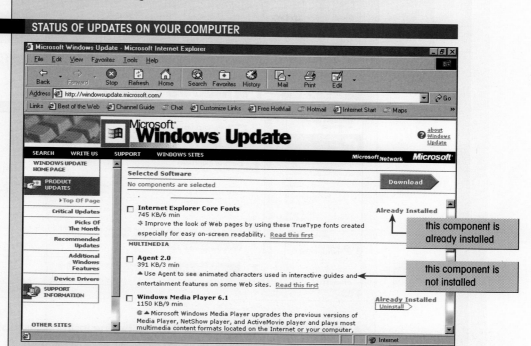

6. Click the check boxes preceding the components you want.

7. Click the **Download** button. The Download Checklist screen appears. Windows Update summarizes the size of the files you chose to download and estimates download time. See Figure A-12.

Figure A-12   LIST OF UPDATES YOU ARE DOWNLOADING

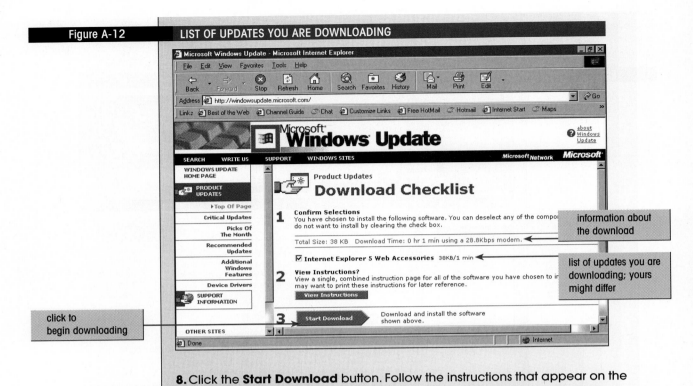

8. Click the **Start Download** button. Follow the instructions that appear on the screen; they are identical to the download and installation instructions you used to download the Internet Explorer software.

Windows Update also makes available additional software programs, often called **add-ons**, that extend the capabilities of Internet Explorer and its components. Some of these additional programs come from Microsoft, and others come from third-party (non-Microsoft) companies that develop and make them available through the Microsoft Web site. You can often download trial versions of add-ons for free.

Figure A-13 shows the add-on categories relevant to Internet Explorer. You can find these listed under the Additional Windows Features subheading on the Windows Update Select Software page. It's possible that Microsoft added or removed add-on categories since this book was printed. To view descriptions of each software program described in Figure A-13, scroll down the Windows Update page, locate the component, and read its description.

Figure A-13	WINDOWS UPDATE SOFTWARE
CATEGORY	**DESCRIPTION**
Internet	Offline Browsing Pack, Dynamic HTML Data Binding, Internet Explorer Browsing Enhancements, Internet Explorer Help, Internet Connection Wizard, Internet Explorer Core Fonts
Multimedia	Agent, Windows Media Player, VRML Viewer, AOL ART Image Format Support, Macromedia Shockwave, Macromedia Flash, DirectAnimation, Vector Graphics Rendering (VML)
Communications	Outlook Express, Chat, NetMeeting
Internet Authoring	FrontPage Express, Visual Basic Scripting Support, Additional Web Fonts, Web Folders Internet Publishing Utility, Web Publishing Wizard
Commerce	Wallet
International Language Support	Support for many languages that appear on Web pages

These add-ons are all available from Windows Update, and you can download them following the steps just described.

REVIEW ASSIGNMENTS

1. Microsoft, like most software companies, makes product information available to the public on the Web. You can download some of it directly from the Web site, but you must order some using more traditional means. Start Internet Explorer, click the Internet Start button on the Links toolbar, then click the Products and Services link, probably located on the left of the screen under the Microsoft heading. (Scroll down if necessary to locate this link.) Click the links for the products in which you are interested. Research several products and note whether you can download them directly or whether you must purchase them separately. Print a product information sheet for one product you've researched, and write a paragraph on the back of your printout that summarizes your findings for at least three products. Figure A-14 shows the Microsoft Product and Technology Catalog page.

Figure A-14

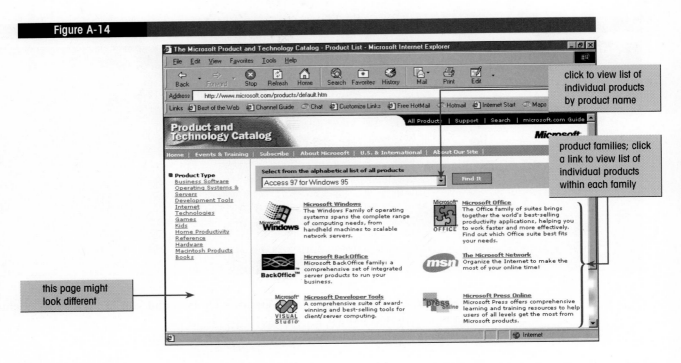

2. Internet Explorer was a free product at the time this book was written. However, usually software companies must charge for their products, as must most companies selling goods over the Web. How are goods sold over the Web most often paid for? What security issues do Internet sales raise? Use the Search Explorer bar or your library to research the sale of items over the Web, and write a one-page report on how companies are resolving consumers' concerns about the safety of selling goods over the Web. Summarize your report by indicating whether or not you would be willing to purchase a product over the Web.

3. Downloading software over the Web can take quite a long time, depending on the size of the software files. When your school or institution provides your Internet service, your connection is usually fast and free. However, when you connect to the Internet from home, you usually use a modem and pay for a dial-up connection to a local Internet Service Provider (ISP). Some ISPs charge by the minute, regardless of whether or not you are calling long-distance, and some offer unlimited connection time for a flat rate. If you plan to spend much time on the Internet (as people who regularly download Internet software do), you need to research ISP dial-up plans. Research at least three of the ISPs in your area, and write a one-page report comparing rates, service plans, and technical support. Of the companies you researched, which would you choose?

WEB PAGES & HTML

Web Pages & HTML

It's easy to create your own Web pages. As you learned in this chapter, there are many software tools to help you become a Web author. In this Lab you'll experiment with a Web authoring wizard that automates the process of creating a Web page. You'll also try your hand at working directly with HTML code.

1. Click the Steps button to activate the Web authoring wizard and learn how to create a basic Web page. As you proceed through the Steps, answer all of the Quick Check questions. After you complete the Steps, you will see a Quick Check summary Report. Follow the instructions on the screen to print this report.

2. In Explore, click the File menu, then click New to start working on a new Web page. Use the wizard to create a Home page for a veterinarian who offers dog day-care and boarding services. After you create the page, save it on drive A or C, and print the HTML code. Your site must have the following characteristics:

   a. Title: Dr. Dave's Dog Domain

   b. Background color: Gold

   c. Graphic: Dog.jpg

   d. Body text: Your dog will have the best care day and night at Dr. Dave's Dog Domain. Fine accommodations, good food, play time, and snacks are all provided. You can board your pet by the day or week. Grooming services also available.

   e. Text link: "Reasonable rates" links to www.cciw.com/np3/rates.htm

   f. E-mail link: "For more information:" links to **daveassist@drdave.com**

3. In Explore, use the File menu to open the HTML document called Politics.htm. After you use the HTML window (not the wizard) to make the following changes, save the revised page on Drive A or C, and print the HTML code. Refer to Figure 8-19 of your textbook for a list of HTML tags you can use.

   a. Change the title to Politics 2000

   b. Center the page heading

   c. Change the background color to FFE7C6 and the text color to 000000

   d. Add a line break before the sentence "What's next?"

   e. Add a bold tag to "Additional links on this topic:"

   f. Add one more link to the "Additional links" list. The link should go to the site **http://www.elections.ca** and the clickable link should read "Elections Canada".

   g. Change the last graphic to display the image "next.gif"

4. In Explore use the Web authoring wizard and the HTML window to create a Home page about yourself. You should include at least a screenful of text, a graphic, an external link, and an e-mail link. Save the page on drive A, then print the HTML code. Turn in your disk and printout.

TASK	PAGE #	RECOMMENDED METHOD
Address, locate	IE 2.32	On Search Explorer bar, click New, click Find a person's address option button, enter relevant information, click Search
Address Book, add contact from a received message	IE 3.20	See Reference Window: Adding a Contact from a Received Message
Address Book, add new contact	IE 3.20	See Reference Window: Adding a New Contact to the Address Book
Address Book contact, delete	IE 3.36	Click [icon], right-click contact, click Delete, click Yes
Address Book contacts, group	IE 3.23	Click [icon], click [icon], click New Group, enter a group name, click Select Members, double-click members you want to include, click OK twice
Address Book contacts, select	IE 3.24	See Reference Window: Selecting Contacts from the Address Book
Attached file, see File		
Audio clip, play	IE 2.21	Click audio link
Background, set	IE 4.36	See Reference Window: Using a Graphic Image as a Page Background
Bookmark, set	IE 5.04	Click Edit, click Bookmark, type bookmark name, click OK
Bullet symbol, change	IE 4.21	Select the bulleted list, right-click the selection, click List Properties, click bullet style, click OK
Bulleted list, create	IE 4.19	See Reference Window: Creating a Bulleted List
Column width, adjust	IE 3.16	Point at the vertical line at the column border, drag the vertical line to the left or right
Connection, abort	IE 1.26	See Reference Window: Aborting a Connection
E-mail account, set up in Outlook Express	IE 3.06	See Reference Window: Setting Up an E-mail Account
E-mail folder, delete	IE 3.36	Right-click message, click Delete, click Yes
E-mail message, file in a folder	IE 3.29	See Reference Window:Filing a Message
E-mail message, forward	IE 3.31	Open the message, click [icon], enter a recipient and contents, click [icon]
E-mail message, open	IE 3.17	Double-click the message
E-mail message, print	IE 3.18	Select message, click File, click Print, check print settings, click OK
E-mail message, receive	IE 3.14	Click [icon], click Inbox folder
E-mail message, reply to	IE 3.17	Open the message, click [icon], enter message, click [icon]
E-mail message, save as a file	IE 3.30	Select the message, click File, click Save As, select a location, select a file type, click Save
E-mail message, send	IE 3.11	See Reference Window: Sending an E-mail Message

TASK	PAGE #	RECOMMENDED METHOD
E-mail message folder, create	IE 3.28	See Reference Window: Creating a Message Folder
E-mail message list, change view	IE 3.04	Click View, point to Current View, click view option
E-mail message list, sort	IE 3.04	Click View, point to Sort By, click sort option
E-mail rule, set	IE 3.34	See Reference Window: Setting a Mail Rule
Explorer bar, view or hide	IE 1.14	Click View, point to Explorer Bar, click the Explorer bar you want to view or hide
Favorites folder, access page in	IE 2.12	Click Favorites, if necessary point to folder, click page
Favorites folder, add page to	IE 2.10	See Reference Window: Adding a Page to the Favorites Folder
Favorites folder, create subfolder	IE 2.12	See Reference Window: Creating a Folder for Favorite Pages
Favorites folder, delete page from	IE 2.17	See Reference Window: Deleting Pages or Folders from the Favorites Folder
Favorites subfolder, add page to	IE 2.14	View page, click the Favorites menu, click Add to Favorites, click folder, click OK
File, attach to an e-mail message	IE 3.25	See Reference Window: Attaching a File to an E-mail Message
File, download	IE 2.38	Right-click link to file, click Save Target As, select a location, click Save
File, view on Web page	IE 2.21	Click link targeting file
File, view when attached to an e-mail message	IE 3.26	See Reference Window: Viewing an Attached File
File associations, check	IE 2.19	Start My Computer, click View, click Folder Options (or Options if you are using Windows 95), click File Types tab, click file type
Font size, increase	IE 4.24	Select text, click $\text{A}^\bullet$
Frame, navigate	IE 1.21	Click the scroll arrows for the frame you want to navigate
FrontPage Express, start	IE 4.06	See Reference Window: Starting FrontPage Express
Header and footer, print on Web page	IE 1.30	Click File, click Page Setup, enter codes into Header and Footer boxes, click OK
Help, access	IE 1.33	Click Help, click Contents and Index
Home page, connect to	IE 1.29	Click 🏠
Identity, add to Outlook Express	IE 3.37	See Reference Window: Adding an Identity
Identity, remove	IE 3.38	See Reference Window: Removing an Identity

TASK	PAGE #	RECOMMENDED METHOD
Identity, switch	IE 3.37	See Reference Window: Switching Identities
Image, insert inline	IE 4.32	See Reference Window: Inserting an Inline Image
Image, modify properties	IE 4.35	Right-click image, click Image Properties, change properties, click OK
Image, save from a Web page	IE 2.36	See Reference Window: Saving an Image from a Web Page
Internet Explorer, exit	IE 1.22	Click ✕
Internet Explorer, start	IE 1.10	See Reference Window: Starting Internet Explorer
Line, change properties	IE 4.29	Right-click horizontal line, click Horizontal Line Properties, change properties, click OK
Line, insert	IE 4.28	See Reference Window: Inserting a Horizontal Line
Link, activate	IE 1.18	Click the link
Link, create to bookmark within open document	IE 5.06	Select text, click 🔖, click Open Pages tab, click Bookmark list arrow, click bookmark, click OK
Link, create to e-mail address	IE 5.29	Select text, click 🔖, click World Wide Web tab, type mailto:*e-mail address* in URL box, where *e-mail address* is address you are linking to, click OK
Link, create to open file	IE 5.17	Select text, click 🔖, click Open Pages tab, click file, click OK
Link, create to Web page	IE 5.24	Select text, click 🔖, click World Wide Web tab, type URL in URL box, click OK
Link, create using drag and drop	IE 5.25	Make sure both Internet Explorer browser and FrontPage Express windows are visible, then drag link from page in Internet Explorer browser to page in FrontPage Express
Links, print table of	IE 1.32	Click File, click Print, select the Print table of links check box, click OK
Map, locate	IE 2.33	On Search Explorer bar, click New, click Find a map option button, enter relevant information, click Search
Message, see E-mail		
Multiple users, see Identity		
Newsgroup, search for newsgroup on specific subject	IE 3.51	Click 📁, type subject
Newsgroup, subscribe to	IE 3.44	In newsgroup list, click newsgroup, click Subscribe, click OK
Newsgroup, unsubscribe from	IE 3.52	Right-click newsgroup in Folder list, click Unsubscribe, click OK if necessary
Newsgroup account, set up	IE 3.43	Click Tools, click Accounts, click News tab, click Add, click News, follow wizard steps
Newsgroup list, view	IE 3.43	Click news server at bottom of Folder list, click 📁
Newsgroup message, post new	IE 3.50	Click 📝, fill out New Message dialog box, click 📤

TASK	PAGE #	RECOMMENDED METHOD
Newsgroup message, reply to	IE 3.49	Open message, click [icon], fill out New Message dialog box, click [icon]
Newsgroup messages, download	IE 3.45	Click newsgroup in Folder list and messages download automatically; to view next 300, click Tools, click Get Next 300 Headers
Newsgroup messages, read thread	IE 3.47	Double-click first message, click [icon]
Newsgroup messages, sort	IE 3.46	Click View, point to Sort By, click option
Numbered list, create	IE 4.17	See Reference Window: Creating a Numbered List
Outlook Express, start	IE 3.03	Click [Start], point to Programs, click Outlook Express
Outlook Express window, change layout	IE 3.04	Click View, click Layout, select layout options, click OK
Radio, listen to	IE 2.24	Click [icon] on Radio toolbar, click Radio Station Guide, click radio station button
Radio toolbar, view	IE 2.24	Click View, point to Toolbars, click Radio
Search, by keyword	IE 2.29	On Search Explorer bar, click find a web page option button, type search word, click Search, click Next to use next provider
Search, by subject	IE 2.31	On Search Explorer bar, click find a web page option button, click search provider logo (or connect to search provider home page), click category
Search settings, customize	IE 2.26	On Search Explorer bar, click Customize, change settings, click OK
Source code, view	IE 4.11	Click View, click HTML
Status bar, view or hide	IE 1.13	Click View, click Status Bar
Style, apply to text	IE 4.12	See Reference Window: Applying a Style
Text, bold	IE 4.23	Select text, click [B]
Text, center	IE 4.14	Click text, click [icon]
Text, change color	IE 4.25	Select text, click [icon], click color, click OK
Text, change properties	IE 4.20	See Reference Window: Changing Text Properties
Text, format	IE 4.23	See Reference Window: Applying Character Tags
Text, indent	IE 4.21	Click within paragraph you want to indent, then click [icon] to shift text to right or [icon] to shift text to left
Text, italicize	IE 4.23	Select text, click [I]
Text file, open from Internet Explorer	IE 2.35	See Reference Window: Opening a Text File
Toolbar, modify button appearance	IE 1.14	Click View, point to Toolbars, click Customize, select the options you want, click Close
Toolbar, move to a new location	IE 1.14	Point to the vertical bar that precedes the toolbar and then drag it to its new position

TASK	PAGE #	RECOMMENDED METHOD
Toolbar, view or hide	IE 1.13	Click View, point to Toolbars, click the toolbar you want to view or hide
Toolbars, customize FrontPage Express	IE 4.07	Click View, then select toolbar options you want
Toolbar button, add	IE 1.14	Click View, point to Toolbars, click customize, click the button you want to add in the Available toolbar buttons list box, click Add, move button into position by clicking button in Current toolbar buttons list and clicking Move Up or Move Down, click Close
Toolbar button, remove	IE 1.15	Click View, point to Toolbars, click Customize, click the button you want to remove, click Remove, click Close
URL, enter	IE 1.24	See Reference Window: Entering a URL
Video clip, play	IE 2.22	Click video link
Web Events page, view	IE 2.23	Click Channel Guide button on Links toolbar
Web page, add for offline viewing	IE 2.15	View page, click the Favorites menu, click Add to Favorites, click Make available offline check box, click Customize, follow wizard steps
Web page, connect to from Address list	IE 2.06	Click Address list arrow, click page
Web page, connect to with a URL	IE 1.24	See Reference Window: Entering a URL
Web page, locate visited using History Explorer bar	IE 2.07	See Reference Window: Locating a Visited Page
Web page, open from disk	IE 1.16	See Reference Window: Opening a Web Page
Web page, print	IE 1.31	Click File, click Print, check print options, click OK
Web page, print header and footer	IE 1.31	See Header and footer, print on Web page
Web page, print linked documents	IE 1.32	Click File, click Print, select Print all linked documents check box, click OK
Web page, save as file	IE 4.08	Click File, click Save As, click As File button, click Save in list arrow, select drive and folder, type name in File name box, click Save
Web page, save as text file	IE 2.34	See Reference Window: Saving a Web Page as Text
Web page, search for on History Explorer bar	IE 2.09	On History Explorer bar, click [icon], type subject, click Search Now
Web page, select from Back and Forward list	IE 2.05	Click list arrow to right of Back or Forward button, click page
Web page, send address or link by e-mail	IE 3.32	Connect to the Web page, click [icon], click Send Page or Send a Link, fill in New Message dialog box, click [icon]
Web page, view collection of best pages	IE 2.03	Click Best of the Web on Links toolbar

TASK	PAGE #	RECOMMENDED METHOD
Web page, work with favorites	IE 2.10	See Favorites
Web pages, move among	IE 1.28	Click ⬅ to move back to a visited Web page or ➡ to move forward to a visited Web page